Which Way Is West

Which Way Is West

A place, or a state of mind?
One man's journey to find out.

Dick Elder

SUNSTONE
PRESS

SANTA FE

Sunstone books may be purchased for educational, business,
or sales promotional use. For information please write:
Special Markets Department, Sunstone Press, P.O. Box 2321,
Santa Fe, New Mexico 87504-2321.

FIRST EDITION

2 4 6 8 10 9 7 5 3 1

Library of Congress Cataloging-in-Publication Data:

Elder, Dick, 1927–
     Which way is west: a place or a state of mind? : one man's journey to find
out / Dick Elder.—1st ed.
     p. cm.
     ISBN: 0-86534-384-5
     1. Elder, Dick, 1927– 2. Stunt performers—United States—Biography.
3. Dude ranchers—United States—Biography. I. Title.

PN1998.3.E43 A3 2002
791.43'028'092—dc21
[B]   2002036487

Published in SUNSTONE PRESS
Post Office Box 2321
Santa Fe, NM 87504-2321 / USA
(505) 988-4418 / *orders only* (800) 243-5644
FAX (505) 988-1025
www.sunstonepress.com

FOR MY PARTNERS

Jim and Twila Dodson

George and Donna Horton

Without you, I wouldn't have had the guts to do it.

George and Geneva Begley

Mel and Janette Schaefer

Without you, there would have been no pot of gold.

ACKNOWLEDGMENTS

During the two and a half years spent writing this book, I agonized over what I should reveal and what would be left unsaid. During the many rewrites, I recognized that the best and most honest story would be to just tell it like it was.

I gave the original 400 page draft to Gerry Shepherd, an editor and author whose judgment in matters literary I respected. She admonished me to cut the trivia and keep the story moving .

By the time I had finished rewrite #10, I thought it good enough to give to Dina Wolff, a professional editor. Dina forced me look inside myself and open up to the reader. This positively impacted both the content and the quality of the story.

My thanks go to my wife and friends who encouraged me throughout this process and to my former partners, Jim and Twila Dodson and George and Donnie Horton who shared those early years with me and helped me fill in some of the fuzzy details.

Finally, and with no apologies, I thank the computer. No way in hell, would or could I have done this work on a typewriter.

FOREWORD

While my intention was to write a history of Colorado Trails Ranch from its inception to the time I sold it, forty years later, I soon realized that the more compelling narrative would be my personal story during a single decade. In 1960, I made the giant leap from security and a comfortable lifestyle to, well, what you'll read about in the following pages.

It doesn't particularly matter to me how this narrative is labeled. Call it an autobiography, a memoir, or whatever. I have elected to write in a style and tell the story as if I were chatting with you, face to face. But, in order to breathe life into the characters you will meet, I have deviated from true autobiographical style by recreating events through scenes with dialog. Though these moments took place some forty years ago, I do have, and please excuse me if I appear to be bragging, a remarkable memory with regard to how people talked in terms of manner, idiosyncrasies of speech, arcane phrases and their dialects. I can recall these conversations with clarity and thus can, with a high degree of accuracy, recreate them for you.

Finally, while I shamelessly admit to flaws in my character, particularly my propensity to fool around (being unfaithful, to be precise), I trust that you will find that I do have some redeeming characteristics. By changing the names of some of the characters, especially those who might be embarrassed or displeased to see their names appear on these pages, I hope that I have exercised a partial redemption.

When the sixties are recalled, most people think about the Viet Nam war, hippies, the counterculture revolution, long hair, free love, drugs, tie-dyed clothes, beads, and rock-and-roll. For me and my partners struggling to stay alive in Colorado, it was none of that.

Traveling through that decade was a marvelous adventure. I hope you too will enjoy the trip.

PROLOGUE

The last echoes of Bob's song had drifted to the far corners of the room. The candle-lit eyes now turned toward me as I mounted the stool next to the antique candelabra.

It was Saturday night and the chuck-wagon dinner and camp fire sing-a-long had ended after the staff and I had sung *Now is the hour when we must say goodbye.* Later, the guests had gathered in clusters and said their good-byes with handshakes, hugs and tears. I had invited the guests to attend a final get-together in the parlor and, despite the late hour, most of the adults and a few teenagers showed up to listen to Bob Bellmaine and me tell ranch stories and sing our songs.

I raised my guitar and ran my thumb lightly across the strings. "This song is about a twelve year old kid whose momma had died and shortly thereafter, his paw married a lady who beat the kid constantly. After one of the whippings, the lad decided to run away, so early one morning, he quietly shoved some clothes and a couple blankets in a cotton sack and slipped out to the horse corral where he saddled a stout gelding. Tying a canteen to the saddle horn and strapping his bedroll behind, the boy headed west to find adventure."

I played a G seventh chord, took a breath and began, *Well, he's little Joe the Wrangler, but he'll never wrangle more, his days with the ramuda they are o're.*

The song frequently elicits a tearful response from the audience because little Joe is killed during a stampede. Bob claims the folks tear up because I'm a lousy singer, but my wife says it's because I sing the old cowboy classic so well. I'm not sure which one of them has it right.

I peered into the darkness and briefly left the moment, suddenly aware of the look of the room we now called "The Parlor." Furnished with antiques, the décor was distinctly late 1800's. I instantly recalled a time when the room had a dirt floor and the walls were ugly gray cement block. During hunting season, we had cut up elk and deer here. Later, when we had a little money, we put in a concrete floor and used the room for a store and game room. Ten years had flown by since Jim, George and I began building the lodge. Ten years! So much had happened. So much had changed.

"Little Joe" was the last song of the Pow-Wow program. I thanked the folks for choosing Colorado Trails Ranch and was just about to say, have a safe trip home, when someone piped up with, "How'd you happen to get into dude ranching?"

I laughed. "Well, that's a long story and it's getting late."

A chorus of voices from the darkened room shouted words of encouragement.

Bob laughed and I couldn't help but chuckle. Every week our guests asked the same questions. How did you start? How did you happen to choose Durango? What did you do before you started the dude ranch and so on? Off handedly, I usually answered that it was just something I had always wanted to do, which was true. Facetiously, I might say that I was a ham actor and half-ass musician and this job provided a captive audience. I guess that's true too. Or I might say that horses had been my hobby for many years and I just decided to turn my hobby into a business. That was definitely true. Most often, however, I'd just let it go with a quip, "It sure beats working!"

A lady sitting on the floor in front of me pleaded, "C'mon Dick, tell us about it."

"Okay." I sighed, sliding an old rocking chair next to the candelabra. Sitting down, I put the rocker and my story into motion.

Go confidently in the direction of your dreams.
Live the life you have imagined.
—Thoreau

Go west young man.
—Horace Greeley

CHAPTER ONE

I grew up a-dreamin' of bein' a cowboy.

The "Depression" was in full bloom in 1934 and I was seven years old when we moved to University Township, near Cleveland, Ohio. Warrensville Center Road, paved with bricks laid by the Works Project Administration (created by President Roosevelt to put people to work) was a mile east of our rented home. East of Warrensville Center Road was the country. Folks who lived in Cleveland said we lived in the "boondocks," or "out in the sticks."

My father's company manufactured artificial grass used to cover open graves and for decoration in store windows. Although times were hard, we had plenty to eat, lived in a nice house and, by contemporary standards, lived comfortably. We owned two cars, a 1933 LaSalle and a 1928 Huppmobile.

One of seven children, my dad grew up on a farm near the little central Ohio town of Shelby, so living out in the sticks was nothing new to him. He was forever taking our family out on weekend excursions looking for a farm to buy. Although we looked at a lot of farms, and they were dirt cheap during the 30s, he never did buy one. That was a disappointment for my two brothers and me because we were certain that once we had a farm, we would each have our own horse.

My mother, born in 1900, was three years younger than my father. She was a loving, caring and very gracious person who, as a stay at home mom, exercised a great deal of influence on her three sons, giving us lessons, by example, on how we should conduct ourselves in polite society.

My dad gave my mother, who knew how to play, a Fisher baby grand piano as a tenth wedding anniversary present. The day it arrived, I started banging on it. I guess it is from her that my musical talents sprung. Within a few weeks, I began composing little tunes and several years later, when my folks thought I was old enough to take lessons, I wasn't interested. Playing the silly simple stuff in the *John Thompson Beginners Piano Book* was boring, and by then, I was making up some quasi complex music. After a half a dozen lessons, I quit. That was one of the dumbest things I ever did because although I can play, I don't play very well. To this day, I cannot read music with any degree of proficiency.

My brother Bob is five years older and Howard is about two years younger than me. On Saturday afternoons, we would go to the movies at the Cedar Lee Theater in neighboring Cleveland Heights. It was a good bet that the double feature would include at least one and sometimes two "westerns." We grew up with the great cowboy stars of the thirties: Hop-a-long Cassidy, Gene Autry, Roy Rogers, John Wayne and Tim Holt. For just a dime, we could see two full length movies, a newsreel, a travelogue, and a fifteen-minute segment of a serial that ended with the hero about to be killed. Large candy bars sold for a nickel, two for seven or three for ten cents. Twelve-ounce bottles of soda pop cost five cents. We would spend an entire Saturday afternoon watching movies, eating candy and drinking soda pop for about twenty cents each.

After the movies, we'd come home, strap on our six shooters and chaps, put on our cowboy hats and vests with the little shiny conches and head for one of the many wooded areas near our house. Armed with boxes of caps for our pistols, we'd replay the movie, running through the woods on our imaginary horses, shooting Indians and generally having one hell of a good time. (It should be noted that shooting Indians in the 1930s was politically and ethically correct in as much as the Indians in the movies were always played by white guys.) At that point in my life, I had never seen a real Indian on or off the screen.

Willie Nelson must have had me in mind when he sang; I grew up a-dreamin' of bein' a cowboy, lovin' the cowboy ways. Yep, that was me all right. My boyhood dreams were much like the movie serials we watched on Saturdays, a continuing saga in which I was the cowboy hero. The venue would always be the same. In fact, I can picture to this day what the cabin of my dreams looked like, what kind of pistols and rifle I used, the name of my flashy paint horse, the clothes I wore and so on. Night after night the story would continue like the weekly serials we watched on Saturdays.

I don't know why, but horses have fascinated me since I was a very small child. Prior to 1934, we rented a house in a suburb known as Cleveland Heights where milk, ice, farm produce and bakery products were delivered by horse-drawn wagons. When I heard the sound of a horse's hooves clip-clopping on the paved road, I'd run out to see the horse and visit with the salesman/driver. If the delivery wagon arrived around noon, the driver would feed his horse oats in a nose bag while he ate the lunch his wife had prepared for him. While they were eating, I'd chat with the driver, keenly aware of the grinding sound the horse made as he chewed the grain. The bakery wagon was my favorite because the driver gave me a cream-filled pastry horn or a soft sugar cookie that he took unwrapped from the white wooden drawers around which flies gathered. Although I looked forward to the baked treats, I enjoyed spending time with the horse even more. I think I understood, even at that early age, that these deliverymen had special relationships with their horses.

One morning, our milkman arrived in a shiny new Divco step van. "What happened to your horse?" I asked.

"No more horses," the man sadly replied. "We gotta drive these new fangled trucks now. You can whistle to one of these dad blame step vans till you're blue in the face, but it won't do no good. They won't come trotting up to ya like my ole horse did. By golly, I sure miss him." So did I.

My brother Bob had a pair of baseball shoes fitted with metal cleats and I would put these on, pretending to be a horse and go clomping around sounding very much like a shod horse on a paved street. Horses were a part of every day life. When I saw a mounted policeman, (There were no female police.) I would give his horse a pat. The affection those cops had for their mounts with their groomed coats and polished tack was apparent. There were hungry people everywhere, but no police horse went hungry.

The many public parks near Cleveland were patrolled by mounted rangers (There were no female rangers.) and each could tell me why his horse was so special. The affection and concern those men had for their horses was not lost on me, even as a young boy.

Seeing a tractor back then was something of a novelty and we would stop and watch, somewhat fascinated. But most farmers were working a hundred acres or less and still relied on horse drawn machinery. A farmer could buy or raise a work horse for very little money and since they had pasture and raised hay (Hay sold for ten cents a bale.) and grain, feeding horses cost practically nothing.

As kids living in University Township, our parents didn't worry about our going some place after dark or taking a streetcar or bus all the way to Cleveland to see a movie. About the only time we'd be indoors was to listen to the adventure serials on our Philco radio. We'd tune in Little Orphan Annie, Jack Armstrong, The All-American Boy, Tom Mix and others. The books we read as kids were mostly tales of high adventure with identifiable heroes like The Radio Boys (the radio being something of a novelty). There were no Radio Girls as the intricacies of the radio were, I assume, beyond the ken of females. Stories about Tom Swift, the Great War (WW I) and books involving airplanes, cars, ships, cowboys and life in the West, attracted our attention.

Children did not require, nor did they get, a detailed explanation from parents as to the 'whys and wherefores' of the many behavior edicts imposed upon them. Frequently the answer to a child's question of why was, "Because I said so." Spankings both at home and in school were more the rule than the exception. Applied sensibly, this kind of discipline resulted in children who were basically well-behaved and respectful. We did as we were told and parents were not the least bit reluctant to tell us how we were to behave. This seemingly dictatorial method of raising children cut across all economic lines from poor and uneducated immigrants to the wealthy. I don't think that any parent ever asked a child, "How do you feel about this?" Of course, Dr. Spock hadn't written any books at that time either.

There were, however, inconsistencies that will seem at odds with what you have just read. I feel the need to tell you about them so that you may find it easier to accept my somewhat less than sterling behavior later in life. It has been suggested by some individuals, that, as a child, I suffered "sexual abuse." I don't believe it for a minute! I enjoyed the hell out of it. Besides, there was no such thing as sexual abuse back then. That is to say, no one ever put a name to it.

As with many families of modest wealth, we had full-time, live-in help whom we called maids. The customary weekly wage for five and a half days was six to eight dollars plus room and board. These maids were the teen-aged daughters of Eastern European immigrants. They knew little of the ways of the world and even less about sex. But, they were inquisitive and easily compromised, as was I. As a result of this unbridled curiosity, the girls and I (my brothers, as well) became involved in exploring one another. We never had intercourse but, we did a lot of touching and feeling and kissing. I knew all about the "French kiss" by age thirteen which doesn't sound like such a big deal by contemporary standards, but trust me, back then it was huge. As a result, my view of the so-called sanctity of marriage and the sexual experience was diminished considerably. For me, it was just something to have fun with and I didn't mind having fun. Was it sexual abuse? I don't think so. Did all of that "fooling around" at that early age foster a pattern of sexual promiscuity? Perhaps. You can judge for yourself as this story unfolds. I relate these fundamentals of my upbringing and the environment of my childhood so that you will have an understanding of my social perspectives and how my childhood experiences colored many of my adult decisions. As they say nowadays, so you will know where I am coming from.

I WAS TWELVE YEARS OLD IN 1939 WHEN WE BOUGHT A HOME in Shaker Heights, an up-scale residential little town. Our large home on the corner of South Woodland and Montgomery was again within a few miles of the *country side*. My fun with maids abruptly ended when I was fourteen and my mother hired a married couple. Shaker Heights had excellent schools that provided a very good education. By my senior year, I could quote from memory all of Hamlet's soliloquies plus the speeches of Marc

Antony and Richard III. I could read, write, solve mathematical problems using nothing more sophisticated than a pencil and paper, and recognize most of the great works of serious composers including Wagner, Brahms, Mozart, Beethoven, Billy Strayhorn, Lionel Hampton and Duke Ellington. With my peers, I engaged in spirited conversation using English, a language betrayed by too many Americans these days. My friends and I frequented such venues as: The Crossroads Cafe, Louis', The Ce-Fair Tavern and The Richmond Country Club. By the time we were seventeen, my friends Tom Fribley, Jack Bailey, Bluey Parino and a gaggle of other guys, had become serious users of beer and casual imbibers of hard liquor and I was no less of an imbiber than the rest.

Ah, ha! Now you are going to trip me up by asking, "What about doing what I was told?" I did say there were exceptions. For what it's worth, here's my excuse; World War II was going full blast when this unsanctioned behavior blossomed. We high school boys were convinced that we would be gobbled up by the draft, sent to Europe or the Pacific where, after fighting heroically, we would be killed. It really didn't matter if we got drunk or didn't do our best in school. In a year or two, we'd be DEAD! The logic of our less than perfect behavior should now be clear. It certainly was clear to us!

My best friend, Tom Fribley and I ran a little business in high school providing music for dances. We had an amplifier, a couple of twelve-inch speakers, a microphone and a turntable on which we played records. For those readers not familiar with the word "record," substitute compact disk.

While we Shaker boys dated and tried to make out with Shaker girls, we never got very far. In fact, I never had intercourse with a girl nor did any of my high school friends. That was something we just didn't do! We might get very close, but intercourse, never! (The phrase, "having sex" did not exist.) I'm not saying this phenomenon was universally true, but it was certainly true amongst the gentlemen and ladies of Shaker Heights High. Any girl, and there were very few, who went "all the way," was unmercifully ridiculed and quickly found herself excluded from polite society.

Because my mother enrolled me in school when I was only four and a half years old, I graduated in January rather than June, 1945. I went straight into the Navy, having enlisted prior to graduation in the Navy's Combat Aircrew training program and subsequently got my Combat Aircrew wings as an aviation radioman/gunner. This, however, is not a "war story" so the only thing you need to know about that time of my life is that I wasn't killed and I was no longer a virgin. You can't beat that Navy training!

Honorably discharged from the Navy in September 1946, I immediately drove down to the Ohio State University in Columbus and enrolled in the College of Commerce and Administration just days before the fall trimester was to begin. You may find it enlightening to learn that my tuition for a full academic year was fifty-five dollars. No, that is not a typo, $55.00 is correct.

During my sophomore year, I met Marye Francis Jeffery, an eighteen year old from Cleveland Heights. Marye was very intelligent, very sweet, very innocent and very virginal when we started dating. I enjoyed being with Marye and after several months of steady dating, an irrevocable event took place. Pregnancy was, in our view, an irrevocable event. There were no options. No gentleman (and I was one) would walk away from a girl who was "in a family way" and no decent girl got an abortion. There were no exceptions. It was a rule set in concrete. You did the *right thing*. You got married and that was that. Many a postwar marriage took place under similar circumstances, so our situation was by no means unique.

My first encounter with Marye's dad, Richard Werner Jeffery III, was in a café near the Ohio State Campus. He was at the university taking courses for his doctorate and Marye seized the opportunity during dinner to tell him that she was going to get married. I was prepared for a big blowup with outrage becoming disbelief, then recriminations with a proper lecture apropos to the situation. To my surprise, he accepted the news without emotion.

The conversation went on to something else. Richard Werner Jeffery was not an emotional man nor did he seem that interested in what was going on around him. At least that was my take on it. On the other hand, Marye's mother, Gretchen, was very aware of everything. She served in Europe as a nurse during World War I then earned a masters degree in public health nursing and worked in that capacity for the city of Cleveland. She was a wonderful woman whom I admired greatly. She accepted the advent of our marriage with good grace.

Marye and I married in a little Kentucky town across the Ohio border. It was just us and a Justice of the Peace. It wasn't very fancy and in retrospect I would have to admit that it was not a particularly joyous occasion. Had that set of circumstances taken place now, there is no doubt in my mind that Marye would have had an abortion and there would have been no marriage.

In January, 1948, our daughter, Nancy Gretchen, was born. When the new school quarter began, Marye attended classes in the morning while I fed, bathed and took care of Nancy. Just hand me a Curity diaper and a couple of large safety pins and I'll show you how it's done. When Marye returned from class in our 1934 Studebaker convertible, I'd drive the short distance to the campus and after my last class of the day, drive some twenty miles to my evening job at a Sohio gas station way out in the country. Since I took a full load of classes every summer when most sensible students went on summer vacation, I was able to get my Bachelor of Science in Business Administration degree in just a little over three years. I couldn't wait to get out of college. I wasn't a particularly good student, although I got A's and B's in the subjects in which I was interested and C's and the occasional D in others.

Going to school from the time I got out of the Navy until I graduated in December, 1949 without the respite of summer vacations, and being in a less than ideal marriage and having a child to worry about was hard and frequently frustrating. I was too damn young and irresponsible to be married and the consequent lack of freedom and the need to provide for my family while still attending college was just a bit more than my personality would allow me to deal with. I was either taking care of Nancy or going to school or working, and that regimen created a physiological overload. Maybe that's too dramatic. Regardless, something was happening that didn't bode well for the marriage. My first extra-marital encounter took place during my senior year.

CHAPTER TWO

There is nothing so good for the insides of a man as the outsides of a horse.

A rmed with what was then considered a prestigious degree, I joined my father's manufacturing company, receiving a generous weekly salary of one hundred dollars. (The minimum wage was thirty-five cents an hour.) Dad had just retooled the plant and the new equipment had so many problems that production was seriously hampered. Being confronted with constant glitches and breakdowns was very beneficial for advancing my mechanical proficiency, although it had little to do with advancing my college degree in marketing. I wasn't particularly enamoured with the job but I sure did learn a lot about using tools, fixing things, and understanding the underlying principals of how things work. Over time, I learned the production side of the business and when my uncle, the shop foreman, left to start his own business, I took charge of the factory.

My dad came to work every day about ten in the morning, looked at his mail, worked on his many charitable responsibilities, then left to have lunch and play cards at his downtown club, returning in time to leave for home by 4:30. He had the final say on major decisions. It was his company after all, but Bob and I ran the outfit.

Ironically, my degree in marketing was of little value since brother Bob, who had not been to college, was the sales manager. Go figure.

In 1950, Marye and I were able to buy a new three bedroom colonial home for $19,000 by taking advantage of a 5% G. I. Loan available to veterans. Marye was pregnant when we moved in but went right to work planting a garden and getting everything ship shape. My folks helped us with money to buy new furniture and the other household necessities. Although we were within the city limits of University Heights, no longer a township, the area was sparsely inhabited. In fact, there was an operating farm directly behind our home, so we considered ourselves to be country folk. There were dozens of vacant lots on our street when we first moved there, but in a year or so, there were houses on most of the lots and the farm gave way to civilization.

On November 3, 1950 our son Mark was born and in July of 1951, my younger brother went off to the army and later was shipped to Korea as an artillery officer. I was fearful I would be called back, as I was still in the Navy Reserve as a combat air crewman and flying personal seemed to be in demand. Being married with two children probably saved me from participating in that unfortunate war. Excuse me, it was not a war; Korea was referred to as a "Police Action." If you ask my brother who was in the middle of it, he'll tell you it was, in fact, an honest to God war!

One evening in early 1953, I was sitting in my favorite chair waiting for Marye to announce that dinner was ready. She prepared a full course meal every single evening, had it ready by six, and no part of it was made from anything instant or frozen. I should point out that this was not an unusual event. That scene was being played in millions of homes all across the country. I was watching the news on our Admiral TV with its nine-inch screen and drinking my favorite Old Forester bourbon, when Marye came in from the kitchen and said, "I've a grand idea for a vacation." *Grand* is a word she would use.

I pulled an Old Gold cigarette from the pack and lit it with the Ronson table lighter (a wedding present). "Okay. I'm all ears."

"A dude ranch."

"A what?"

"A dude ranch called the Jack and Jill Ranch. It caters to singles, but I was told that some married couples go there as well. I think it would be a lovely change, something entirely different. You can forget about the factory, you can ride horses and—"

"A dude ranch? Why in the hell would I want to go to a dude ranch for God's sake?"

AT THE JACK AND JILL RANCH WE MET PETER MCALLENAN who was called *Rocky*. I have no idea why he was called "Rocky" except that the management wanted all the wranglers to have *cool* nicknames. Rocky was the single most important influence for my becoming totally involved with horses. In my view, he defined the term "horseman." When Rocky sat on a horse, you couldn't tell where the horse ended and the rider began because it was all one beautiful picture with horse and rider in perfect harmony. This oneness of horse and rider is something that every serious student of equitation strives to achieve but few ever attain. It was a thrill to watch that man ride and see the horses respond to his skill. After my first session with Rocky, I knew that this was the way it should be done. To emulate the man became my goal. Peter McAllenan was the most incredible *horseman* I had ever seen, and fifty years later after having been around hundreds, perhaps thousands of riders, I can still say he ranks in my top ten.

Our week-long vacation at the ranch opened my eyes to many new and wonderful experiences. It was a revelation! No, more than that, it was an epiphany. While horses and riding were the center-piece of their program, there were many activities available that kept the guests busy and happy from breakfast until bedtime. I loved the trail rides, especially those guided by Rocky, who allowed me to ride a neat little mustang called *Popcorn*. Hanging out with the "cowboys," (albeit very few were *real* cowboys), was a kick. They, like Little Joe the Wrangler in the song, didn't know straight up about a cow, but they wore the western outfits and rode horses.

The lively program at Jack and Jill suited that young, mostly single crowd. Ranch guests enjoyed singing around the campfire, and late night entertainment called Pow-Wows. Singing after lunch and dinner in the dining room that may seem square now, but at the time, it was thoroughly enjoyed. The ranch held horse shows, awarded riding trophies, presented stage shows with staff as cast, provided many sports opportunities and offered a variety of entertainment. It was magic and I was hooked! When we returned the following year, I was absolutely convinced that I had found the perfect lifestyle if I wanted to lead a meaningful life. Many of my "original" ideas that I employed later on in life originated at Jack and Jill Ranch.

I had been having stomach problems since my senior year at Ohio State University and the pain was getting worse. Finally, Marye insisted that I see Donavan Baumgartner, her family doctor. After a complete physical, he sat me down in his office and explained the strict diet he wanted me to follow, which included a lot of rice but excluded coffee and liquor. I hated that! Then he leaned forward in his chair and in a solemn voice said, "In addition to changing your diet and cutting out the drinking, I want you to do something that I think will be the most important part of this regimen. Do you have any hobbies right now, something that you enjoy and do frequently?"

I shook my head. "No, not really. Well, I do like riding horses and I try to ride several times a week, but that's not a hobby is it?"

"Well, it certainly could be. Doesn't horseback riding require your complete attention? Seems to me that if you're paying attention to your horse and thinking about what you're doing, you won't be thinking about things that tend to upset you and may be the root cause of your stomach problems."

I couldn't argue with that logic. Peter McAllenan had told me how important it was for a rider to always stay alert to what the horse was doing. The more I thought about it, the more I convinced myself that getting involved with horses could be my salvation.

Veterinarian Dan Stearns and I met one day at Andy Durek's stables where I frequently rented horses. I asked him and Andy to be on the lookout for a horse that would suit me. Several weeks later, Dr. Stearns told me that Calumet Farms had a two year old mare at Thistle Downs race track that was having some knee problems and they wanted to "put her down." Dr. Stearns thought this filly would make a nice riding horse. If I would agree never to race her, Calumet would sell her to me for a token price. I bought the thoroughbred mare, *Flying Mite*, a grand-daughter of the great Triple Crown Winner, *Equipoise*.

Flying Mite and the Jack and Jill Ranch changed my life completely and irrevocably.

CHAPTER THREE

The rider's grave is always open.

I needed a place to keep my new horse and the problem was solved for me right next door. My neighbor introduced me to her brother, Sonny Breman, a slim young man who always wore Levi's, cowboy boots with spurs and a cowboy hat. Curious, I asked him about his choice of garb. He told me that he trained and showed quarter horses. That got my attention. He said he rented a nice six-stall barn on Johnny Cake Ridge Road in Willoughby Hills and would rent one to me.

I figured that Sonny was someone I needed to get close to and, in a little, while we became riding buddies. Sonny's primary show ring event was cattle cutting, which basically is sorting cattle on horseback. I sold *Flying Mite* the following year and purchased a young Quarter mare named, *Moab Cole,* a daughter of *Babe Mac C*, the first AQHA (American quarter Horse Assn.) Champion. By this time, I was totally committed to learning all I could about horses and riding. I intently watched others ride and took note of their methods then pestered them with questions that usually began with, *why?* I read every available horse-related book I could lay my hands on, including some written hundreds of years ago. I asked Sonny to help me train the mare for working cattle so that I could compete in cutting horse classes. We built a cutting pen, kept six to eight head of steers on the place to work the horses, and we frequently hauled our horses together to horse shows. Sonny also introduced me to reining classes and other western show events. It wasn't very long before *Moab Cole* and I were bringing home ribbons and trophies every week. When the doctor told me to get involved in a hobby, believe me, I got involved to the point where my regular job was interfering with my hobby. That presented some problems, because showing horses meant I would sometimes miss a few days at work, and that didn't sit too well with my brother and dad.

In November, 1953, my daughter Lauren was born. She was a beautiful baby with a sweet personality. I knew that I should spend time with her, Nancy and Mark, but between riding horses, going to horse shows and working five days a week at the factory, the time I spent at home with my growing family was minimal. When I came home from riding, I would either pour out a generous portion of Old Forester or drink half a bottle of my other favorite beverage, Harvey's Hunting Port. I was, to be honest about it, a lousy father and a piss-poor husband. I was self-indulgent to the point that the only thing that was important was my intermittent extramarital romantic interludes, brought about, I suppose, by some need, whether imagined or real, for intimate female companionship that I concluded was not available at home. Or, perhaps it was available at home, but I refused to recognize it. I reckon you could say that I had a bad case of the *greener pastures syndrome.*

The forty-five minute drive out to Willoughby Hills to ride my horse every evening was getting tedious. I was keen to get out of University Heights and buy some acreage out in the country where I could keep horses. In 1957, we purchased a property in scantily populated Chester Township, in Geauga County. The four-bedroom home, the four-stall barn with tack room and hay storage, the large riding arena and the five acres of lawns and fenced pasture, made the place just about perfect. With the horses there, I was able to ride every day, go to horse shows on the weekends and participate in all sorts of horse-related activities. I and two of my children, Nancy and Mark, got involved with the Geauga County Sheriff's Posse and within a year, I headed up the Geauga County kids riding program and wrote their horse owner's hand book.

Living out in the country, potluck dinners with friendly neighbors, and endless riding on sparsely traveled dirt roads, made our Sperry Road home perfect. Sonny and I were participating in horse shows almost every weekend and I was riding and training virtually every day after work. I met Kent Vasco, a young vet who was looking for a place to board his polo pony and I agreed to let him keep his horse in my barn. Kent and I hit it off from the start and we began to pal around. Kent loved horses and horse owners, especially rich horse owners with social standing. He had a tendency to be somewhat of a snob in that regard. We had interesting conversations about equine anatomy and physiology, diseases, lameness, and training problems. I would frequently go with him on farm calls to assist him as he treated his equine patients.

On July 1, 1958, a big bay gelding I was training fell over sideways landing on top of me. I should have checked with a doctor and had x-rays taken immediately. However I put it off, as I had a commitment to judge the big July fourth horse show at the fairgrounds in Chesterland. I was on crutches and it was mighty painful, but I judged the show. The next day I checked into a hospital where they informed that I had a fractured hip and femur.

After a month in traction at St. Luke's Hospital in Cleveland, I was released wearing a leather and steel appliance that was supposed to hold everything in place until the bones mended completely. I couldn't go to work for over a month after leaving the hospital, but I did manage to go with Dr. Vasko on many of his calls.

During one of our trips to see a sick horse, Kent suggested that we start an equine hospital. He had located a large barn that he thought would be perfect. I'll refrain from boring you with the details and simply say that we both put up some money and established the non-profit Northeast Ohio Equine Institute in a large barn not very far from my Sperry Road home.

We were accomplishing some noteworthy outcomes, even with difficult cases that other vets might have refused. Kent was the head of surgery and I was the administrator. In practice however, I did all kinds of things. I held cassettes for x rays (which was stupid even with the lead apron and gloves), and assisted in the O.R. as a scrub nurse, assistant surgeon, or anesthetist. I prepped, sutured, retracted and got both hands in and held organs while Kent did his thing. Over time, I learned many veterinary skills, and I loved it!

One afternoon, Kent took me along to see a horse that had been stung by a swarm of bees. Immediately upon our arrival, a young girl came running up sobbing that we had to do something without delay because her horse was down and wouldn't get up and she was afraid he might die. Had she called the same day the horse was attacked, there may have been an opportunity to save him. However, several days had passed and now it was too late. Knowing that the horse was terminal but understanding the need for the young owner to feel as though she had done everything she could to save her beloved friend, Kent made it appear as though he was doing something beneficial. In spite of the seemingly heroic regimen, the horse died. The young girl was devastated and Kent, being a soft hearted sucker, empathized. Sally's vet bill came to several hundred dollars, so she asked Kent if there was something she could do to work it off. Feeling sorry for the grieving girl, Kent invited her to dinner.

I guess my humor was not at its best after spending a month in the hospital. Although I don't recall the precise circumstances, my guess is that I was feeling sorry for myself, acting like a jerk, and taking it out on Marye and the kids. In any case, we decided that it would be best for Marye and the children to get away from me. I recall that we talked about divorce but decided not to act on it, hence the hiatus to cool off. My wife and children went on an extended stay with my in-laws in California.

Kent, Sally and her girlfriend were to pick me up, but we decided to barbecue some steaks and spend the evening at home. After our meal, Kent went off with Sally, to console her I suppose, while I and the other girl, whom I judged to be in her early twenties, went downstairs to the recreation room. I built a fire, and then sat next to her on the sofa. She told me about her family emigrating to America after the U. S. government granted special visas to those Hungarian "freedom fighters" who had escaped during the revolt against the Soviet Union. The warmth of the fire, the flush of the bourbon I was sipping, and the charming personality of this girl inspired romance, not that I ever needed much inspiration in that regard. Before long, we were kissing and feeling but Sonja was not about to go further.

No doubt about it, Sonja was a peach with light blond hair, lovely blue eyes and a very attractive figure. During the next few months, I saw a lot of Sonja and I think I fell in love with her, but I was still married with three kids and that was a fact of life that I could not ignore, in spite of my penchant for self-indulgence. In the end, I knew I had to bring my family back home. In spite of tearful remonstrations from Sonja, I went to California where Marye and I came to some sort of understanding. There still remained the underlying problem exacerbated by the lack of a loving relationship. Given the circumstances of our marriage, I doubt that there ever existed the bond necessary for our marriage to prosper. There was no appropriate resolution other than a truce that allowed the marriage to continue for the benefit of our children. That course of action, really non-action, turned out to be no resolution at all.

After Marye and the children returned, I continued to see Sonja. I just could not give her up. Was that a good idea? Probably not.

CHAPTER FOUR

Late-night may not be the best time to make life-changing decisions.

On April 26, 1960, our son, Richard Bradley was born. I think he was conceived while I was in California collecting the family for the return to Ohio, proving yet again my lack of maturity in matters sexual. Our other children had arrived at intervals of three years, which suggests that there was some thought given to family planning. Now, this baby showed up six years after Laurie was born.

A month or so after Brad arrived, I was working a horse in the arena when my daughter Nancy ran out of the house yelling, "Doctor Vasko is on the phone."

"Okay. Tell him I'll call him as soon as I get this horse cooled down."

I was taking off the saddle when Nancy came back out and said, "Doctor Vasko called back and said he was coming over to get you. It's an emergency. Some horse has a broken leg."

Kent arrived and we hitched up my Circle M trailer in case we needed to haul the horse back to the hospital.

At our destination, we found the animal, a large gray thoroughbred ex-jumper. He was standing quietly in a pasture behind the stables. It didn't take long to figure out the problem: a fracture of the left hind leg between the hip and the stifle joint. This was exactly the sort of injury that usually ended with a shot to the head or a lethal injection, but it was the type of injury our hospital was dedicated to repairing.

We informed the owner that this was going to be a pretty touchy situation, that we could not guarantee a good outcome, and further, that the horse may still have to be "put down." (A euphemism for *killed*) In spite of the risks, the owner wanted us to do all that we could for the animal.

The problem was getting the horse into the trailer. It didn't have a ramp, which meant that the horse had to step up about six inches, put his two front feet inside, and then walk up, which he was unable to do.

Leaving Kent with the horse, I drove back to the hospital, dropped off the horse trailer and hooked on our mobile operating table. It was dusk when I arrived back at the farm and positioned the table close to the horse. Sedating the old gray, we placed his three good legs on the foot board, put the body bands around him and finally the thick cotton leg ropes. The table had a hydraulic tilt mechanism, so that as we began to lay the table down from its vertical position, we simultaneously tightened the body bands and leg ropes to keep our patient in position on the table.

When the horse was secure with a tarp covering everything except his head, we took off down the highway. Picture this: A twelve hundred pound horse lying on his side going down the road on a table with wheels. Although he was sedated, every now and then he would raise his head and neck and have a look around. People in passing cars gawked, unbelievingly.

It was a long night in the operating room. When the fracture had been reduced, and a walking cast applied, I washed the plaster off my hands and called two friends, George Horton and Jim Dodson. I told them what was going on and asked if they could come over and give us a hand. A short time later, they arrived, and around eleven we had the old gray in a sling in the recovery stall. Kent went home, but George, Jim and I drove over to George's house where his wife, Donnie, having been awakened by our arrival, got out of bed and made coffee and steel cut oatmeal.

We sat in the living room enjoying the late night snack while watching Johnny Carson chat with Jonathan Winters on the TV. Suddenly, I blurted out, "I wish to hell I had gone to vet school instead of business school because I really do enjoy that cutting and slashing stuff." The guys just looked at me but made no comment. I continued, "Doing surgery on horses is exciting! I love it! Vasko is letting me get more involved. Tonight, on that fracture, I was clamping and tying off bleeders and having a hell of a good time."

George looked at me and nodded, but Jim spoke up. "You ought t'do it full time then if you enjoy it so much."

"Hell, I'd love to if we had enough business but Kent and I still have to subsidize it." I laid my spoon down and looked around the room. "I'll tell you one thing and I ain't shitin' you. Sorry Donnie. One of these days I'm gonna get the hell out of that damn factory and get into something that has to do with horses."

George swallowed a mouthful of oatmeal. "Like what?"

"Oh, I don't know. Maybe a dude ranch. Something like that Jack and Jill Ranch Marye and I went to. I'll tell ya, that was fun and the people working there were havin' as much fun as the guests."

Jim's face lit up. "Now, there you have something. A dude ranch! By gosh that'd be all right, ya know it. The three of us could quit our jobs, buy us some land out west someplace and go to ranching. Besides the dudes, we could have cattle and horses and that sure would beat the heck out of sellin' x-ray machines." Jim was sitting on the edge of his chair waving his arms around, his blue eyes shining. Getting to his feet and walking toward the TV, he said, "Can't you just see it George? It's the answer to the whole thing." Jim reached out and switched off the TV.

"Hey, what the hell you doing? Turn that back on. I'm watching that." George rose from his chair but Jim laid a hand on his shoulder and pressed him back.

"Listen." Jim said holding George with one hand and turning toward me, "This is more important than Johnny Carson."

Reaching up, George pushed away Jim's restraining hand. "For Christsake Jim, what are you talking about? You gonna tell me that you're gonna quit your job with Picker, give up your horses, the Sheriff's Posse, your friends and all that and go off on some dude ranch fandango, just like that? Don't make me laugh! Besides, you'd never get Twila to go for it."

"I don't see why not." I interjected. "What the hell is so great about selling x-ray machines? Outside of the one he sold to Vasko, he hasn't sold any others and he's been fartin' around with that job for more than a year now?"

"Wait a sec. It takes a while to get started on something like that," Jim said defensively.

I smiled, aware that I had misspoken. Jim was sensitive about his job. Recently, he had become a regular luncheon companion, meeting me at a café near our factory. I rather enjoyed our lunches, even though the conversation invariably came back to the same theme, his job selling radiology equipment.

Jim was my age and an easy going kind of a guy. He had a pleasant face, blue eyes and wavy blond hair. He stood around five foot eight and had a muscular body. I guess you'd characterize his build as "stocky." I met Jim in 1957 when we had been thrown together as riding instructors for the Geauga County Junior Sheriff's Posse. At first, we simply tolerated each other. He thought I was a know-it all and I thought he was a little dense. Later though, we developed a mutual respect when he learned that I really did know quite a little about horses and I learned that he had a lot more on the ball than I had first assumed.

Jim's wife was a young lady I greatly admired. Twila was a pretty girl with marvelous dark blue eyes. She was eight years younger than Jim. When she was peeved with Jim, her voice would raise to a high pitch ending in a screech. Jim said she was one of the best hog callers around. Twila had a pleasant nature and an abundance of good sense, which was just as well, because she knew how to put the brakes on Jim when he got carried away. Jim, I'm afraid, didn't always exercise the best judgement, but Twila did.

"Don't get your balls in an uproar," I said quietly as I could hear Donnie rumbling around in the kitchen, "All I meant was that I don't think selling x ray machines is what you want to do the rest of your life. Christ knows we've talked enough about it over lunch. In fact, that's about all you do talk about. And when it comes down to it, you both know that I've had a belly full of that damn factory. I don't see myself working down there the rest of my life or even another year, so there's nothing wrong with what Jim says. Why couldn't we quit our jobs and buy a dude ranch? Why the hell sit around here growing old, working at jobs we don't like? What's the point of that?"

Now George was on his feet. "I can just see you Elder, giving up your big salary to go play cowboy. Don't make me laugh! Jim, maybe. You, not a chance! You're no different than me and a lot of other guys. Sure, we'll talk about going out west or someplace to get away from the rat race and we'll moan about our lousy jobs, but the truth is, we aren't about to do it. I've got eighteen years with Thompson and I can retire in two more and I'm not even forty yet."

"I can understand why you wouldn't want to leave your job George," Jim said. "You've been at it so long and besides, from what you say, you kinda like it anyway."

"Don't kid yourself." That from Donnie who had returned a few moments earlier. "You ought to hear George rave about some of the things they do down there."

"Look," I said, putting a match to a cigarette, "I'll be honest with you. If the Northeast Ohio Institute could make it, you know, provide me with some kind of a living, I'd quit my job pronto."

"What would your dad and brother say to that?" Jim interjected.

"They probably wouldn't like it but they'd get over it. I'd bring my brother Howard over from Great Lakes Sash and Door and train him to do my job before I left the company. Hell, he'd be good at it. The likes that business crap and the money he'd be making compared to what he makes now . . . I know he'd like that. Don't you worry. He'll go for it, no problem." I looked up at Donnie and smiled. "No problem" was George's pet saying. A faint trace of acknowledgment crossed Donnie's face. "No problem" summed up George's attitude toward life. Whatever the job, be it fixing a roof, repairing a motor or coping with the day to day impact of marriage, it was no problem. It was also an illusion. I may be wrong, but I think that deep down Donnie had known it for years.

I can't remember exactly how I met George. It may have been at a horse show I was either riding in or judging. He lived in a lovely old frame house on the highway about three miles from my home. George's wife, Donnie, short for Donna Mae, was about the same age as her husband. She was a small, slender, attractive woman who always appeared as though she had just gotten dressed up. She was never messy or rumpled. Her blouse collar stood up stiffly with nary a wrinkle. She could be scrubbing a floor or painting a wall, yet remain neat as a pin. I always marveled how every thing about her was so well organized and that included her home, which she maintained in her image with everything in its place. She collected little glass and china pieces that she displayed wherever space permitted. Early American was the theme for her home and early American, I suspect, was the pattern for her life.

George loved Donnie; I'm darn sure of that. I didn't discuss it with him, but I think he felt the way to nurture Donnie's love was to make himself a hero in her eyes. He had to be the knight in shining armor and so he developed his perpetual "no problem" attitude. Of course, I could be mistaken, as neither George nor Donnie were intimate with me when it came to personal and family matters.

When we first met, George and I had an almost immediate kinship. He is the kind of guy you feel comfortable with right from the start. About three years older than me, he was slim, about five nine, bright blue eyes and an attractive face that was quick to smile. I think that when we met, I was extremely impressed. He just exuded manly attributes of self-reliance, sort of a can-do attitude and an almost eager openness that immediately won me over. He was an electrician by trade, who went to work for Thompson Products, now called TRW, before World War II. He served in the Army Air Corps during the war, came home a hero and married little Donna Mae Herbert whom he had dated since they were teens. After leaving the Army, he returned to Thompson Products and rose in the ranks to a department supervisor. When we met, he was the head of the Meter Testing Department.

Like his wife, George was not just neat but noticeably neat. He would never leave the house until he had shaved, whether he needed it or not. Typically, he would say, "Gimme a minute to knock off these whiskers." When he dressed to go out, his attire was always fashionable with suit pressed and not too old, shoes shined and of the latest style, shirt highly starched and always the right tie. His car was never a Ford, Plymouth or Chevy. He preferred the more up-scale Oldsmobile station wagon and it was always kept spotless and in perfect condition.

At first blush, it appeared as though Donnie and George enjoyed the perfect relationship. They were fastidious in everything they did. Never were cross or disrespectful words spoken between them, at least not in the company of others. They were the most concerned of parents. Their two boys, Bruce and Scott, were about what you would expect from an All-American Family and not unlike those Nelson boys on TV. That evening in the Horton home however, it was becoming evident that everything was not quite so "no problem."

Donnie sat down on a three-legged stool in front of the fireplace. "George," she said, "I think that the best thing you could ever do would be to leave Thompson and start something new. You're in a rut and have been for years and furthermore, you know it. We need a change. Don't you honestly believe that this whole family needs a change?" There was pleading in her voice.

George looked at her, his eyes mirrored the disbelief he felt. "You," emphasizing the YOU, "would leave your home, everything?" He jumped to his feet, taking in the room with a sweep of his arms, "Everything, just like that? Just pick up and ship out? Well, I don't believe it and I don't think you do either." I'm sure he thought that Donnie was embracing an idea that didn't originate with him and worse, slashing at his knight's armor in front of his friends. That was the worst part; his own perfect wife was tearing the fabric of their perfect marriage. He sat down, deflated. George gazed at his wife for a long moment and in a whisper added, "We have a good life. Why would we want to change it?"

"Do we?" Donnie looked unblinkingly at him. "Is it really so great, so wonderful that you couldn't give it up, or would you be afraid you couldn't do anything else. Is that it?"

"No, that's not it at all." He looked at her intently for a moment, then cast his eyes about the room and said, "I could do it alright, I mean leave Ohio, no problem. It's just that it would be a big move. You know, darn near twenty years on a job, the house, kids. You know, it's not something a guy does just like that."

"A guy does it if it means improving his life and making his wife and family happy."

"You're not happy now?" George asked, in a tone of disbelief.

Donnie didn't answer but neither did she avoid his eyes. I rescued her. "I think that there are degrees of happiness, George. Sure, you may be content right now, but won't you concede that maybe, just maybe there are things you could do in life that would bring you more happiness because they were more fulfilling or more of a challenge? And what about Donnie? Maybe she's looking for something more to do with her life than she's doing now. Let's face it, being around the house all day can't be one of the world's great experiences, can it?"

And so the conversation went. Jim was hot to trot and why not? He had no children, lived in a rented home, and financially had little to loose. It was a different story for the Hortons. Nevertheless, Donnie was warming to the idea and George, who was not about to be left out, would soon come around. He was a very good politician who knew when to fight and when to join.

As for me, going into the dude ranch business was not a new idea. I had been thinking about chucking the family business for several years. Marye and I had recently had another in a series of destructive episodes which resulted in another separation. I felt that since we were probably going to divorce someday, what was the point of staying in Ohio in a job I hated. I had written to several ranches about employment opportunities as a horse wrangler and riding instructor, but nothing came of it because I didn't have the guts to pursue it. In that respect, I was no different than George. I certainly could understand his reluctance to abandon his comfortable lifestyle, jeopardize his hard-earned assets and head off into the unknown. But George Horton was not a man to concede to any weakness of character whether real or imagined.

Later, with fresh cups of coffee in hand, we found ourselves standing around the gleaming white enameled kitchen table upon which Donnie had spread a map of the western United States. By this time, the conversation had turned to where we would buy our dude ranch.

Donnie put her finger on the map, "Here is where we should go. See, the Prescott area has mountains around it. It's beautiful there."

"What about in Arizona?" Jim asked. Donnie reminded Jim that Prescott was in Arizona. We laughed.

"No, I mean farther south around Phoenix or Tucson. You wouldn't have to worry about winter down there."

We all viewed the map suggesting one place and then another. I placed a finger on the map and said, "Okay, how about this? Right where these four states come together."

"Let's see." Jim leaned over my shoulder for a better look. "What's the name of that town you got your finger on?"

I raised my hand. "Durango. Durango, Colorado." None of us had ever heard of it.

CHAPTER FIVE

Anytime you have a 50/50 chance of getting something right, there's a 90% probability you'll get it wrong.

The very next day, I wrote a letter to the Durango Chamber of Commerce asking them to send me a list of realtors who dealt in ranch and farm properties. Although I sent letters to every realtor on the Chamber's list, I only received one answer, from A. A. Ball Realty, which stated that they would be happy to locate properties that might suit our purpose.

Over a period of several weeks, Ball Realty sent descriptions of three properties. One was the *Red Ryder* ranch located in the Blanco Basin near the town of Pagosa Springs, about fifty miles east of Durango. Another property that looked interesting was the *Columbine Ranch,* some twenty miles north of Durango. The third was *Camp Silver Spruce*, a boys camp fifteen miles northeast of Durango on the Florida River.

Shortly after receiving the information, the three families held a meeting at Dodson's house. Central to our deliberations was this question: Were we really serious about quitting our jobs, leaving friends and family and moving to Colorado? It obviously wasn't an easy decision for any of us because, aside from our perceived expertise with horses, we would be heading into a huge lifestyle change in a field that none of us knew much about. We understood that it made more sense to buy an established dude ranch and have the former owners teach us the business for a period of time, rather than buy a piece of land and start from scratch. Many knowledgeable people advised us to only consider buying an established ranch, as it would take years before a start-from-scratch operation became profitable and we might all starve to death waiting for that day.

The reality of a move to Colorado was discussed at great length. Regardless of the obvious hurdles and pitfalls, we continued to make plans. When shards of doubt chipped at our resolve, they were swept away with confidence. We felt certain that winter jobs would tide us over when we needed additional funds, yet we did not investigate the Durango job market, nor did we try to learn the details of the Durango economy. In the wintertime, we assured ourselves, we could find work and save the money to use for construction the following year. Based on no solid evidence or criteria and having done very little research, we talked ourselves into believing that we had a solid plan. In retrospect, those early meetings remind me of the time when my brother and I decided it would be fun to jump off the garage roof using umbrellas as parachutes. Once up there, we both realized that the jump would be a disaster. Nonetheless, we stood there mouthing words of encouragement, neither wanting the other to think he was afraid, and then with a whoop, we jumped. It *was* a disaster!

I remember talking to Kent Vasko about our plans. I think he thought he was listening to a lunatic. He considered me to be a straight thinking guy with business savvy, definitely not a starry-eyed nitwit. He could not believe that I was actually serious about moving to Colorado.

Kent leaned across the table, "Listen Dick, use some common sense will ya? You're gonna go out there and obligate yourself to some bank for the next how many years? There's Marye and kids to think about."

"Hey, Marye is all for it. She thinks that starting over in a new place with a new life may salvage our marriage. I don't know. Maybe it might get us back on track."

"I wouldn't count on that, especially if things get tough. And they will get tough, because there's no way you can make this work unless you find some dumb son-of-a-bitch who'll give ya a couple hundred thousand dollars that you don't ever have to pay back. For Christsake, wake up! You people are either dreaming or you're all drunk."

It wasn't so much what he said or the way he said it. It was the nagging realization that he might be right and was only trying to help me avoid a tragedy. What were we thinking about anyway? I started having some serious doubts.

I brought these concerns to the table when the three couples met again. To this day, I don't know why we didn't abandon the idea given the abundance of very good reasons to do so. We kept minutes of all of our meetings right from the start, so I know for sure what was said and who said it. I took movies with my 8mm Bolex camera at a couple of those meetings, and you can tell that we were desperately trying to examine and evaluate every obstacle to our plan. The confidence we had in each other and in the project leaps right off the screen.

During a meeting, we decided to assign responsibilities for the six adults. Everyone, and that included the older children, was going to work. Marye was a great cook and baker, so she was the obvious choice to manage the kitchen. Twila Dodson was a secretary, so she would be in charge of the office. Donnie Horton was a fastidious housekeeper, so it seemed natural to us, if not to Donnie, that she would be the head housekeeper.

Jim Dodson said he would learn how to cut meat. (He actually went to his friend's meat market a number of times and learned how to be a butcher.) Jim had other talents we needed too. He grew up on a farm in Pennsylvania, so he knew something about farm machinery and farming. His job at our ranch, aside from meat cutting, was to work in maintenance and grounds, drive equipment plus lead trail rides and guide hunters. Oh yes, we planned a full scale big game hunting program as we had *heard* that the area around Durango had excellent deer and elk hunting. Jim's ranch name was *Ponhoss*. I have no idea how he came by that handle, nor do I remember what it means.

George, who we now addressed by his new sobriquet, *Hap*, was to be in charge of the horse operation plus work in maintenance and wherever else he was needed. George was an ace electrician plus he had many other skills. As you now know, he was a "can do" kind of guy. Even if he didn't know squat about something, he'd figure out a way to do it. His "no problem" attitude usually worked. He would say, "No problem," even when he knew it was going to be a huge problem. I liked that about him. He was exactly the talent we needed.

The minutes disclose that everyone agreed I should be the manager which, thanks to my marketing degree, would include promotion and advertising. Additionally, I was to teach riding and do whatever else needed to be done.

Within a month, the idea evolved from silly to serious. Financing remained the big hurdle. How much could each family contribute? "Aye," as Hamlet so aptly put it, "There's the rub." The "rub" was that I was the only one who could contribute any significant capitol. Jim had been working for Picker X-Ray for about a year and between his earnings and Twila's, they were just getting by. Jim said he'd sell his Ford pickup and horses and could probably invest three thousand dollars. The

Horton's owned their home in Chesterland and I'm sure they had some savings too. They offered ten thousand. I figured we'd sell our house for thirty-five thousand, which would net fifteen after paying off the mortgage. We would sell one of the cars, the horses, except for my show horse, *Moab Cole*, the horse trailer, furniture and some other stuff which, when added to our savings, would add up to about sixty thousand dollars. However, the minutes state that I only offered thirty five thousand dollars. I guess I was hedging my bet by holding something in reserve. Between us, we had agreed to invest a total of forty-eight thousand dollars in cash and other assets.

In retrospect, it's hard to believe that we were seriously considering buying a dude ranch, even taking into account the value of money and the relatively low cost of real estate in 1960. Were we naive? Were we crazy? Were we just plain stupid? The answers have to be, yes, yes and definitely, YES!

Regardless, we decided that Hap Horton and I would meet with the realtors and check out Durango and the three properties. That trip turned out to be a defining event, because after that, there was no turning back.

If we had the slightest idea about what was really going to happen, I'm quite certain that there would be no story to tell.

CHAPTER SIX

Hey Sarge, want a parachute?

George and I boarded a United Air Lines DC-8 bound for Denver on September 10, 1960. Neither of us had flown on a jet before. The trip to Denver was miraculously smooth and quiet and it wasn't long before George was asleep. I glanced at him and wondered if he'd go through with our plan when it was time to cough up the money and make the big move. I didn't wonder about Jim; I knew a team of horses couldn't keep him from Colorado.

I tried to sleep, but all I could do was think about my two partners. George was complex. Jim wasn't. George had concerns that constantly worried him. Jim had problems too, but he didn't seem to worry much about them. George didn't like to talk about his problems because he was the "no problem" guy. Jim, on the other hand, was very open with me. No topic was off limits. George, at times, could be superficial and perfunctory, while Jim was much the opposite.

In addition to our frequent lunches, Jim and I rode our horses over miles of dirt roads and forest trails in Chesterland. Driving his new Ford pickup along some back country road, he'd see a sign: "Fresh Baked Pies," and he'd stop and buy one. With a slice of warm pie in hand, he'd look at me and break into a broad grin, the space between his two front teeth dark with berries. With blue eyes twinkling he would exclaim, "This is the life, huh? Goin' on down the road eatin' warm pie. We sure have us some good times don't we?" Jim loved the simple pleasures. Unlike George, the less cluttered, uncomplicated and straight-forward things were, the better Jim liked it. I enjoyed his company and was flattered by his respect for my judgment. When things got especially bad between Marye and me, Jim became the one to whom I confessed. Though he rarely had any answers, he never made any judgements. It was good to be able to air my problems with someone I could trust. What Jim lacked in education and worldliness, he made up by being constant and in all ways, genuine. At times, George might bluff with his "no problem" responses, but Jim didn't even know how.

The pilots' voice on the PA startled me. I looked out the window and saw the flaps moving out from the trailing edge of the wing. George's eyes popped open and he was totally awake, a residual from his flight crew days in Air Corps bombers. He looked at his watch, "Gosh, this is some airplane. We're in Denver in less than three hours."

I smiled. "Sure as hell beats your old Liberator, don't it?"

After lunch in Denver, we lit up and smoked in silence. I squashed the butt and looked at George intently. "You sure you want to do this?"

His eyebrows shot up. "What do you mean? We settled all of that. Sure I'm sure. What the hell do you think I'm doing sittin' here in Denver? I told you before—"

I raised my hand. "I know, I know. But I still have the feeling that this may be just a game with you. I'm worried that even if we do find a place we like, you'll be back at Thompson Products fartin' around with meters again."

"Horse shit," he hissed, mashing his cigarette furiously into the remains of a piece of black bottom pie. "We had it all out that night at Jim's house. Now, I said I would quit my job and throw in with you guys and I meant it. And please don't tell me again about all the goddamn sacrifices we're going to have to make, I know all about it!"

"Don't get your balls in an uproar," I said softly. "It's just that this means a lot to me and I don't want to get it screwed up."

"No problem."

"You're sure, absolutely sure?"

"I said, no problem and that's what I mean."

I repeated his words. "Okay. No problem." So the die seemingly, was cast, at least for the moment. George's sense of gallantry, (Yes, I think that's just the right word.) would not let him turn back now.

Out on the street, George laid his arm across my shoulders and said brightly, "Come on. Let's see if we can find something interesting to do until the plane leaves."

Late in the afternoon, we boarded a DC-3, a twenty-one passenger, twin engine, tail-dragging relic that first went into commercial service in the thirties. Out on the runway, the pilot revved up the starboard engine then shut it down and returned to the terminal. George looked out the window, beads of perspiration were accumulating on his forehead and upper lip. "There's something wrong with this son-of-a-bitch. That engine sure ain't right." He should know, he spent enough time listening to those big Pratt and Whitney engines during the war. The curtain to the cockpit parted and the stewardess, as flight attendants were called then, told us they were experiencing some *radio trouble*. George pulled out a handkerchief and wiped his face. "Radio trouble my ass."

I laughed and poked an elbow into his ribs, "You want a parachute, Sarge?"

"T'ain't funny McGee. I had my share of scary flying in the Air Corps. I'm not looking for any thrills on this trip."

The flight from Denver to Durango was a "milk run" that took about four hours. That flight now takes less than an hour. It was getting dark and we were informed that we would be flying at a higher altitude for safety reasons which, when translated, means so we don't auger into a mountain. The cabin was neither pressurized nor equipped with oxygen. As a result, we both fell asleep. I awoke as did George, when the wheels of the main gear touched the ground. A short distance later, the tail wheel settled down on Durango's single runway and we taxied to the little terminal building.

The A. A. Ball Realty agent had patiently waited to meet us, in spite of our late arrival. She kept looking at the plane as if expecting someone else to disembark but when she realized that we were the only passengers, she walked up to us and said, "Mr. Elder, Mr. Horton?"

"Are you with Ball Realty?" George asked.

"Yes. I'm Betty Jean Weinland and this is my husband, Grady." She smiled extending her hand. "Frankly, I was expecting someone a bit older."

"So were we," I said. We laughed. Betty Jean was a tall brunette. She was wearing a dress and high heeled shoes which showcased her attractive legs. Betty Jean had a pretty smile that enhanced her good-looking face and she spoke with the slightest touch of a Southern accent. She appeared to be in her late twenties. She told us that she had gone to work for Ball Realty just a short time before and we were her first clients. She no doubt felt that these two young guys dressed like cowboys would be wasting her time. Grady, short for Graden, a family name, was a jovial kind of a guy wearing a suit and tie. He was a bit shorter than Betty Jean and kind of on the "round" side.

Grady drove us to the Strater Hotel in a new Dodge sedan. The hotel had been built in the late 1800s and named after its founder, Henry Strater. Betty Jean and Grady thought we should have a drink or two after our long journey and they escorted us to "The Diamond Belle Saloon" where a young man dressed in period attire was playing ragtime tunes on a rinky tink upright piano. The bar room décor was turn of the century, or a reasonable facsimile thereof. Locals and a smattering of tourists were sitting around drinking and talking but no one seemed to be paying the slightest attention to the piano player who, despite the indifference, hammered out his ragtime selections.

We sat in the back of the room and ordered drinks from a scantily garbed cocktail waitress. Grady warned us that since the local elevation was 6,500 feet, alcohol would have a profound effect on us. He told us that it might take a few days for us to get acclimated to the high altitude and the very low humidity. He advised us to drink plenty of water and to be careful out in the sun as the combination of altitude and very clear air increased the chance of sunburn. I was a guy who could drink a half a bottle of Old Forester in an evening, but halfway through my second bourbon and ginger ale, I started feeling light headed. Consequently, I probably didn't give my best attention to Betty Jean, who was telling us about the three properties she planned to show us over the next few days.

It was after midnight when we finally fell into our beds in a third floor room with a high ceiling, ancient furniture and a transom over the door (a little window that could be opened for ventilation). The room rate was $3.50 a night! It was, we were told, one of the "modern" rooms with a bathroom. The $2.00 rooms, the clerk explained, did not have bathrooms and were not so deluxe. In case you are wondering about the rooms without bathrooms, no, you didn't use a chamber pot; you used the bathroom at the end of the hall. If you don't know the term, *chamber pot*, look it up.

CHAPTER SEVEN

If music be the fruit of love . . . stop playing!

The piercing shriek of a train whistle woke us. A vintage narrow gauge locomotive was backing up to couple with a line of wood-sided coach cars. Thick black smoke billowed from the little engine's high stack while white steam curled around its wheels. It was as if we had been transported back to 1880. This train appeared a few years before in the movie, *Around the World in Eighty Days* and would later have a role in *Butch Cassidy and the Sundance Kid*.

Betty Jean picked us up in her Dodge and after riding for more than an hour, we arrived at the Red Ryder Ranch east of Pagosa Springs. The place was located on a dirt road that led to the Blanco Basin. Neither owner Fred Harmon, author of the *Red Ryder* comic strip, nor anyone else was there to show us around. The price, Betty Jean informed us, was $65,000 for 300 acres and the well-maintained and attractive buildings. After a brief look-see, we concluded that it wouldn't be suitable for a dude ranch. How did we come to that decision? Damned if I know. It was much like the guy who, in the process of buying a new car, looks under the hood to evaluate the engine. He hasn't the slightest idea what he's looking at, but nonetheless, believes he is able to make a definitive judgment.

During the drive back, we determined that we needed to be reasonably close to Durango because it had air service, and the narrow gauge train, and Mesa Verde National Park was only 40 miles away. Pagosa Springs, on the other hand, had nothing much to offer tourists and it wasn't all that easy to get to. Moreover, the bubbling natural hot springs made the town smell like a giant leach field gone bad. Consequently, without further investigation, we convinced ourselves that as a prerequisite, the location must be close to Durango. That, my friend, is how we conducted our market research.

The following day, we headed north on Route 550 to see the Columbine Ranch. The Animas Valley was populated with cattle ranches and small farms where second cut hay was being mowed and raked into windrows. From the high mountains to the valley floor, the Rio de Las Animas Perdidos (River of Lost Souls) traveled a twisting route. Gaining elevation, we saw aspen trees turning from summer green to fall yellow. The Twilight Peaks, Engineer and Spud Mountains towered into the clear blue sky revealing their bald tops above the timberline. I had never seen anything quite so impressive and dramatic. My Bolex movie camera ran out of film before we were half way to our destination.

The 180 acre Columbine Ranch was about twenty miles north of Durango and at first glance we knew it wasn't what we were looking for. The disappointment on Betty Jean's face was unmistakable when, after a hasty look, we said we had seen enough. The owners were asking $65,000 but we were too unenlightened (dumb may better a better word) to realize that even that was more than we could afford.

That evening we ate at *The Western Steak House.* George had the steak dinner with a beverage and dessert, for $1.10, while I had a big bowl of chop suey for sixty-five cents. That's right, chop suey at the *Western Steak*

House. The place was owned by a Chinese guy named Woodrow Wong. Several of the cooks were relatives, hence a menu that included Chinese food along with Mexican dishes and typical cowboy fare. We left a two bit (25 cent) tip. Most folks would have left a dime, but not us; we were big time ranchers!

We went back to the Belle after dinner and sat around sucking up local flavor. It was an odd mix of people, most of whom were men. Some wore business suits and ties and there were cowboys dressed in blue jeans, broad-brimmed hats and boots. Two Indians moved from table to table, trying to sell their handmade bracelets, rings and other jewelry. Another old Indian had a load of fine Navajo saddle blankets he was trying to sell for eight bucks each. (Similar blankets sell for several hundred dollars now.)

Captain John, the piano player, finished the ragtime tune he had been beating to death on the old upright, swiveled around and said he was going to take a break and would be back in twenty minutes, not that anybody gave a damn. George gave me a nudge and said I should play. I shrugged it off, but he kept insisting. Then he stood up and addressed the crowd, "You folks wanna hear some real good piano playin'?" They started clapping and carrying on. George told them, "My friend Dick here sure can play. Go on Dick, get on up there and entertain these people."

I got up on the little stage, sat down and tried a few runs to get the feel of the keyboard. I played one song and got a nice hand and was just getting into my second when Captain John came trotting up to the piano yelling, "Hey you. Get the hell off of there!"

I stood up and was just about to jump off the stage when a fellow in a suit sitting with a group by the window jumped to his feet and yelled, "Go on John. Let the guy play. He's good." This outburst elicited a lot of laughter, further displeasing Captain John. "C'mon, get down." he growled. "You ain't gonna be playin' no more, so get the hell off of there." Then for emphasis he added, "Get me?"

"Fine." I said, jumping down and returning to our table where Hap Horton was obviously loving every bit of this episode.

"Okay. If you won't let him play, I'll sure let him play," said the fellow in the suit. Turning toward the bar he yelled, "C'mon folks, everybody is welcome to come to my house. I've got a damn good piano and lots of booze." With that, he and his friends, one of which was a very attractive young gal, began walking toward the door. Well, I'll be a son-of-a-gun if about half the people in that saloon didn't get right up and follow him out. George and I couldn't believe what we were seeing. It was like an old B western movie. Then the man came back to our table and said, "C'mon boys. I ain't kiddin'. We're going to my place." He grabbed my wrist. "Come on."

"Say, pal, we don't have a car here," George told the man.

"That's okay. I'll get you a ride. By the way, my name's Larry McDaniel." We introduced ourselves and then we joined the crowd out on the street. Larry returned with a very tall stout man. "This is Fred Close. He owns French Hardware over there," said Larry McDaniel, pointing to a two story building on the other side of Main Avenue. "He'll give you a ride to my place."

Fred Close and his wife drove us to Larry McDaniel's home. Larry was busy putting out bottles of whiskey and beer. He put a box of pretzels and a half used bag of potato chips on the table, then escorted me in to something like a sun room where stood an old Chickering upright piano. I sat down and started to play. Larry listened for a minute then said, "Hey, I want you to meet my girlfriend. I'll be right back. Keep playing. I like that style."

People gathered around to listen and soon began shouting requests for songs. Suddenly, I heard yelling and swearing and then some banging like furniture was being knocked over. I was just about to go see what was going on when George came running in and said, "You won't believe what's happening in there. Larry was looking for his girlfriend, you know, that young chick that was sittin' with him at the Bell?"

"Yeah, yeah," I said impatiently. "What about it?"

"Well, it looks like Larry walked into the bedroom and found his girlfriend fooling around with some guy. He's madder then hell. Took a poke at the guy and they got into a free for all. The girl locked herself in the bathroom and won't come out. Shit, I don't blame her. I think our friend Larry would knock her block off if he could get to her. He laid a pretty good one on that guy. Knocked him right over a chair. It was pretty darn Western."

Things quieted down after awhile and the folks drifted out. Larry was embarrassed and apologized for his less than diplomatic behavior. Horton told him, "No problem."

It was quiet in the car riding back to the hotel. Fred broke the silence, "Damn shame. Larry should have known better then to tie up with that kid. Why the hell do guys do stuff like that anyway?" I was tempted to tell him why but kept my mouth shut. Fred mused, "What's he thinkin' about, especially him bein' a lawyer an all."

Now I spoke, "Larry's a lawyer? That's good to know, because we'll probably be needin' a lawyer before we leave Durango."

George looked at me and smiled. "I believe we just found one."

CHAPTER EIGHT

Some Groves are not trees.

We were back in the Dodge with Betty Jean again heading up Main Avenue. At 15th Street she turned right, crossed the narrow gauge railroad tracks then turned left and exclaimed, "Okay. Now we're on the Florida Road." She pronounced the word in Spanish as was the local custom: *Floor-ee-da.* "It's about twelve miles from here to Camp Silver Spruce. On your left is our little ice skating rink and on the right, our big ski area." She laughed, "It's just a dinky thing but it's fun in the winter and they light it up at night so it gets lots of use."

Driving on, we discussed weather conditions in the area, what the different seasons were like, was there a rainy season, how much snow and so on. The pavement suddenly ended and we found ourselves driving over a very dusty, bumpy road. Climbing a long hill, we found ourselves surrounded by a semi-dense forest of predominately pine, fir and spruce. Looking to the south from our vantage point on the high road, we could see the Florida River and just beyond, rising majestically above it, a sheer cliff, a mosaic of fall colors that resembled a gigantic patchwork quilt. George and I did our share of oohing and ahhhhing. I suspect that Betty Jean was pleased to learn that we were not total neanderthals and could appreciate nature's beauty.

We crossed an old one lane steel bridge and continued past a lovely little red house with a green roof surrounded by mammoth cottonwood trees. George thought the scene reminded him of an old-fashioned calendar picture. A few hundred yards farther we passed a large metal barn and a log cabin. Betty Jean explained that this was the old "Pillow place," whoever Pillow was. The log cabin, she told us, was the original homestead cabin built around 1885.

The narrow dirt road curved through the bottomland, then crossed another narrow bridge that appeared to be older than the first with a surface made of thick wooden planks that rattled as we drove across. Leaving the bridge, we drove along a stretch of road with high rocky walls to our left and the river to our right. The road was very narrow here and I wondered what might happen if a car came around one of the curves. I reasoned that one of us would either be in the river or up on the rocks. As it turned out, no other cars were on the road that morning.

We passed the Flood Ranch with its fields of hay and oats tucked between little hills that extended southward to distant high cliffs. The Spear A Ranch was next with its long pastures sandwiched between the Florida River and the road on which we were traveling. Rounding a bend, Betty Jean pointed to a log cabin on our left. "That's what's left of the old Coney Cove Dance Hall. The Conway's built it oh, somewhere around the time of the First World War. They built it to use as a dance hall and for making moonshine whiskey because Colorado had prohibition back then. The Conway boys figured a dance hall way out here would be a good safe place to sell whiskey." She chuckled, "The reason they got away with it was because most of the deputies loved to come out here to dance and have a good time. They weren't about to shut it down. Y'all talk to some of the old timers in town, they'll tell you all about Coney Cove and the good times they had up here. Well, here we are."

Turning, we saw a lopsided wooden sign straddling the drive that proclaimed, *Camp Silver Spruce*. One side of the sign was attached to a large post while the other was nailed into an immense pine tree which explained why one side of the sign was considerably higher than the other. George got us laughing when he said, "Too bad they didn't water that post more. Maybe that sign would have stayed level." We were still laughing when Mrs. Groves and her son Bill walked up to the car.

Betty Jean started to open her door but Mrs. Groves laid her hand on it and in a not too pleasant voice said, "Hold on Miz Weinland. Don't bother gettin' out. We're not selling the camp!"

Betty Jean blinked then almost shouted, "What?"

Mable Groves was a woman of about sixty, maybe older, with gray hair and a medium build, perhaps five-feet six inches tall. She spoke in a commanding voice. She seemed to be the type of woman who was used to giving orders and having them obeyed. "You heard what I said, Miz Weinland. We are not going to sell the camp." She said each word slowly to make certain that we would understand her intent.

George and I looked at each other. Betty Jean spoke, "I don't know what to say . . . I mean, I had it all arranged with Bill here and . . ."

Bill Groves was a tall, good-looking guy in his thirties. He spoke slowly with a trace of a Texas accent when he popped his head in the window and said in a low voice, "Y'all get outta the car. We'll get this fixed up pronto. C'mon. C'mon boys, y'all just hop on outta there and I'll show you 'round."

Mrs. Groves had her hand on the car door again. "We ain't showin' nobody nothin'. I told you Bill, when you first told me about this hare-brained idea of yours that I wasn't gonna let you do it."

"Now, Mama, just settle down. It won't do no harm to show these folks around. They've come all the way from Ohio just to see the camp."

Betty Jean jumped right in with, "That's right Mrs. Groves. These gentlemen came all the way from Cleveland, Ohio to look at your camp. Bill and I had talked all of this over weeks ago and he told me that y'all were interested in selling the camp. I sure wouldn't have brought these gentlemen out here if I knew y'all weren't interested in selling."

George and I got out of the car and stood there like a couple of dummies, not sure what to do, while Mrs. Groves and son were going at it big time. Bill was reminding his mother that his idea was to sell the old camp and then build a new camp on land they owned across the road, but Mom Groves remained adamant. She said that if he sold the camp he wouldn't build anything anywhere. It was getting downright embarrassing for us, especially since she spoke to her full grown son like he was a juvenile. After awhile, Mrs. Groves broke off the argument and walked over to where the three of us were standing. "Look here," she said in a somewhat more conciliatory tone, "We ain't gonna sell this camp. You heard me tell him that didn't ya?" We shook our heads in the affirmative. "Tell ya what. I'll let ya have a look at the Coney Cove propity 'cross the road there. That should make ya a good place ta build ya a dude ranch. Besides, this place was built to be a boy's camp. I don't think it do for a decent dude outfit anyway. Don'tcha reckon folks would be wantin' somethin' better'n this?" She made a large sweep with her arm, indicating the buildings scattered about.

Glancing around, we could see the place wasn't too elegant. In fact, it was a tumble down bunch of buildings. I said, "Sure, we can do that. We can take a look. We're here anyway, might as well."

Betty Jean was very much into it now. I believe she

thought her first big commission was sailing down the river, but now her prospects were looking up again. She was smiling and so was George.

Bill shook his head and looked very sad. "Mother, [not Mama this time] if we sell that property, I won't be able to build my new camp."

Mrs. Groves shot right back with, "And that's exactly why I wanna sell it. Once it's gone, you kin concentrate on what your Daddy left ya. There's a big plenty kin be done right here. If ya want somethin' better, git after it! Ain't no need to be goin' 'cross the road ta do it. Besides, there ain't no river on that side and the camp needs a river for fishing and floating and what have ya. So, just take these here folks 'cross the road and show 'em 'round."

With Bill reluctantly leading the way, we crossed the Florida Road and took a walk of a mile or more to what Bill *thought* was the northern boundary line of their property. North of that point, Bill explained, was United States Forest Service land, about a million or more acres of it. There was so much to see and admire, we simply couldn't take it all in. Shearer Creek ran the length of the valley. On either side were beautiful walls of rock covered with vegetation of all kinds. And the trees! Good God, thousands of them! It was spectacular! Being in that valley was like a journey into some remote and unknown place. Were we impressed? Hell yes, we were.

When we returned, Mrs. Groves and Betty Jean were standing next to an old pole corral behind Coney Cove. Mrs. Groves seemed a bit more relaxed.

"How may acres have you got here?" I asked Mrs. Groves.

"Three hundred and fifty, give or take and we want $35,000 for it. That's a hundred dollars an acre." She did the math for me.

"No, Mama. It's over four hundred acres." That remark from Bill started a brand new argument that lasted ten minutes. Each one was telling the other why they were so positive about the total acreage.

Finally, realizing this show could go on until sundown I said, "Okay, okay. How about this? Suppose we were to buy whatever it is you own on the north side of the road for $35,000, but if it turns out to be less than say, three hundred and twenty five acres, we'll renegotiate the price." The Groves chewed on that for awhile, then Mama agreed. I remarked that we wanted to have a good look at the entire property before we signed anything and asked if they knew where we could rent a couple of horses. Bill gave us the name of the owners of the Spear A Ranch, located about a half-mile to the west.

We advised the Groves that we would check on the horses on the way back to town and if they would rent us two, we'd come back the next day and ride the property then give them a yes or no. Bill said that he would show us a way to ride up to the top of the high ridge that lay just south of the river and from there we could see the entire property all the way back to the National Forest. I liked that idea, so we agreed that after we got the horses we would meet him.

At the Spear A Ranch, Mrs. Delany agreed to rent a couple of horses for two dollars an hour. Driving back to town, Betty Jean Weinland was a happy camper. She said that maybe we were in luck after all, because having a beautiful piece of land that backed right up to the San Juan National Forest, might be better than buying a place with buildings. With just land, she concluded, we could build exactly what we wanted. While George and I agreed with her concept, a little voice in my head kept reminding me that without exception, everyone with whom we had consulted had cautioned us to buy an established ranch with a good earnings record and a solid client base.

BETTY JEAN ARRIVED THE NEXT MORNING WEARING SLACKS and walking shoes instead of her customary dress and high heels, and drove us to Camp Silver Spruce where we picked up Bill Groves and traveled the short distance to the Spear A Ranch. Emma Lou Delany explained that her husband, Weldon, was out "checking cows" but he had saddled a couple of horses for us and they were tied up at the hitch rail next to the barn. After telling us where we were to meet, Betty Jean and Bill took off. George and I walked down to the barn and there we saw a pregnant chestnut mare that I guessed to be in her tenth month, (Mares carry for twelve months.) and a mustang-looking little dark bay gelding. We checked our cinches, put on the bridles, mounted the horses and started up the drive. The pregnant mare was huffing and puffing before we ever got to the cattle guard at the road. There was a wire gate off to one side of the cattle guard and George stepped off his mare to open it. My little bronc decided that he couldn't wait for no damn gates, so he took a big leap and we cleared that darn cattle guard by a good two feet. That little infraction took me by surprise, but I stayed with him and held him from running off by riding around in circles until George had fastened the wire gate and remounted.

I had been scribbling notes about our trip in a little spiral notebook and this is some of what I wrote that day:

We turned south on the Texas Creek Road which wound its way up the mountain behind Silver Spruce Camp (across from Coney Cove). It was a pretty steep climb and by the time we got to the place where Betty and Bill met us, my horse began to settle down. It's hard to describe it but the path from this point up was nothing but good size rocks. Actually there was no trail.

Bill and Betty started climbing on foot and had to

stop often. The horses however, stepping on, over and in between rocks, brush and down timber, made it up with only one stop for rest. About half way up, we had to get off and reset our saddles. Mine had slipped back a good nine inches. At the top we tied up and took pictures. What a view! We could see the entire property. It was just like looking at a map. We also could see the mesas (flat areas) that Bill described to us yesterday.

Back on horses again and down the slope. At one point Hap's horse's hind feet hit a big flat stone and the horse skidded on her tail a good ten feet. Hap said his feet were dragging on the ground. We rode down to the Florida Road and over to Coney Cove. Everytime a car passed us, my horse either climbed a hill or jumped into the bar ditch. Hap sure laughed. I didn't.

We rode up into the meadow just north of the barn when the rain hit. You have no warning as the sun keeps on shining and the sky appears to be clear. The rain stopped as suddenly as it had started so we rode on about a mile when it started to rain again, so we ducked under a huge pine tree. The west mesa proved to be much larger than we expected and could grow a lot of hay etc. Back at Coney Cove, Bill said we had brought them good luck because this was their first rain since June.

We rode the horses back down to Delany's place. My little bronc was plumb tired and didn't feel like doing any acrobatics over the cattle guard. As we were pulling the saddles off the horses, Weldon Delany came strolling down from the house. "How'd you boys make out?" I tried to figure out the accent.

"These heah ponies do ya a good job? I'm Weldon Delany." He offered his hand as we introduced ourselves. "C'mon in and have ya some coffee or maybe you'd like a cold beer."

Betty Jean pulled in the drive just then and pointing to her car I said, "Sure would like to Weldon, but here comes our ride to town and we'd better not keep her waiting."

"By God, she's a looker, that's fer sure. Ah,'scuse me. Sure didn't mean nothin' by that, ah, all I mean is a she's a, a right fine lookin' lady. That one of y'alls wife?" Weldon said in a half whisper.

"Naw." I was talking like Weldon now, "She's the real estate lady been showing us 'round."

George looked at me and smiled. He'd seen me do this thing before. I'd listen to someone speak for a minute and then be able to imitate the sound and style.

"But, since we're gonna be neighbors directly," I continued, "why I reckon you'll be seein' a whole lot more of us then maybe you care to."

"That'd be fine. Y'all come by anytime. The latch string'll be out."

"Where you from Weldon?" George asked.

"Pahuska, Oklahoma."

We got into the car and George said, "Interesting sort of a guy, wasn't he."

I chuckled, "Yeah, by God. He sure 'nuff is."

CHAPTER NINE

A fool and his money are soon parted.

At the livestock auction in Durango, we learned that 7 to 15 year-old ranch horses were selling for $65 to $125. We chatted with the local forest ranger, called on the postmaster who assigned Box 363 for our mail, and talked with Jim Bodine, a building contractor. I believe one could conceivably call that research.

That evening, George and I talked about the Coney Cove property. We discussed how we would go about developing the ranch, where the buildings could be situated, the best place for the corrals and so on. We talked into the late hours, becoming more excited as we explored each new twist and turn. George was hooked on the idea now. We agreed to make an offer on the property. Even if we couldn't raise sufficient money to build the ranch right away, we would at least have the land, and that would be a good start.

The next morning, along with Betty Jean Weinland, who had given up on the fancy dress altogether, we drove back to the camp for a chat with Mrs. Groves and Bill. We told them we were interested in buying the land and agreed that we would pay $35,000 for all the land they owned north of the Florida road. The way the offer was written, it allowed us to renegotiate the price downward if the total acreage was less than 325. Interestingly, no provision was made should the parcel have more than 350 acres. An earnest money deposit of $5,000 was to accompany our offer and the balance was to be paid in annual installments of $5,000 plus six percent interest on the unpaid balance. The Groves required two other provisions: In the event we ever operated a camp for boys or girls, the land and improvements would revert back to them. They also reserved for themselves, one half of the mineral rights. We didn't want to run a kids camp, so that was no problem, and we agreed to the mineral rights reservation. The simple truth is, we didn't know squat about mineral rights. I guess we assumed that the word *minerals* meant gold or lead or something like that. It would have been very helpful to know that mineral rights included oil and natural gas. Our *market research* and Betty Jean failed to provide that information.

Amazingly enough, Mrs. Groves accepted our offer. I wrote a check payable to Camp Silver Spruce, Inc. for the earnest money deposit and handed it to her. Betty Jean gave Mrs. Groves and me a copy of the agreement. She kept the original. We all shook hands, congratulated each other and after ten minutes of small talk, we departed.

Betty Jean was busting to tell Lawrence Hickman, the owner/broker, about her big sale. In the office, Mr. Hickman seemed very pleased and he showered her with praise. He then carefully read the purchase agreement and asked if Mrs. Groves had shown it to her attorney before signing it. Betty Jean related what had transpired, including her observation that Mrs. Groves seemed to be in a big hurry to close the deal and get our check. Hickman had concerns about some of the legal details and decided to check it out at the court house. He seemed especially concerned that Mrs. Groves had not shown the agreement to her lawyer.

At the Sage café, Betty Jean stopped to talk to several

men, one of whom was Barney Spaulding, a general contractor who had moved to Durango from someplace in Texas. While she didn't know much about him, she had heard that he did good work.

Barney was drinking coffee with two men, both wearing carpenters' overalls. He looked to be about forty or so, and had a pleasant suntanned face with a wide smile.

Betty Jean slid out of her seat, walked over to Barney's booth and said something to him. Returning, she told us that she had asked Barney to stop by our table before he left, which he did. After introductions, we explained what we wanted to build. He said he had a lot of experience building all kinds of things in Texas. His quiet southern voice was building with enthusiasm with each new sentence as he told us that he would be *very* interested in working with us. We talked a while longer and asked him if he would like to come out and have a look at the "Ranch." He said he would be more than happy to meet anytime. He handed his card to George and left.

Upon our return to the office, Lawrence Hickman told us that he had looked up the Coney Cove parcel north of the Florida Road and discovered that it contained 458 acres, more or less. He repeated the number emphasizing the four. That, Hickman told us, was not even close to the 350 acres stated in the Purchase Agreement. About that same time, as I later learned, Mrs. Groves was having a meeting with her attorney, Howell Cobb, who also checked the plat and told her that she was off by 100 acres. He also wanted to know why she failed to show him the agreement before signing it.

As we were about to leave the real estate office, Hickman received a call from Howell Cobb. They discussed the discrepancy in the acreage and Cobb told Hickman that the deal would have to be renegotiated because Mrs. Groves insisted on another $10,000. Hickman relayed the message and asked us what we wanted to do. I said that we would have to think about it, as we had not planned to spend that much money for land. George agreed that we should put the deal on hold.

Back we went to Camp Silver Spruce. I told Bill and his mother that we were not interested in the deal if they had to have an additional $10,000. Mrs. Groves looked at me unblinking but said nothing. I broke the silence. "So, I guess I'll just take my check back and we'll put everything on hold for a while, okay?" Mrs. Groves didn't answer. We stood there, looking at one another like a couple of mutes. At length, she told me that she didn't have our check.

"You don't have our check? Whadda you mean? Are you saying you just don't have the check here or—"

"No! I don't have it 'cause I went and cashed it. That's how come I don't have it. That's simple enough, ain't it?"

"You cashed our check then?"

"That's what I just said, didn't I? I took it to the Burns Bank yesterday before I went to see Cobb; he's my lawyer. I wanted to find out if it would be good so I had 'em call your bank in Ohio to find out, you know, if it would cash out all right. Well, your bank said it was a good check so I just went ahead and deposited it."

She started to walk away. I said, "Now, wait just a minute. If you endorsed that check and deposited it in your account, it means you accepted our offer. You can ask your lawyer. He'll tell you that once you endorsed that check and cashed it, well, that showed that you accepted our offer."

A heated conversation ensued. Mrs. Groves was one mad son-of-a gun. I assured her that the three elements of a legal contract had been satisfied: offer, acceptance and consideration. (After all, I had taken business law at Ohio State.)

Dropping the *western* accent I had affected, I spoke in a very calm and conciliatory voice, "Look Mrs. Groves, we can make this deal stick. I think your lawyer will tell you the same, but neither George nor I want to start off out here on the wrong foot, especially with you folks as our neighbors. So I'll just let you make the decision to either go ahead with our deal or return the money and forget the whole thing. I can tell you right now that we can't afford to spend $45,000 for land. The truth is, we decided before we even came out here that we would not allocate more than $25,000 for raw land. [I made that up.] So we're definitely stretching our budget to go the thirty-five. You think about it and let Mrs. Weinland know what you want to do. We'll be in town a few more days, so before we go you can return our deposit or agree to the terms of our contract. Okay?"

George looked at me with admiration. He had just witnessed a beautiful piece of diplomacy or maybe it was just excellent acting. Betty Jean had tears in her eyes. Perhaps she thought her big sale was saved after all. Mrs. Groves blinked. The next day we learned that the Groves had agreed to the original contract price.

Hap Horton and I bought 458 acres with a log cabin and a barn for $35,000. Later, we discovered that the ranch actually had at least 500 and maybe as many as 600 acres. We were never totally certain, as no ground survey of the entire property was ever made. Additionally, it was never totally clear where our northern boundary line was located. Neither we nor the U.S. Forest Service had the desire to incur the expense of an extensive survey.

Now that we had the land, the rest would be easy. Well, that's what we thought anyway. All we needed to do was build some buildings, get a string of horses, find a good source of water, and launch operations. Heck, we were as good as there. Unfortunately, I think that in our euphoria we forgot one other extremely important item: Money!

CHAPTER TEN

Show me the money!

eorge and I met contractor Barney Spaulding at the ranch. We discussed all sorts of things with him and he gave us a lot of ideas.

For example, he told us that since local coal sold for just $6.00 a ton, we would be wise to consider using it instead of propane to heat the building. Observing a huge rock slide, he suggested incorporating rock into our building plans. After selecting a site for the main building, we started looking for cabin locations and found some beauties.

Barney said he would work up some preliminary drawings so we would have something to submit to a bank for loan purposes. After spending several hours with him, George and I agreed that he seemed to have "a lot on the ball."

I made some notes of our meeting that morning concluding with:

> . . . *every time you are near the creek you smell the most fragrant aroma . . . very hard to describe. The three of us talked about everything from rough sawed siding to door lintels, fireplace treatment and central heating. Small game darted here and there all over the place and we did see fish in the stream. One thing that*

really tickled us was when ol' Barney said just as earnest as could be, "If you fellas didn't pay over $100,000 for the land, you did all right." Hap and I just looked at each other.

That evening, over dinner George and I rehashed the days events and tried to get serious about finances. Quoting from my notes:

Financing could be a rough problem which would require some very deep consideration. However, we would cross that bridge as we came to it with as much beforehand preparation as possible. Regardless of whether we build the [dude] ranch or not, this property is probably the best investment we will ever make.

That last line was prophetic! Though much of what we talked about was, in reality, pure nonsense, speculation and wishful thinking, my prediction regarding the land proved to be right on the money.

Before we left Durango, George and I did a lot of running around to check on as many things as we could think of. We called on John Murphy at the REA (Rural Electric Association) to inquire about electric service, the cost to put in the poles and so forth. Since financing was much on our minds, Betty Jean offered to introduce us to Mr. Stalons, Chairman of the Board of the Burns National Bank. My notes of that meeting state:

Beautiful bank—very modern and plush, ol (sic) boy says he bought it [the bank] for his daughter and son in law to fool with. Mr. Stalons is a very nice, straight talking man who is very interested in our project and said "it is needed"—without getting into specifics he thought he'd have no trouble [arranging a loan]. We must submit our plans to him & he'll let us know what can be done. We talked for about ¾ of an hour and both of us were very encouraged—at least he did not take a negative attitude.

This is the final entry in spiral notebook #2 made during our flight to Ohio:

One thing Geo & I both agree on is that we will probably never again spend such a wonderful & eventful week. We're approaching Cleve, but our hearts & thoughts are in Durango. A week ago we were strangers in town and now we feel very much a part of it. The mountains, the sky, the wonderful people and The Head Ranch are calling us back. RDE—Sept. 18, 1960.

The HEAD Ranch? That's what we were calling it. **H**orton, **E**lder **A**nd **D**odson. Pretty ingenious, huh?

DONNIE, MARYE AND THE DODSONS MET US AT THE AIRPORT eager to hear every detail. We assembled that evening at the Horton home and George and I took turns reading from the spiral notebooks. We tried to recount the flavor of the area and describe the schools, churches, stores, homes, and countryside.

The movies I had taken helped to convince them that the land we had purchased was not only a great property on which to build a dude ranch, but the price we paid made the deal fantastic. I showed them scenes of the Narrow Gauge Train, the First Presbyterian Church on Third Avenue, plus pictures of elementary schools, the junior high and the high school. We went to a local horse show and I filmed that too. The interesting thing about that horse show was the poor quality of horsemanship. Being a horse show judge, I could be blamed for being overly critical, but George saw it as well. Of course, there were many scenes of the ranch, including some of Barney Spaulding standing in front of his green Ford pickup talking to George. The images that seemed to interest our wives and the Dodsons most were those I took of possible locations for the guest cabins and the main building which we were calling "The Lodge." It was my impression that everyone was wildly enthusiastic about the project.

Since we had purchased the land in our individual names, it was necessary to transfer the title from Horton and Elder to a new company. My uncle, Harry Elder, was an attorney who, with Larry McDaniel, worked on the transfer of ownership to the yet unnamed corporation. We hadn't decided on a name, although we had tossed around about a dozen. At that time, the name *de jour* was, "The Head Ranch." We thought it was such a clever name but most folks we tried it on were not impressed, so we abandoned it. Other names we considered were: Ho-El-Do Ranch, Coney Cove Ranch, B. R. Guest Ranch, Mountain Valley Ranch, Shearer Creek Ranch and others. In the end it was my little daughter, Laurie, who suggested the name we adopted. Here's how that came about: One evening, my family was sitting around listening to the Norman Lubboff Choir singing, "The Colorado Trail." It was one of a dozen or so tunes on a record album entitled, "Songs of the Old West." Five-year old Laurie suddenly popped up with, "Why don't you name the ranch after that song?" At our next meeting, the three families officially named the ranch, "Colorado Trails Ranch," and our theme became, *The Colorado Trail.*

When I told my brother Bob and my parents what we planned to do, my dad said that I was "nuts." Of course, I was. We all were. Who could argue with that? However, the important thing is that we didn't *know* we were nuts.

I remember a conversation I had with my father in his office one afternoon. He was tilted back in his chair with one foot propped up on the bottom drawer of his desk. The corner of that drawer was worn down from years of abuse from his right shoe. He had his ever-present Cuban cigar (They were legal back then.) clamped between his molars and he pursued the conversation without ever removing it. Every few minutes, he would spin the wheel of his Dunhill lighter and apply fire to the charcoal end of the cigar, take a few puffs and talk some more while the cigar, unattended, went out. Frequently, the ash would grow long and drop onto his shirt. It's just a guess, but he probably lit and re-lit each cigar a hundred times. Meanwhile, the end of the cigar he held in his mouth would be chewed to a pulp. It's no wonder he only lived to be seventy-three. Well that, plus he didn't eat his vegetables.

I diligently explained to my father exactly what we planned to do and how we planned to do it. Lighting the cigar and talking at the same time, Dad said, "You can't make a living being open only a few months out of the year. That's nuts." There's that word again. "You'd have to have a hundred people a week to even begin to make any money and you know Dick, that's not being very realistic, is it? In fact, your whole plan is nothing more than a lot of speculation. You think you'll do this and you think you'll get that and it's a whole lot of what you think is going to happen. It's all wishful thinking and that's a lousy way to plan for a new business. Wouldn't it be better if you could say, I know instead of I think?" He actually took the cigar out of his mouth, which alerted me that he was about to say something *really* important. "I'd feel a whole lot better about all of this if you could tell me that you know where the money is going to come from. You know, how you will advertise for people, and maybe most important of all, that you know something about the dude ranch business besides horses."

Of course he was right, but that's the trouble with fathers. They're damn near always right and when things go wrong, they can say, "See, I told you so." To his credit, one thing my Dad never did after I became an adult was tell me to do or not do something that would have a profound effect on my personal life. He might give me some advice but he wouldn't say do this or don't do that.

One time he told me, "When you give someone more than advice, actually tell them what they should do, then you are responsible for the outcome." So even though he said I was nuts, he never said, "Don't do it!"

The families held a meeting on November 20 and another on the 26th at Horton's house. Here's a synopsis: I presided and Twila Dodson took the minutes. I said that we would need about $100,000 to get the ranch built and ready for guests. We had been assured $45,000 from the three families. We had been promised $15,000 to $20,000 from potential investors, leaving about $40,000 we still needed.

Stating that during the winter the men can get jobs in the city [like Durango was a city], *George suggested pooling all wages.*

We were advocating communism which, in the 1960s, was not something an American would be inclined to do. The minutes prove it:

Regardless of money invested, all investors [the three families] *are to have equal say-so in all affairs of the business.*

The plan was totally sophomoric (not to mention unrealistic,) yet I was totally for the concept. This, in spite of the fact that I was putting up most of the money!

The November 26 meeting refers to me as, "Acting Chairman." During this meeting, we discussed what vehicles the ranch would require. I find the following downright amusing if not imbecilic:

Dick Elder presented facts on possible purchase of a bus from the GM Truck Division which accommodates 42 people. For this bus, which Dick described as being in good condition, the asking price is $825.

We had not even begun to build the ranch nor did we have any idea where the money would come from, and we were seriously talking about buying a 42-passenger bus that we would not need for at least several years. Was my Dad wrong when he said I was nuts?

Additionally, the minutes describe my meeting with David Englehorn, an architectural student I met at Ohio State University.

This architect is going to work on a plan [for the lodge building] *and will work on a cost plus basis to a maximum of $1,000. We agreed to have Dave draw up plans. George reminded us that we needed to agree upon a completion date for the building and Dick reminded the group that Barney would like to get started right after the spring thaw in early April.*

Does it strike you that we were putting the cart before the horse? We were contemplating beginning construction in early 1961 and yet we did not begin to have sufficient funds to complete the job. Furthermore, we had no idea where we would find the money, except that Mr. Stalons of the Burns Bank had told us that he didn't think there would be a problem getting a loan once we submitted construction plans. There's that word *think* again.

I love the final sentence of the minutes, as it highlights the genuine good feeling we had toward one another.

After having drawn names [for gift giving] *and discussing plans for Christmas, the meeting was adjourned at 11:30 P. M.*

The next meeting was held on January 3, 1961. We spent much of the meeting discussing the purchase of a large truck and what kind of a pickup we should buy, yet no one ever mentioned anything about MONEY! Absolutely nothing was said about acquiring additional investors or what happened with those persons who had made promises to invest. There is just a brief line stating that, "We have received a letter from C. L. Hickman regarding insurance loans and he will try to set up a meeting with Jefferson Standard Insurance Co." There is over a page of notes devoted to vehicles and a short paragraph about Dave Englehorn's plans for the lodge. We talked about insurance, approved Larry McDaniel's bill for legal services in the amount $186.65, noted a letter from Fred Close, regarding sources for refrigeration equipment, and a line that I was to meet with the S. S. Kress Company to discuss kitchen planning. Amazingly, there was not a single sentence devoted to the subject of how we were going to finance the building of a dude ranch.

My uncle Harry had put in many hours doing legal work for us, which is why I had to laugh as I read the final paragraph of those minutes:

A discussion followed regarding payment of Harry Elder for professional services rendered. Dick explained that Harry insisted upon receiving no payment for same. It was moved by Jim Dodson that a gift, to show our appreciation, be purchased not to exceed $50. Seconded by Mary (sic) Elder and unanimously passed.

Fifty dollars! The man did several thousand dollars worth of legal work and our gift to him was not to exceed fifty dollars. Well, at least you can't say we weren't frugal.

CHAPTER ELEVEN

Heading into the sunset.

We met at the Dodson's house on February 15, 1961. I explained my meeting at the Institutional Equipment Company where I was advised that they would design a kitchen layout for around $50 to $75. Jim said that he had found a 1957 GMC four-wheel drive van (similar to a SUV) for around $1,000 and he brought us up to date on his meat cutting training. George told us that he had located a 1957 International two-ton truck priced at $1,400 with an enclosed box that he thought would be perfect for hauling furniture to Durango. We decided to buy both vehicles. Marye said she met with a woman who gave her pointers on managing a commercial kitchen.

There is a short paragraph in the minutes stating that the three men had been talking to prospective investors, but none had committed to buying stock. Nothing in the minutes suggests that we had any solid prospects for obtaining money, either invested or borrowed. Regardless, the last paragraph states:

The meeting was concluded after setting a tentative date of departure [for a trip to Durango by George, Jim, and me] *for the week of February 17th at an approximate cost of $200 for each man.*

On Saturday, February 18, we had a sale at my house combining all the stuff the three families were not going to take to Durango. The "Garage Sale" concept was unknown back then, so the sale was advertised as an auction. We hired Ed Kempf, a professional auctioneer who placed large ads in several local papers. For the Elders, it was just about a total sell-off of darn near everything we owned. We sold most of our furniture, keeping only a few chairs, three beds, and the Jensen console piano. I really couldn't part with that piano because I loved to play, plus we would have a use for it at the ranch. All of the horses were sold, except my quarter mare, *Moab Cole*, who I entrusted to Joan Seibert, one of my more dedicated young riding students. She agreed to keep the mare until I could arrange to bring the horse to Colorado. We kept the saddles, tack and other horse related supplies but sold my Circle M two-horse trailer and 1954 Buick sedan. We didn't sell our 1958 Pontiac station wagon, as we planned to use it as a ranch vehicle. The Horton and Dodson families added their goods to the sale inventory. We had a heck of a good sale, although most items sold below their true value.

A few weeks earlier, our house, which we had purchased in 1957 for $32,500, sold for $35,000. Selling most of our possessions would prove to be a mistake. The purchase of the GMC and the International were also mistakes, but minor compared to some that followed.

The following day, February 19, we loaded the International with the piano, furniture, clothes, horse equipment, tools, etc. from my place plus a refrigerator, an electric range and other household items from Dodson's home. The three of us were to drive the truck to Durango, fix up the old log cabin and get things ready for the Dodson and Elder families. George and his family would remain in Ohio and join us when we were ready to begin construction on the lodge. Precisely where everyone would live was undefined at the time, but initially we decided that the Dodsons and Elders, a total of four adults and six children, would live in the Coney Cove cabin. That ancient remnant of a dance hall had less than eight-hundred square feet of living space, and we intended to inhabit it with no less than ten living humans.

After the three of us returned with the big truck, the Elder and Dodson families planned to drive back to Durango in two vehicles. Jim would take the GMC with a U-Haul trailer and I would drive our Pontiac station wagon. Meanwhile, George would keep his job with Thompson Products. When we were ready, George would drive the International truck, loaded with doors, windows and mill work from my Uncle Ed's lumber company, while Donnie and the two boys followed in their station wagon. That was the plan.

When the truck was fully loaded and farewells had been said, the three of us drove off, heading west into the sunset. Our heavily laden, red International Harvester A-164 truck was bound for Durango, Colorado, some eighteen hundred miles away. We figured it would take us no more than three days to complete the expedition, but we were dead wrong. It took a week! That trip, with the three of us jammed into the cab, sitting on an incredibly lumpy and uncomfortable bench seat, was the worst driving experience of my life.

During our journey to Durango, Mr. Murphy's Law prevailed. Everything that could go wrong with that friggin' truck, did go wrong. We spent a hell of a lot of time and money in gas stations and truck repair shops. I remember being about twenty-five miles east of Garden City, Kansas when a universal joint on the drive shaft failed. We coasted off the highway on to a farm road. The motor was working fine, the clutch, which had been repaired the day before, was fine. In fact, the truck was running perfectly for the first time since the trip began. We thought that the old Binder, an affectionate name for International trucks, would make the rest of the trip without further incident. Imagine how depressing it was when we broke down again. Picture it: Three guys on the road for five days, crammed in the cab of a broken down truck, needing a shower and some bed rest, out on the Kansas plain and not a house in sight.

The western sky lit up with the setting sun. We figured we would have to spend the night right where we were, as we hadn't seen a single car since we stopped. But, I guess luck was with us, because an old pickup truck came chugging down Highway 50. The driver saw us, turned, and pulled up alongside our crippled truck.

The pickup was a half ton pre-World War II Chevy. The driver was sixty or so, with a well-worn face covered with gray stubble. A beat up straw hat was pushed back on his head revealing a shock of gray hair. His shirt (I'll never forget it) was faded blue with large white polka dots. It looked like his wife had made it from an old dress or maybe a flour sack. The old guy poked his head out of the window and in a country accent that Hollywood would kill for, exclaimed, "Howdy. Name's Leonard. You boys gottcha some trouble there?"

Jim told the man that we had a busted drive shaft and asked if he could get a tow truck in Garden City to come out and haul us to a garage.

Leonard eased out of his pickup saying, "Don't reckon y'all be needin' no tow truck. Why, ain't but twenty mile or so to Garden. I'll just tow you to a garage ma'self. Heck fire, no trouble 'tall. Glad to hep you boys out."

We looked at the man in disbelief, shifting our eyes from him to his little truck. No way was he going to be able to tow our truck with that half ton 1940 Chevy.

We told him we appreciated the offer, but we thought it would be better to get somebody with a good size tow truck to haul us to town

The man laughed, "Shit fire boys, was y'all a thinkin' I was gonna try ta pull you with this here outfit?" He chuckled, "Nah, I'll just scoot on back to my place and git n'other one. Don't you worry none. It'll pull your rig just fine." Getting back in his truck, he leaned out the window and with a big grin said, "Won't take me but a half hour at the most. Now don't y'all be a goin' nowhere 'till I git back, ya hear?" He laughed and drove off, showering us with dirt and gravel.

When the dust had settled, George looked at Jim and me, "Now ain't that something? There's a real character for ya."

After Leonard left, several cars and a few semis passed but none stopped. We sat on the front bumper smoking cigarettes, eating candy bars and Lance cheese crackers with peanut butter. We liked those crackers and fortunately, kept a good supply of them in a bag behind the seat.

Some thirty minutes later, a pickup turned off the highway and pulled up next to us. We were surprised when the driver turned out to be Leonard because the truck he was driving looked about the same as the first one.

Backing up to our truck, Leonard wrestled out a fifteen feet long chain and hooked it up. Eyeing Leonard's pick up, George said, "Gosh, I don't know about this. I mean, do you think your truck can pull us? What is it a three quarter ton?"

"Don't you worry none 'bout it. It's a thirty-five hunert [one ton] with ninety good horses and a four speed box. It'll pull y'all just fine. Let's go."

We arranged some horn signals so Leonard would know whether he needed to slow down or speed up. I was worried that if we didn't keep the chain tight and got to jerking it around, we might just pull the hitch right off his truck or worse, we could ram him. I told Leonard to take it easy. He suggested that one of us hop in the bed of his pickup and keep an eye on the tow chain to make sure it didn't go slack.

Jim jumped into the bed of Leonard's truck. George wanted me to drive. I wasn't wild about the idea, but slid behind the wheel, fired up the engine, checked the brakes and signaled for Leonard to start.

That poor old Chevy had a hell of time getting us moving. The back end kept fish-tailing as the rear wheels spun on the loose gravel, but on the blacktop, we were okay and traveling at forty. Going up the hills was hard work for that little Chevy with Leonard doing plenty of gear changing. Going down the hills was scary as hell. Several times we came darn close to banging into Leonard's outfit, but Jim did a good job, much like the guys who guided our plane in for carrier landings during the war.

I just don't have the talent to describe that trip driving fifteen feet behind that Chevy pickup, but I'll tell you this: I was covered with sweat by the time we made the garage in Garden City. I shut down the engine and just sat back. My hands ached from the tension of holding the wheel. Jim and Leonard unhooked the chain while George and I lit up a couple of his brand. I caught sight of George just staring out the windshield and said, "Hap, what the hell are we doing here anyway?"

Looking straight ahead, he took a long drag on the Lucky and slowly let the smoke roll out his mouth and nose. "I was just thinking the same thing. We must be crazy. If this is a sample of how we're gonna build the ranch," he pulled off his hat, scratched his head then shook it from side to side, "I just don't know. Ya think this gol darn truck is ever going to hold up long enough to get us there? Damn! We've spent a fortune on it already."

"I don't know. I was wondering about it myself. All I know is, it damn sure better get us to Durango." As an after thought I added, "Hell, it's got to take us back too, you know."

Jim opened the door and stuck his head in. "Well, we made it. Kinda scary there in places wasn't it? Couple times I thought sure as shootin' you was either gonna bash into us or pull that darn pickup in two." George and I said nothing. "What you guys been talkin' 'bout?"

George flipped the butt of his Lucky out the window. "Nothin,' just shootin' the shit."

We offered Leonard twenty dollars for towing us to Garden City but he refused to take it. "Tell ya what you kin do fer me. You kin give me one of them tailor mades." We all grabbed for our packs but he took just one, the Philip Morris Jim offered. After accepting a light and taking a few appreciative puffs he said, "Shit fire boys, if'n a man cain't do a good turn fer a feller what needs a favor, then piss on him. Ain't that right? One a these days, I jest might be out there on that two lane broke down an maybe you boys be a-comin' by and hep me out. I reckon it all evens out."

We invited Leonard to join us for dinner, but he declined that too. We told him that we sure would be pleased to return the favor sometime and thanked him profusely. Jim shoved a pack of Philip Morris in Leonard's shirt pocket as we said good bye. Leonard sure saved our bacon that evening but more than that, he gave us a lesson in western hospitality that I have never forgotten.

CHAPTER TWELVE

Let the games begin!

D amn near broke in spirit and money, we left
Garden City the next afternoon with a new universal joint and over a hundred dollars less in our
bank account. Driving across the plains of eastern
Colorado to I-25 was as downright dreary as traveling
Route 50 across the plains of western Kansas. We were
anticipating the next catastrophic event, but to our surprise, the International performed without incident as
we headed south and then west on Route 160 at
Walsenburg. At dusk, we began our ascent of La Veta
pass. The narrow two-lane road was incredibly steep and
barely clung to the hillside. At the top, Jim pulled into
the parking lot of a little café where we enjoyed the best
meal of the entire trip. At the summit of La Veta Pass, we
were introduced to homemade flour tortillas and delicious green chile, hot enough to start a forest fire. I've
been addicted to the stuff ever since. Generous slices of
fresh baked pie and cups of strong coffee topped off our
meal. After visiting the little outhouse behind the café,
we were ready to face the downhill drive and the next
hurdle: Wolf Creek Pass.

George took the wheel after dinner and made the drive
down the west side of the pass. That, believe it or not,
was scarier than the climb up. If George had not used the

gears just right to keep us from going too fast, he would have burned up the brakes, we would have gone over the side on one of those treacherous curves and the rest of this story would have been written on three tombstones. It wasn't very long before we saw a sign, "Wolf Creek Pass summit 12 miles." This pass wasn't as steep as La Veta, but in 1960 the narrow two lane road had more twists and turns than a pretzel. At the top, there was a place where weary truckers could check their brakes and take a little rest before the spiraling ride to the bottom. We stopped, and as if orchestrated, all three of us simultaneously reached for cigarettes.

It must have been near midnight when we got into the little town of Pagosa Springs some fifteen miles west of Wolf Creek Pass. Durango was only sixty miles away and we were getting excited. The old Binder, quite unexpectedly, was running like an eight-day clock. Though we were dog tired, we decided to finish the trip. Because of the number of long steep hills we encountered, the sixty miles to Durango took over two hours. We arrived in town about the time the sun was coming up and parked the truck in a weed-filled lot behind the Strater Hotel. It sure felt good to get the hell out of the cramped cab and to know that we had finally reached our destination.

George called Barney Spaulding to inquire about the plans for the lodge and also asked him about car rentals since we couldn't run around town in the International. Barney advised that he would have some plans to show us in a day or two. He also said we could use his old Ford station wagon. This was Jim's first encounter with Barney and he later remarked that Spaulding sure seemed like a nice guy but something of an "eager beaver." We arranged for a room on the second floor of the Strater Hotel. The room had three narrow beds, and like the other rooms on that floor, was designed to accommodate cowboys who became too drunk at the Diamond Belle to return to their outfits.

Our intention was to rent a house until we had Coney Cove ready for occupancy. At A. A. Ball Realty, Betty Jean said she had located a nice house at 2403 Columbine Avenue owned by Eugene Brooks, and after looking the place over, we agreed to rent it for $90 a month. Jim drove the Binder to the house where we unloaded all of the furniture. The last item off the truck was the piano, and while carrying it into the house, Jim hurt his back and ended up at Mercy Hospital where he spent the next three days.

George and I busied ourselves with the many details involved in the move such as electric service, telephone, propane delivery and so on. We called on our new "buddy" Larry McDaniel and asked him to help us with the fuzzy details involved in starting up a business.

The law offices of Bradford and McDaniel consisted of three rooms. Larry had one, another housed the senior partner, Byron Bradford, and their secretary, Mrs. Balliger had the third. The offices were located in the ten hundred block of Main Avenue on the top floor of a two-story building above some retail stores. Larry sat at right angles to his desk in front of an old manual typewriter where he typed the essence of our conversation using the "hunt and peck" method. Occasionally he would stop, run his tongue across his upper lip, gaze out of the window for inspiration and then type some more. It was not the most expeditious method, but like most lawyers at that time, he charged by the job and not by the hour. My recollection is that our bill for the legal work that day was probably no more than twenty-five dollars.

Finishing our session with McDaniel, we drove to the ranch, entered an unlocked Coney Cove and discovered that the toilets, water heater and bathroom sink were gone. The water pump, which had been laying on the kitchen floor, was nowhere in sight and the 250 gallon propane tank had been removed.

We walked across the road to Camp Silver Spruce hoping to find someone there who could shed some light on the whereabouts of the missing items, but the camp was deserted. George looked in a window of the recreation building and exclaimed, "Well, I'll be damned! Hey Dick, come over here. Have a look at this, will ya?"

There, in plain sight were our two toilets, water heater, and sink. "What the hell you suppose this is all about?" George pointed, "What do you bet that's our propane tank sittin' over there."

Back in town, we stopped at the real estate office and asked Lawrence Hickman what we should do about it. He advised us to call Bill Groves in Texas. We called Bill who told us that he didn't think those things were included in the sale. When I suggested that I was sure he knew that they were included, he changed his story insisting it was his mother who had the fixtures and propane tank removed. I told him that I planned to call the sheriff if he didn't return the stolen items. The next day the missing items were left on the back porch of the cabin. It was clear that Mrs. Groves suffered from what is now called, "seller's remorse" and it appeared that we were not going to be good neighbors after all.

We visited with Jim at Mercy Hospital every evening and shared what we had accomplished during the day. In three days, Jim rejoined us. Armed with some ideas from Barney Spaulding, we went to work on Coney Cove. We built a couple of walls to make bedrooms and since the building had a very high ceiling, we were able to add two more bedrooms by constructing a second floor. The cabin configuration now consisted of two small bedrooms upstairs, two more on the first floor, a kitchen, a living room/office and a bathroom with two toilets, a tub and two sinks.

There was much more work to be done before Coney Cove would be fit for occupancy. However, we heard a weather forecast advising that a large storm was on the way, so we decided to leave before the snow trapped us. The day we left, it started to snow, so rather than use the route through Kansas, and to avoid all the mountain passes, we agreed that it would be safer to head south to Farmington, New Mexico and then east on a southerly route. Naturally, we didn't think to figure out how much longer the trip would be. No, we just took off trusting the truck would hold together for another couple thousand miles. In spite of the lumpy seat and the crowded conditions, we enjoyed the sight-seeing and, without a load, the truck sailed along at a blazing fifty miles an hour. Going through Santa Fe to Interstate 40 and then on to Amarillo was uneventful. However, west of Oklahoma City something happened to the truck. I can't remember exactly what the problem was, but it must have been serious because we barely made it to the International garage. It was late in the afternoon when we arrived and the mechanics were ready to leave for the day. However, one mechanic took pity on us and said he would stay late and try to get us going.

The shop was huge with white walls and a very high ceiling. The smell of gas, diesel fuel, oil and exhaust fumes filled the room. I stretched out on a wooden bench in the shop and closed my eyes. Immediately a jumble of thoughts cascaded across my mind. Maybe this dude ranch thing wasn't such a good idea after all. A myriad of crazy thoughts put my subconscious into overdrive and I couldn't turn it off. Suddenly, I was sweating, my heart was racing. Was I having a heart attack? Great, I thought, I'm going to croak in some goddamn truck garage in Oklahoma City. I started to cry, I couldn't help it. I was going to die and never build my ranch or do anything else. Jim must have heard me. "Hey Buddy. What's the matter? You okay?"

I opened my eyes and saw Jim leaning over me, his face close to mine. "Are you alright?" I jumped up. "Sure, I'm fine. Must have had a nightmare or something.

Maybe the fumes in this damn garage got to me. Anyway, no, I'm fine." I was back to normal in a few minutes. That was my first anxiety attack. Sadly, it would not be my last.

Around noon the next day, with the repair completed, we left Oklahoma City on I-44 to St. Louis then on I-70 through Indianapolis, Columbus and Cleveland to Chesterland. What a trip! My 1957 hip injury was causing a great deal of pain throughout most of the journey, and by the time we returned, I was walking with a pronounced limp. So much for touring the country in a '57 International A-164. You may find it hard to believe, but I actually drove that truck to Durango several more times. That should further reinforce the contention that we were a bunch of lunatics. I had the seat rebuilt and made other repairs, but when all was said and done, it was still the same old red Binder. It was not, and never would be, a comfortable, smooth running, air-conditioned, seventy-five mile an hour down the freeway sport utility vehicle. No, as Leonard might have put it, not by a jug full.

CHAPTER THIRTEEN

Which Way is West?

Kent Vasko, the Hortons, members of my family and some of our friends were on hand to say farewell and wish us luck. Good luck was certainly something we were going to need and lots of. Jim, Twila and their two young boys arrived in the GMC with the remainder of their household possessions packed in a U-Haul trailer. After hugs and kisses, I pulled out of the driveway with Jim right on my tail. Durango, here we come!

I had no regrets, but I'm sure the kids and Marye had misgivings about leaving Chesterland and their friends. Truthfully, I didn't care about any of that. I was going to become a Colorado dude rancher and nothing and no one was going to stop me now. In retrospect, I must admit that it was very selfish. Everything I had done since buying *Flying Mite* was centered around horses. Everyone else lined up for my time and my affection and frankly, I gave them very little of either.

The trip west was a hell of a lot more comfortable than the previous one. I took the same route through Kansas as before, pointing out all the places we had broken down or where we ate or slept and so on. By the time we got to Garden City, the family was not interested in hearing any more of my "here's where" stories.

Wolf Creek Pass presented the only trouble we encountered. As luck would have it, the snow started falling just as we finished lunch east of the pass at a little café in South Fork. Before long the wet road became icy and snow packed. Directly in front of us, having difficulty maintaining traction, was a truck hauling a trailer load of motor boats. Suddenly, the trailer started to slide toward the ditch but the driver overcorrected and his outfit scooted plumb across the road and over the side, crashing down the steep slope. That's when I lost traction. Jim pulled up behind me, as did several other cars and trucks. We peered over the side of the hill and saw twisted pieces of boats scattered amongst the trees and the truck on its side, where it had been stopped by a large fir tree. Luckily, the driver was able to crawl out the window and climb back up to the road.

With his four-wheel drive, Jim pushed my Pontiac all the way to the summit without causing hardly any damage to my car or the Jimmy. Car bumpers were built a lot stronger back then, thank goodness and thank goodness *Ponhoss* was one hell of a driver. The trip to the bottom of the pass was tedious, but otherwise uneventful.

The drive through Pagosa Springs and the sixty-miles to Durango went by quickly and once in Durango, we drove directly to our rented home on Columbine Avenue. Twila thought the house was very nice. Actually, it was a bit more upscale than their little home on Heath Road. For Marye and my children, it was something of a let down when compared to our big home on Sperry Road.

After unpacking the cars and trailer, Jim and I went outside and sat on the front steps. Jim pulled out a pack of Philip Morris and offered me one but I declined and reached for a Camel. Jim said, "Gosh. I don't know. Ya think we did the right thing? I mean, moving out here and all? It don't look like Marye is any too happy with the house and all." He took off his cowboy hat, hung it on his knee and shaking his head from side to side, continued, "I sure hope this works out 'cause there's no turning back now, is there?"

I let my breath push slowly through my lips. "I guess not."

We sat there silently for a while, then he turned to me and whispered, "Ya know what I'm thinkin'?" Jim paused and pursed his lips. "I hate to say it, but you know, if Marye don't think this place is that great, what's she gonna say when she sees that broken down cabin we'll be movin' into? Have ya thought about that?"

I ground the butt with my boot. Exhaling the last of the smoke, I gave Jim a little grin, "You know what I'm gonna say? I'm gonna say, here's our new home. This is where we're gonna live and work and do what we said we were gonna do and that's all there is to it. That's exactly what I'm gonna say."

"Ya think she'll go fer it?"

I stood up and brushed off the seat of my Lee Riders. "Course she'll go fer it. Where the hell else is she gonna go?"

As Jim had predicted the night before, my family's first look at the ranch didn't go near as well as I had thought it might. I actually believed that once they saw the ranch, they would be all excited and overlook the shortcomings of their new home.

First of all, the drive from Durango to the ranch wasn't too inspiring, at least from Marye's point of view. The Florida Road which I proudly pronounced in Spanish, *Floor-ee-da* for the benefit of my newcomer companions, was a dirt road, and I do mean *dirt*! It wasn't a graveled road or maintained, just an old dirt road that had been scratched out with horse-drawn equipment some fifty years earlier. The three county commissioners didn't concern themselves with it, especially since none of them lived on it. Back then, you could always tell the county roads a commissioner lived on by how well it was maintained.

Driving along, being careful to dodge the bigger rocks whenever I could, I pointed out various sights that I thought were beautiful or spectacular in some way. I was hoping the kids and Marye would be impressed enough so as not to notice the teeth jarring ride and the fine dust boiling up inside the car. Although the kids seemed to be all eyes, Marye just sat there without comment.

After driving the uncomfortable fifteen miles, we passed Texas Creek Road, rounded a curve and pointing to a hillside on our left, I exclaimed, "This is where the property starts." The family obediently turned their gaze. "And all of this you see on the left side of the road for the next half-mile is part of our ranch." (Big emphasis on the *our*.)

Past the next curve, and with excitement in my voice, as I *was* excited, I almost shouted, "And here's the ranch house. It's the old dance hall that was built before World War I that I told you about. How about that?"

The look on Marye's face said it all. I was excited as hell, but Marye was horrified as she realized that the two families would actually be living in this tiny relic of a cabin.

I pulled off the road in front of Coney Cove. In the yard behind the cabin, we saw a battered Ford pickup. Standing next to the truck with one foot resting on the running board, was a grizzled old cowboy wearing Levi's, a faded chambray shirt and a rumpled sweat-streaked cowboy hat. I took particular notice of his high-heeled cowboy boots into which his jeans were tucked, revealing the entire boot top. The boot pulls were long with the name, *Sammy*, inscribed on each. This style is called "Mule ear boots." (How do you suppose they came up with that?) I opened the car door and was about to get out when Marye said, "Who is that man?"

"I have no idea."

"You better not go out."

"Why not?"

"You don't know who he is or what he wants. Let's leave and come back later." I just looked at her. "Come on. Let's go," she insisted. Her tone had a slightly frantic edge to it.

I said, "Take it easy. I'll see what he wants. You can lock the doors."

I stepped out of the Jimmy and walked over to him. "You the feller what bought this outfit?" he inquired.

"That's right."

"I'm Sam Carson," he said, sticking out a rough looking hand. "Right pleased to meet up with ya." We shook hands.

"Dick Elder. Were you waiting to see me?"

"Yep," Carson replied, "I hear tell you boys is gonna build ya some kind of a dude outfit. That right?"

"You heard right," I offered.

"Well sir," said Sam, turning his head away to spit a stream of brown tobacco juice, "I own a pretty fair bunch a good saddle horses, got all the tack fer 'em too. Ya know, blankets, hair pads, headstalls, the whole nine yards. It's good stuff, not ole junk like a lot a them dude wranglers use. Tell ya how come I come up to see if you was here. See, I was at the Belle [The Diamond Belle Saloon] last evenin' and I heared that lawyer feller . . . can't think of his name right off,"

"Larry McDaniel?"

"Yep, that's the one. McDaniel. Anyways, he and 'nother feller was talkin' 'bout y'all buyin' the boys camp. Now, the reason I come up here to see ya, I was a-wonderin' if you boys will be needin' some horses."

"I reckon we'll be needin' some ponies after we get the place built," I said, using my very best western jargon. I pulled a pack of Camels from my shirt pocket and offered him one.

"No thank ya. Don't smoke them tailor mades. Mostly jest chew a little Red Man or maybe a King Edward." He chuckled. I guess he thought that chewing a cigar as opposed to smoking it was funny. My dad was a serious cigar chewer and I never thought that was particularly funny, but I smiled anyway.

Just to let him know straight off that I wasn't some green horn that just fell off the turnip truck, I lit a stick match with my thumbnail. Of course, my savvy western lingo plus my authentic cowboy garb should have told him right off I was the genuine article.

Carson said, "That'll be fine then. You jest let me know when and where you want 'em, and I'll sure deliver 'em right to ya with all the tack like I said. And I guaren-god-damn-tee they'll be good dude ponies too." He was about to say more but decided to drain his mouth first.

"How much you gonna ask fer fifty head if we kept 'em fer four months?" again, in the western vernacular.

"Whadaya say to sixty-five dollars a round? That be 'bout right? Now, that's with the tack and fresh shod and brought right on up to yer pen."

"I'll sure talk it over with my partner."

Taking a small note pad and a stub of pencil from his shirt pocket, he wrote down his name and phone number, tore off the page and handed it to me. "I'm down there in Aztec. [New Mexico] Me and brother Bob own a tradin' post down there."

"Okay. Maybe me and my partner will come on down and look over your string. Both of us been ridin' and trainin' horses for a long time so we got us a purdy good idea as to what kind a horses we'll be needin'." That was pretty good I thought. Let him know he can't pawn off a bunch of crow bait broncs on us.

Sam grinned a little and said, "Heck fire, I'm gonna treat you boys right, sure nuff. We don't have 'em settin' in some dry lot waitin' 'round. Know what I mean? But I kin take you boys out to a couple places where some of 'em are and you kin kind a git an idear 'bout 'em. Heck fire, you kin ride 'em if ya want."

"I'll call ya." I offered my hand. "Thanks for coming on up. Glad ya did."

Sam opened the door of his pickup and started to get in, then turned around and with a grin said, "Say, you know what the definition of a dude is?"

"Yeah, I think so."

"I ain't talkin' 'bout no dictionary book definition. I mean the r-e-a-l, honest to God, definition."

"Okay. Maybe not. What is it?"

"Well sir," said Sam with an ever widening grin, "A dude is a feller what'll look at a beautiful sunset then turn right around and ask ya, 'Now, which way is west?'"

We laughed, Sam more than me. He was still chuckling as he drove off in the old truck, raising a cloud of dust that hung in the still spring air.

CHAPTER FOURTEEN

*A coney is a type of rabbit. Coney Cove
is a type of misery.*

I went back to the car, rapped on the window, and
Marye unlocked the door. Nancy, Laurie and Mark
piled out and started running around the yard;
Bradley had remained with Twila. I put on my happy
face, grabbed Marye's hand and said, "C'mon. Let's have
a look at our new home."

"Well? Who was that man you were talking to?"

"Sam Carson. He wants to rent horses to us."

"You just walk up to a man that looks like that and
have a conversation? What if he just shot you? Where
would I and your children be then?"

"Shoot me? Jesus, Marye, he's just an old cowboy
wantin' to rent me some horses. That's all. We're in a different world now and you gotta change your thinkin."
Then, wanting to get off that subject I added, "Okay, I
know this doesn't look too good right now and you're not
going to be very impressed with the insides either, but
we're gonna fix it up and it will be very nice by the time
we're done with it. You'll see."

Marye muttered something about talking to strangers.
Dragging her by the arm, I opened the door. Marye
heaved a long sigh then another as we moved about the
house. In every nook and cranny she saw empty liquor

bottles. The last occupant, Mrs. Groves' oldest son, Forest was an alcoholic who apparently loved to hang on to his empties. Marye viewed with dismay the mess and filth, not the least of which was sawdust and wood scraps that we had failed to clean up prior to our hurried departure. Coney Cove, as the old log cabin was called, was not remotely habitable, even after the work we had done on it. The cabin had four small rooms on the ground floor plus two more upstairs. The kitchen had an ancient wall-hung kitchen sink. There were no cupboards or anything else, just the sink. The bathroom was a jury-rigged addition, quite small and heated by a non-vented propane heater. It was lit with a match and one hoped the gas ignited right away because if it didn't, you stood a damn good chance of being close to a small explosion. The bathroom, as well as the rest of the cabin, had wood flooring. The oak floors might have been a plus, except they were filthy.

When the building was used as a dance hall, the part still standing was an entry room to the main hall. The Groves, in a half-ass effort to partition the one big room, had thrown up a wall and covered it with something like Celotex sheathing, a soft wall board commonly used as an insulation layer over house framing. It was a sorry sight and I certainly could understand and appreciate the disappointment Marye must have felt coming, as we had, from a very nice home.

"Do you really think that the Dodsons and all of us are going to live in this little place? What were you thinking? My God Dick, it's not sufficient for one family, let alone two. Will you please open your eyes and take a good look at it, for goodness sake? There is nothing you can possibly do to make anything out of it but what it is right now, a damn dump!" Marye never used swear words so it was abundantly clear that she was furious. Fighting off tears she exclaimed, "You tell me, what is Twila going to say when she sees this place? You brought us all the way out here for *this*?" She quickly took another tour of the cabin. "We sold our beautiful home and most of our possessions for this?"

"I know, I know, but. . ."

"You don't know anything and this house, if you could possibly call it a house, is proof. I want to go back to town."

"I'm telling ya, by the time we fix it up, paint the walls . . ." I was talking to her back as she walked briskly out the door.

The kids came running up. "Can we go in?"

Marye took Laurie's hand. "Not right now. We'll all come back again after Daddy and Jim burn down this wretched cabin and build a proper home."

It was very quiet in the car during the drive to Durango. By the time we arrived at the house on Columbine, I was feeling very depressed. Marye gave Twila a word picture of our ranch home and Twila, her big blue eyes wide with horror (I guess that's what is was) just kept shaking her head from side to side and making little clucking sounds. I got in the Jimmy, drove downtown and saw our Pontiac parked near the Western Steak House where I found Jim drinking coffee at the counter. Jim opened the conversation with, "Well?"

"Well, what?"

"What? What do ya think? How did the trip to the ranch go? What did Marye think of Coney Cove, that's what?"

Woody Wong ambled over and I ordered a coffee. "Wassa matta. Ah, you not a look so happy," he said in his familiar dialect.

Jim looked up at Woody, "I think he's having a little problem today with his wife. Don't think she's real happy with her new home." He looked over at me, smiled then added, "That about the size of it?"

"No, that ain't the size of it! It's a hell of a lot bigger size than that." There was an unmistakable edge to my voice. "I don't know what she expected to see. Damn it!

We told her about the place, she saw the movies I took of it. Shit!"

Woody hurried off, not wanting any part of this conversation. We sat silently until Jim remarked, "Well, ya know, you only showed the outside of the cabin. You didn't take any pictures of the inside so . . ."

"So what! Listen, Ponhoss, it's not going to make any difference now. We're here and that's that." I took a quick slug of coffee, burning my mouth, "C'mon, let's get out of here."

"Where we goin?"

"Over to the Sage Café to see if we can find a carpenter to help us finish fixing up Coney Cove. We're gonna have to get crackin' on it right away before I end up gettin' divorced." I laughed, "Come to think about it, that's something I should've done before we came out here." Jim shrugged his shoulders but didn't comment.

At the Sage Café we found John Walkington, who had recently moved to Durango from Kansas. After a two-minute interview, we hired him. I remember only two things about John: One, he wore stripped overalls and two, he would frequently end his sentences with "and that's all they are to it." As for his carpentry skills, it's axiomatic that you get what you pay for, and we paid John ninety-cents an hour.

We were installing a furnace in Coney Cove when Vern Woodward, a friend from Ohio and his dad Herb arrived in our International truck loaded with building materials. Herb was a master stone mason. The two talented Woodwards had other building skills as well, including carpentry and plumbing. They built cabinets for the kitchen, removed the old sink, and built a counter top along the length of one wall in which they placed a new two-compartment kitchen sink with a new faucet.

By the time we finished with it, Coney Cove was habitable, with most of the rodents exterminated and the skunks under the house driven out by placing large quantities of mothballs in their dens. If you can imagine a room freshener made from skunk stench and mothballs, then you would have a reasonably accurate olfactory impression of what our home smelled like. Regardless of our precautions, the skunks came back every now and then and Nancy would refuse to go to school because her clothes smelled like skunk.

The water system that served Coney Cove cabin was located across the Florida Road at the bottom of the hill, close to the river. It wasn't a regular well by any means. What we had was a hole about five feet in diameter, maybe four feet deep and lined with river rock. Water from the river seeped into the well through the surrounding rocks and dirt. Additionally, a trickle of water, coming from the side of the hill, was channeled into this so-called well. It didn't occur to me at the time, but that trickle of water might have come from the leach field next to the cabin.

The well water was delivered by means of an electric pump through a three quarter-inch galvanized pipe that went up the side of the hill, under the Florida Road, and then to the house, where it entered under the bathroom. The electric wire for the pump was in the same trench as the water pipe.

Hot and cold water pipes ran under the bathroom to the bathtub, which was set with the faucets on an *exterior* wall. From the bathroom, the water pipes were placed in the ceiling and traveled to the kitchen, then down an *exterior* wall inside the cabinets to the sink. I have underscored *exterior* because this was a log cabin without insulation and exterior walls get very cold in winter. Is this more information than you need regarding the plumbing at Coney Cove? No it isn't, because to appreciate the endless problems we had with water, both trying to get it or get rid of it, you need this technical background.

The place where water goes after you flush a toilet is typically called the septic system, used when city sewage is not available. I say typically, because our system was far from typical. A proper system consists of a septic tank and a leach field. We had neither of these amenities. The sewage simply drained into a hole filled with rocks with a wooden cover over the top. Water from the hole normally filtered into the ground unless it had been raining. In that case, it just oozed out onto the surrounding grass and I must assume, down the hill and into our well. Are you beginning to get the picture? The kitchen sink had its own septic system consisting of a fifty five-gallon drum with some holes drilled in the sides to allow water to seep into the surrounding ground. This drum was buried just a few feet deep and quite close to the house.

The fact that some of the water and drain pipes were either exposed to the weather or located on outside walls didn't seem to be a problem when the camp used Coney Cove. The pump was removed from the well and all the pipes drained when their season ended in September. After the first hard freeze, we had a wake up call, and I do mean big time. We had enough sense, coming from cold country, to know that it was essential to insulate the pump and the pipe going up the hill. We knew we needed to use heat tape and insulate the water pipes under the bathroom so they wouldn't freeze. We did that. We didn't know that the pipe under the road wasn't buried very deep and when the county road graders plowed the snow, the cold would move down to our water pipe and freeze it solid! If we were lucky enough to have water coming into the house, the pipes in the ceiling would frequently freeze so that we had no water in the kitchen and no water for the bathtub. Since temperatures would dip below freezing in the crawl space under the bathroom, the drain lines would freeze as well.

When any or all the above happened, we broke ice in Shearer Creek for water, and used the great outdoors for a toilet. For much of that first winter, we were living in a cabin without bathroom facilities or water. Ah, but there's more. In spite of the new furnace we had installed, the house was always cold. The only heat for the two bedrooms on the second floor was whatever might come drifting up the stairs and that was precious little. If I had a glass of water by my bed at night, the water would be solid ice and the glass cracked by morning. Judged by any standard, living there was far from easy. Remember the little space heater in the bathroom I told you about? Many a morning one of us would go to light that thing and end up with the hair singed on our hands, arms and sometimes, head.

All of the aforementioned notwithstanding, we did get the cabin ready, and on May 6, we left our rented home on Columbine and moved into our new home called, Coney Cove. Whenever we mentioned that name, folks would say, "Did you say *Cozy Cove?*" To which we would reply, "No, it's *Coney* Cove. There's nothing *cozy* about it."

CHAPTER FIFTEEN

Delany rides again.

After looking over the rather simplistic renderings of the lodge building submitted by contractors Jim Bodine and Barney Spaulding, we knew we needed something a lot better. We had no conceptual idea as to appearance, size or floorplan, so I called upon my old college friend, Dave Englehorn, who worked for a Cleveland architectural and engineering firm. Dave came up with a very good plan for the lodge that gave us what we wanted in terms of looks and layout. Furthermore, he included a complete set of "specs" and working drawings for a flat fee of $1,000.

The two-story building would contain 5,600 square feet of usable space. The exterior would have native stone and rough-sawn posts, beams and siding. Principal features included a 50 foot-long covered porch on the second floor, accessed from a 2,000 square foot dining room. Dave designed a huge native stone fireplace and chimney placed at one end of the dining room, an open beam high ceiling supported by large exposed trusses made of rough-sawn fir, a wood floor, paneled walls and lots of windows. The kitchen was 20 x 40 feet with stairs to an 800 square foot basement storage area. Another set of stairs in the dining room led to an 800 square foot room we planned to use for a store and recreation room. A coal-fired furnace using baseboard convectors would provide heat. (Coal sold for $6.00 a ton.) The plan called for four bedrooms and a bathroom above the kitchen.

We met Jim Akin, a contractor, whom we liked because of his down-to-earth attitude, apparent knowledge of commercial construction, and his familiarity with the local building trades. He was a long-time resident of La Plata County and had a verifiable background in construction. Conversely, Barney Spaulding was new to Durango and his overly aggressive manner made us apprehensive. After reviewing the bids based on Dave Englehorn's plans, and noting that Spaulding's bid was significantly higher, we gave the job to Jim Akin. That proved to be one of the better decisions we made that year. On April 25, 1961, I signed a contract with Jim for his direct costs, plus a flat fee of $4,000.00 payable in $1,000 dollar increments as the work progressed.

When we told him that we had selected Akin, Barney, who obviously needed our job to survive, was devastated. Sometime later, we read in the *Durango Herald* that Barney was found dead in his car up in the Hermosa Cliffs, north of Durango. A note found in the car confirmed the suicide. Barney's death had a profound effect on me. Somehow, I felt that I had let him down, particularly since I had spent so much time with him. Every time I drive north on highway 550 past the Hermosa Cliffs, I think about Barney and can't help but believe that if I had hired him, he might still be alive.

REMEMBER DELANY, THE GUY DOWN THE ROAD FROM WHOM we rented horses? Well, we began to spend time with him and his wife, Emma Lou. Jim and I worked a few of his cattle round ups and drank coffee at his kitchen table while listening to tales of monumental things he had done. He told us about the time in South America, when he killed a man with the bucket of his back hoe—on purpose! There were stories about how he had "whipped the shit out of guys" who had crossed him. No question, Delany was a feisty bastard and probably had his share of brawls, but most of his stories we recorded under the heading of "Pure D bullshit." Most certainly, he was fun to be around and I loved that Oklahoma accent which, no matter how hard I tried, I just couldn't help parroting.

When we were ready to build a road from the Florida Road to the lodge site, Delany told us that he, "had, by God, a goddamn D-8 Cat [a large Caterpillar bulldozer] tha'd sure as shit [spoken like *sheet*] do ya a job. And, by God," a term he used a lot, although I seriously doubt that God had anything to do with this guy, "I can get that son-bitch on up here in jig time if'n ya want." He let us know too, that he was "by God" a first rate Cat skinner (Bulldozer operator). He said he'd charge us twelve bucks an hour for him and the machine and, he added, "get her done, by God, quicker'n any son-bitch you can git a holt a."

We told him he was hired and Delany said he would have the Cat shipped out pronto. I couldn't put my finger on it, but there was something sort of suspicious about the deal. He never would tell us exactly where the Cat was coming from, or how he acquired it. Things like that made us wonder and worry. But the twelve bucks an hour sounded real good, so we didn't ask too many questions. Fact is, we didn't ask any questions.

We got a call from Delany about ten one evening. He said he heard from the trucker who was on his way up the Florida Road with the dozer and that he was going down the road toward town to intercept the driver and guide him up to the ranch. A little later on, he called again to tell us that he and the Cat were about four miles west of us parked on the Florida Road near "that ole log place 'tween them two bridges." He asked us to come down and give him a hand.

Jim, Vern Woodworth, and I jumped in the Jimmy and hustled on down. The D-8 Caterpillar bulldozer was on a lowboy trailer parked between the two bridges. I asked why they hadn't brought the machine on up to the ranch.

"This here chicken-shit driver's 'fraid to cross the fuckin' bridge," Delany explained. "Says it's too fuckin' heavy fer the goddamn bridge."

The chicken-shit driver, his face red with anger, mouthed between clenched teeth, "I ain't no chicken shit. Not one bit ya ig'rant li'l sharecropper! See that sign right there? The bridge is posted four ton. If ya wasn't such a fuckin' moron and could read, you'd sure as hell would know that. I ain't about ta take no chances havin' that bridge cave in on me. Ya think I want my rig to be sittin' in the damn river and me end up payin' fer a fuckin' bridge?"

If Delany had been operating a back hoe during this exchange of compliments, I have no doubt he would have swung the bucket smack into the skull of that driver the way he said he killed that guy down in South America. Before Delany and the driver could get at each other, Vern stepped between them and told Delany to just take it easy, unload the Cat and find a good place to drive it across the river. Once on the other side, it could be reloaded on the lowboy and hauled up to the ranch.

In an effort to make a bad situation worse, the semi driver said, "I'm quit of the whole goddamn binus. Soon as I get paid, I'm haulin' ass out a here."

This bit of information set Delany off like a fourth of July rocket. He claimed he didn't have the money on him. The money, he said, was at the ranch where the driver was supposed to be in the first place and second, since the Cat wasn't delivered to where it was supposed to be delivered, Delany, "wasn't so goddamn sure [he'd] pay the sonabitch." Delany had jumped up on the lowboy and had been releasing the boomers securing the tie-down chains while this running word battle was going on. Between outbursts of identifying the driver's lineage, Delany had fired up the Cat's pony motor and was, at that moment, engaging the main engine. Vern, Jim and I stayed in the middle trying to keep the two men separated. Just as the driver was about to climb up on the lowboy and jerk Delany out of the cab of the Cat, Delany jammed the outfit in gear, drove off the trailer, gunned the engine and headed for the bridge. The semi driver, yelled, "Jesus H. Christ! Is he crazy? You boys sure as hell better stop that sonabitch. That bridge ain't gonna handle that Cat no ways."

We ran after the cat waving our arms and yelling for Delany to stop, but he couldn't hear us over the roar of the engine and the shrieking of the rusty tracks. Wood shards went flying as the track cleats dug into the bridge planks and the bridge sagged and swayed under the weight. We held our breath as we watched in panic, but the bridge didn't collapse! Delany made it across and stopped on the other side. He looked back over his shoulder, waved, then dropped the blade, set the throttle to idle and hopped down.

"What I tell ya?" Delany yelled, acting like a triumphant boxer. His bravado didn't play well with the rest of us.

"Geeze Delany, if that bridge had folded, we'd all be in deep shit. What the hell you do that for? Look at that," I said pointing to the chewed up bridge planks. What are they gonna say about that?"

"By God, they ain't gonna say shit 'cause they ain't gonna know 'bout it if we haul ass outta here."

We assured the driver that he would be paid but he refused to drive his rig over the bridge, claiming that Delany had weakened it. Besides, he concluded, his rig weighed more than four tons even without a load. Delany said he didn't need to be hauled, that he would just drive the dozer to the ranch and that's exactly what he did.

All I can say is, it's a darn good thing the Florida Road was a dirt road or we would have ended up buying La Plata County about four miles of chipseal paving or, and this is more likely, we would have ended up in jail.

CHAPTER SIXTEEN

Fire in the hole!

Jim and I spent a lot of time blowing up beaver dams in Shearer Creek. It was risky work, since we didn't know shit from apple butter about using dynamite. It was necessary because water was covering a lot of good pastureland.

We called the Game and Fish Department and asked if they would send a state trapper. They told us to hire a trapper or do it ourselves. We couldn't find a trapper, so we bought some traps and set them. We managed to trap a few very large beavers, but trapping took way too much time.

The only other way to get rid of beavers, we were told, was to destroy their dams and hutches (underwater homes) and prevent their rebuilding. You can make a hole six feet wide in a beaver dam, and the next morning it will be repaired. However, if you persist by blasting large holes in their dams every day, thus draining the ponds, eventually the beaver will move to a place where they can have a little peace and quite.

We purchased a case of 70% ditching dynamite from French Hardware and the first time we used the stuff, Jim got such a terrible headache, he thought he was going to die. Since he was making up the charges, we figured he got the headache because he was handling the dynamite, so we switched jobs. I made up the charges and Jim, wearing rubber gloves, placed them in the dams. With all the explosions we caused, I'm sure many beavers suffered worse headaches than Jim did.

We bought a pair of special pliers with a pointed handle for punching holes in the dynamite. The jaws were designed to put a crimp around the percussion cap. The pliers had a cutter to cut the fuse wire. With my trusty buck knife, I'd wicker the end of the fuse, carefully push it into a metal percussion cap, then crimp the cap around the fuse so it was water tight. After cutting off a length of fuse, I would feather the end with my knife, exposing some of the black powder inside the fuse wire. Knowing how long to cut the fuse and knowing how *fast* the fuse would burn is pretty darn important if you want to keep most of your body parts. I was careful to note the speed and length of the fuse on each charge I prepared.

After I had the fuse prepared with a cap, I'd poke a hole in a stick of dynamite (Yes, you can do that.), shove the fussed cap into the hole, and secure it with masking tape. The number of sticks of dynamite I used on any given blast depended on how deep and how wide the dam was.

When we first began this work, we were timid with our charges but we soon discovered that we had to blow a very large hole so that the water would drain quickly. Of course, the beaver would rapidly make a repair, but if we blew the repaired area the next day and maybe the day after that, they would get discouraged and move.

After making up the package of dynamite, I'd hand it off to Jim, who was in the water wearing a pair of fishermen's waders. He'd punch a hole in the dam with a long steel tamping bar then slip in the package of explosives making sure to hold on to the end of the fuse so it didn't get wet. Next, Jim sealed off the hole with some mud and rocks wedging the end of the fuse in dry timber. If we wanted a wider opening, he would insert whole or partial sticks of dynamite on either side of the fused package. The concussion from the blast would detonate the dynamite placed nearby. The demolition guys call this method of setting charges propagation, and it sure does work. I guess we considered ourselves "demolition guys" because after a couple of days, we began using the word.

When he lit the fuse, Jim yelled, "Fire in the hole!" (That's another one of those demolition guy expressions.) I'd check my watch and let him know the time of explosion. If Jim was way out in the stream, I'd fuse for five minutes but normally I'd cut the fuse to allow for a three-minute delay to explosion. Fuse wire was expensive and we sure didn't want to waste it. After the first few charges, we learned that three minutes is enough time to get out of the way. Occasionally, Jim's waders would get stuck in the mud or fill with water and he'd have to decide whether to "pull the fuse" (abort the explosion) or work his way out of it. Since Jim is still alive and in one piece as I write this forty years later, I reckon you know he always made the right decision.

One thing that's really worrisome is when the fuse ignites normally, shooting a little finger of flame from the end of the wire, but then the flame goes out. You just can't go waltzing back out in the water to check it, because the fuse may still be burning and you would end up floating downstream in small pieces. So you wait and wait until you feel sure it's safe, then wade out and put in another fused half-stick on top of the first package and light it off.

It was cold and raining on the fourth day of blowing beaver dams. Jim, while setting a charge, slipped and fell in the water. By the time he got himself upright and made his way back to dry land, he was completely wet. With teeth chattering he muttered, "I gotta go down to the house. I'm freezing." We jumped in the Jimmy and drove down to Coney Cove. The car had barely come to a stop when Jim jumped out and headed for the cabin.

I yelled after him, "I'm gonna go back up and blow a few more. I've got the other pair of waders in the truck." Jim turned around, "No, wait a minute. Won't take me long to get dried out. You don't want to do that by yourself. C'mon in the house and getcha some coffee, then we'll go back on up."

"Don't worry about it. I'll be okay. Go on and get out of those wet clothes." Jim started to protest, but I stuck the Jimmy in gear and roared off.

At the cabin, they later told me, they were listening for the explosions. After each one they would give a sigh of relief because they knew I had to be okay, otherwise there would have been silence. Jim told me that it was hell waiting between blasts, not knowing if I had been blown up on the previous one.

I think that we must have blown over thirty of those beaver dams using several cases of dynamite. Interestingly, I don't think that all that blasting ever killed so much as one beaver, but they did move out and take up residence elsewhere.

Over the years, I got pretty good at setting charges and later learned how to use primer cord and a detonator, which is a much safer way to handle dynamite. However, I'm compelled to advise the reader that dynamite is not something amateurs should ever fool with. We sure as hell were amateurs, even though we used words like *propagate, fused package* and *fire in the hole!*

CHAPTER SEVENTEEN

Sometimes a Cat is called John Deere.

In spite of the fact that we thought that Weldon Delany was a world-class bullshit artist, we soon discovered that he was also a world class Cat skinner. He was absolutely fearless. He'd drive that damned old cable dozer down hills that were steep as a cow's face. He was good; he was fast, and he sure didn't baby his dozer, if, in fact, it really was his dozer.

Early in the morning, after pumping diesel fuel in the tank, pulling dip sticks to check oil levels and greasing the fittings, he'd fire up the pony motor, a small gasoline engine that was used to start the main engine. In those days, in order to get diesel fuel to ignite, you had to turn on the glo-plugs and when they were hot, throw the lever that engaged the pony engine to the main engine. When the main engine was firing, the pony would be disengaged and shut off. The point of this short form diesel engine course may be obscure but needed, as it gives insight into the way things were. Back then, just about everything we did was a lot harder to do and took a lot longer than it does now. Today, for example, I would simply turn the key to start most any diesel engine.

In the chill air of early spring, I watched with pleasure as Delany started the D-8. When he engaged the pony motor to the main engine, perfect rings of white smoke would rise from the stack as the engine labored to fire. Pufff, puffff, pufff, then the vibrant sound of the engine exploding into life. The resonance of the engine, the smell of diesel fumes hanging in the air, and the white rings of exhaust expanding larger and larger as they drifted toward a cobalt blue sky is a memory as fresh as today. I especially loved the rich smell of the earth as it rolled and folded in front of the dozer blade. That's a smell I still love. Some years later, I learned to drive various kinds of equipment, but I'm best with bulldozers. Hardly a time goes by that I don't think of old Weldon Delany when I climb up the tracks and sit down in the cab of a "Cat," even if the Cat happens to be a John Deere or a Case.

We had planned to build the lodge and cabins at a site we had selected and photographed during our first meeting with Barney Spaulding. It was about a quarter mile north of the Florida Road near Shearer Creek. Fortunately, we abandoned that plan because the cost of building a road, the inconvenience of being that far back in the woods and the prospect of having that much road to plow in the winter, woke us to the realities of it. We went on a hunt and Jim Dodson found the perfect site.

Delany's first job was to build a road up to the new location. The road he built is basically the road that is used to this day. In that part of southwest Colorado, the formidable contours, combined with a soil composition that is encumbered with rocks and boulders, makes the land quite difficult to work. One would think that with his big machine, Delany could quickly pioneer a half mile of road, but he constantly ran into rock, some in big flat slabs, some just rubble and some boulders as big as a Volkswagen. Many of those larger boulders had to be "shot" with dynamite, while others he was able to dislodge and push away by working them with the edge of his blade. He needed to be careful, as he could inadvertently dislodge one of the big boulders above and start a little avalanche that could wreck his tractor and kill him. I seriously doubt, however, that he ever worried about his mortality in spite of some pretty exciting near misses.

After completing the road up to the lodge site, Delany's next job was to excavate the lodge basement. The lodge building was to be built near the edge of a hill overlooking the Shearer Creek valley. Dave Englehorn's design worked perfectly on the site. The structure nestled into the slope of the hill so that there was a full basement under the back two-thirds of the building, while the front one-third was entirely above grade.

The hillside in front of the lodge was thick with oak brush, chokecherry bushes, assorted vegetation and rocks, and we wanted it cleared off. For the life of me, I can't remember why we thought it should be cleared, because within a few years it all grew back. We asked Delany if he thought he could clear it with the Cat, because even though the trunks of scrub oak are only a few inches in diameter, they are tougher than hell.

Delany's D-8 was built before hydraulic rams were used to raise and lower the big dozer blade. His Cat had a blade that was raised by a cable; it had no downward pressure except for its massive weight and a couple of points on the leading edge that once in the ground, would help force the blade downward. Delany knew that he couldn't uproot scrub oak by pushing the trees with the dozer blade, because the trees would just bend and pop right back up again. Being the macho skinner that he was and a bull-headed bastard to boot, he might have said, "piece of cake," but back then, nobody said that. What he did say was, "Well, by God, if'n a Cat'll clear that she-it, then by God, I'm the skinner what can do it." He aimed the Cat downhill and there wasn't a stick standing when he was finished.

I sent a letter to my dad on April 21, 1961. Since he saved every letter my family sent, I am able to share their contents with you. Here are some excerpts:

Everyone is healthy and happy and enjoying their new surroundings. The kids are getting along good in school and making more friends daily. Bradley is walking. Mark is on his class track team. How he does all that running at this altitude is beyond me. Jim and I have to take frequent rests as we run out of wind.

Jim and I are putting the finishing touches on our house at the ranch. We are proud of it as neither one of us are carpenters; it's amazing what you can do if you just have to. Marye is our cook and the food bill for both families is averaging $1.00 a day per person.

Made several good contacts for hunting guides and packers this week and made a tentative deal with the fella that rents horses to the camp to take that string after camp is over, about 30 head for $1.00 a day per horse. Hunting around here is a very lucrative business as they [hunters] pay $150 per week depending on the services rendered. There are some packers here that virtually do nothing else all year.

From that letter and the many others I wrote during that time, it is clear that I tried to maintain an optimistic outlook, putting the best spin on each and every adverse situation with which we were confronted. I wasn't about to let the family know the desperation I frequently felt, brought on by episodes of anxiety and depression. Events would overtake me and I would feel helpless. Fortunately, I managed to overcome those feelings and get on with it, but I knew, even then, that I was paying a price, and so were those around me.

We now concerned ourselves with finding sufficient water to take care of our anticipated requirements. You would think that this was something we would have looked into *before* buying the property. We had simply asked Bill Groves about water and he said we wouldn't have a problem. What he didn't tell us was that he had twice drilled for water and come up dry both times. Our land sat on a layer of Mancos shale that reportedly went down 600 feet. We tried getting water by drilling at several locations but never had any luck. I told my dad that we would try to "dig a well and hope for the best." This is a significant statement because in early May we planned to start construction of the lodge and had already dug the basement for it. Yet, we had no assurance that we would be able to come up with the water we would eventually need. How utterly stupid was that? But wait, there's more of the same kind of intellectual retardation. I told my father, "On the money front, I still have no definite commitment as yet." No money and no water. Did that stop us? Hell no!

I talked to Ralph Atlass about investing in our ranch. I was told that he was the son of a very wealthy Chicago family who had recently purchased the radio station, KIUP. Mr. Atlass and I had a number of meetings. I showed him plans and did the whole sales pitch about investing with us. He seemed quite interested and for a brief time, I thought he would buy $25,000 worth of stock but when I asked for the check, he backed out. I talked to insurance companies and individuals, both in Durango and in Ohio, with no success. George Horton was working on leads in Ohio, but like our wells, he too was coming up dry.

Jim Akin staked out the foundation work for Daleny. One afternoon, after the digging was well along, Akin had to run into town so he assigned one of his men, Shorty Porter, to take readings on the *instrument*, which is what they called a transit or a builder's level. Since Delany was close to the required depth, Akin told Shorty to, "Keep a keen eye on the instrument and take frequent readings so the Skinner don't dig too deep." I'm afraid Shorty wasn't much of a hand as a surveyor because he allowed Delany to dig the basement over two feet deeper than the plans required. We didn't know this, of course, until we were building the basement walls and found out that in order to match up to the back part of the building, they needed to be ten feet instead of the planned eight feet high. That was an expensive mistake, but only one of a series.

Herb and son Vern, who we now called Woody, built forms for the concrete footers and worked the concrete when it was poured. Next, they laid up the cement block foundation walls, the interior block walls, the two fireplaces and the chimney. Eventually, all the exposed exterior block and the chimneys would receive a stone veneer.

Because of the weight of the walls, and especially the weight of the fireplaces, the footers (also referred to as *footings* in some parts of the country) were extensive, but Herb knew his craft. He and Woody worked together, albeit with occasional outbursts of high caliber profanity from Woody, brought on by differences of opinion about how something should be done. Getting the fireplace foundations just right was crucial because when finished, the two fireplaces and their chimneys, made of eight inch cement block with a veneer of four to six inches of native stone, would weigh a bazillion tons. Actually, I have no idea what they weigh, but I think a "bazillion" tons is pretty close.

Jim Akin brought some interesting characters to our job. You already read about Shorty Porter and his lack of surveying skills. He had a pronounced Texas twang when he spoke that sounded as if most of his words were transported through his nose. Based on his nickname, you probably have determined that he was short, and in that assessment, you would be correct. I'd say he stood about five-feet four. Shorty was a fair hand as a framer, but that's about it. At times he could be a royal pain in the ass.

Claude was a laborer and a gofer, although we didn't use that word back then. His job was to help the carpenters by keeping them supplied with materials, stack lumber and perform other unskilled work. He sometimes operated Akin's ancient gas-powered cement mixer. I first met him when he pulled into the yard in a beat up old truck. He was a scrawny kind a guy, five feet eight or so, in his late fifties. My first impression led me to believe that he spent too much time looking down the neck of a whiskey bottle. My second thought was that it would take him about six shots to drive home a sixteen-penny nail, not counting the blows he missed or nails he bent over. He saw me as I was coming out of the Cove and asked, "Ya know where Akin's job's at?"

I walked up to him. "You work for him?"

"Yep. I'm his laborer." Then with a wry grin he added, "And a damn poor one at that."

At the time I wasn't quite sure how to take that remark, but after I got to know Claude, I also began to savvy his weird kind of humor. Truth is, he was a damn fine laborer and right handy to boot.

Akin had a husky young fellow of Swedish ancestry on the job by the name of Arvid Alexander. I didn't know his name was Arvid because he called himself Swede, as did everyone else. Swede had a big round head topped with short blond hair. The skin around his pale blue eyes was heavily lined from squinting in the sunlight and from laughing all the time. When he'd laugh, it was a big laugh you could hear all over the job. Swede was a lot smarter than he let on. If I pointed to something on the blue-prints, he'd laugh and say, "Now Dick, I don't know nothin' 'bout no funny papers." But he could read those prints. Swede drove Akin's flat bed truck, hauling materials from the lumber yards in Durango and Bayfield. He lent his muscle when we needed it and once in awhile, he actually used the True Temper framing hammer he always carried in the loop of his white overalls.

The real star of Jim Akin's team was Homer Hartley, a quiet man who was about my age. I'd say he was close to six feet tall, slim with wavy black hair that he kept neat and I don't believe I ever saw the man needing a shave.

It was Homer who told me that Swede's first name was Arvid. He referred to Swede as "Aardvark" and thought it very funny.

Homer grew up working hard. By the time he was a young teen, he probably knew more about the building trades than most journeymen. An eight hour day on the job could go by without Homer saying more than a few words or a sentence or two. When Dave Englehorn's plans were a little vague as to some detail, Jim Akin would always pow wow with Homer Hartley. Jim would say to Homer, "Looks like we've got us another fuzzy detail here," and then Homer would figure it out. Although Homer hired on as a framing carpenter, he could do it all from layout to finish. Whenever presented with a tough design or detail he would say, "Looks like a lot of trouble," but then he always, and I mean *always*, was able to figure out a way of building it. He worked with me on nearly all the construction jobs we did at Colorado Trails. He also helped me design and build my home, my daughter Laurie's home, plus several outside jobs I took on. No one in La Plata County could build a log house like Homer Hartley. His log homes were absolute works of art. He was as good with a chainsaw as Delany was with a bulldozer.

Jim Dodson and I worked at every kind of job, doing whatever was needed. Sometimes I worked with the masons bringing cement block to them or, using a tool called a striker, I smoothed the mortar joints between blocks, shoveled sand, lye and Portland cement into Jim Akin's old cement mixer and made "mud" for Woody and Herb. Sometimes I ran a radial arm saw or a skill saw cutting out lengths of lumber as the carpenters called down measurements from the scaffolds above.

Johnny Soder, a big teenager whose parents were neighbors of ours back in Chesterland, came out and gave us a hand. He fancied himself something of a carpenter because he had helped his dad build a shed or something. Back then, the retractable tape measure hadn't been accepted by carpenters and they continued to use the wood folding ruler, which they carried in the ruler pocket on the right leg of their overalls. Johnny had a brand new pair of white carpenter's overalls and he too used the folding ruler. The problem was that Johnny didn't know how to *read* the damn thing. This is how Johnny called out the measurements to the man on the saw: "I need a one by six, two feet three inches and up to the little red dot." In spite of our best efforts to teach Johnny how to read a ruler, he never did savvy what all those little lines between the numbers meant.

When it was time to build the three big trusses that would hold up the roof, we all pitched in. If Jim Akin had the equipment, building and erecting those trusses would not have been such a difficult task. Typically, a large truss is built on the ground then hoisted into place with a crane. We had no crane. We built them a stick at a time in the air. All lifting was done by manpower or with the assistance of a gin pole, which is nothing more than a tall pole with a pulley at the top. The object to be lifted is tied to one end of the rope and the other end is pulled by as many men as necessary. Whenever we needed muscle for the gin pole, everyone stopped what they were doing and pitched in.

Placing the huge beams between the trusses was mighty scary for Dodson and me who, unlike the regular carpenters, had no experience. We crawled along the top of the truss trying to keep from falling. We only did this because we were more afraid of being called "chicken" than we were of falling forty feet

One day, a couple of guys in suits drove up to the job in a sedan. They informed me they were from Union Local something or other and wanted to know if all of our carpenters were union men.

"Hell, I don't know," I told them. I walked over to the building where the men had just begun framing. I yelled,

"You guys belong to the union?" No one answered, so I asked again, "No one?" There was a brief discussion amongst the workers, then Claude yelled that he and Shorty were union.

The union rep said, "You can't have both union and non-union people working on the same job, ya know. These other guys you got here need to join or else you gotta replace them with union workers."

"That so. Hmmm." I thought for a moment then said, "Tell ya what. Since I only have two union guys and six non-union guys, countin' me and my partners, I reckon what I'll do is run them two union fellas off and hire me a couple of non-union carpenters."

"Now, wait a minute. You can't do that."

"Well sure I can, why the hell not? Didn't you just tell me I couldn't have union and non-union workers on the same job?

"Yeah, but . . ."

"But nothing. If I can't have both, then them two union guys gotta go and that's the long and short of it."

The union reps talked to their members and then got in their car and drove off without saying another word, and that was the last time I ever saw a union rep. Work was hard to come by in the building trades and I guess these guys didn't want to make any waves and get their members kicked off the job.

After a frugal yet satisfying dinner prepared by Marye, who by now was into the swing of things, Jim, Woody, Herb and I climbed up Eagle Ridge looking for suitable stone to use the next day. We worked up there until it got dark, loaded the truck and hauled the rock back to the Lodge and stacked it. I mention this so you'll know we weren't just sitting around after dinner listening to the radio or playing cards.

If you were to ask Jim Dodson about that time in his life, I'm quite sure that he would tell you, as I would, that it was a time of very hard work, of long hours seven days a week, of stress and fatigue. There was no privacy, no luxury and very little comfort. Everything we did, we had to do the hard, slow, labor-intensive way because there was never enough money and very little equipment to assist us in our work. But, I would bet Jim would tell you, as I would, that it was one of the most satisfying and productive times of our lives.

CHAPTER EIGHTEEN

*We arrived at the bank with nothing
and left with most of it.*

Writing checks for materials, payroll and everything else, I watched with alarm as the checkbook balance dropped like an anvil in a water tank. After our routine rock picking after dinner, we had a meeting to once again *seriously* discuss finances. Since we had not been able to entice anyone into buying stock, it was decided that the time had come to borrow some money from the Burns National Bank. Mr. Stallons, the Chairman of the Board, had given us verbal assurances that there would be no problem getting a loan once we began construction and had committed substantial funds of our own. You can imagine our surprise when Mr. Stallon's son-in law, Don Delano, the bank president, said there was no way he could approve the loan.

Jim and I sat there with our mouths open in shocked silence. I leaned forward and carefully explained what Mr. Stallons had promised us. The lodge building, I explained, was about two thirds completed and paid for with our own money; therefore, we felt that we had met the requirement.

"He shouldn't have told you that. He didn't know what he was talking about. He has no authority to make those decisions. A loan like you want would never get past the bank examiners."

I jumped in, "Wait a minute. My partner, George Horton and I sat in this bank with Mr. Stalons, showed him our plans for the lodge and told him what we were going to do, how much money of our own we would be putting in and how much money we would need to borrow. He's the Chairman of the Board for goshsakes! We had no reason not to believe him when he said there would be no problem getting the loan! Now you're sayin' he had no authority to tell us that?"

Delano tilted his chair back and cupped his hands behind his head. "I'm sorry as hell boys, but that's exactly right. Look, he bought the bank for his daughter and me. He doesn't know anything about the banking business. If he did, he never would have told you boys you'd get the loan just like that. It doesn't work that way. What my father-in-law likes to do is come down here, sit at his desk over there and read the *Wall Street Journal*. He doesn't do much else and he sure doesn't pass on loans."

It was all I could do to keep from jumping across his desk and grabbing him by the throat. "Listen, I've worked with banks before and when a bank officer tells me he's gonna do something, then by God that's what's supposed to happen." I realized that I had lapsed into a Weldon Delany dialect. "Why the hell do you think we put our money in this bank instead of across the street at the First National?" Without waiting for an answer I continued, "I'll tell you why. Because we thought we were dealing with reputable people who would stand by their commitments and as far as I'm concerned your father-in-law gave us a commitment!"

Don Delano spoke in a quiet and calm voice, "Now, just take it easy Mr. Elder; no need to get all excited."

"No need? Really? I suppose you wouldn't get all hot and bothered if you were sitting on this side of the desk." I took a deep breath, and sat back in my chair, realizing that getting mad wasn't going to help matters. "I'm sorry, it's just that we're up against it now and . . ."

Delano interrupted, "Listen boys, I'm as sorry as I can be about it. If you would have spoken to me, I would have told you right off that we couldn't provide a loan when another party has a first mortgage on the land. You need to get the folks at Silver Spruce to agree to a second mortgage because no lending institution is going to take a second position. You need to believe me on this. I know what I'm talking about. Believe me, I will help you when you make it possible for me to do so. I have to answer to the bank examiners and they have some very definite rules we are required to follow." Delano pushed his chair back and stood up and put out his hand.

Jim shook his hand and said something but I didn't hear it because I was already going down the steps to the lobby and heading to a teller's window when Jim caught up with me. "How do ya like that?"

"Not one goddamn bit." To the smiling teller I said, "Look up and see what the balance is for Colorado Trails Ranch, Inc. please." She walked over to a row of file cabinets and came back with a piece of paper on which was written the dollar amount we had in our account. She passed the slip of paper over the counter to me.

"Thank you," I said and walked over to the high table where the counter checks and other materials were placed in neat little bins. I took a withdrawal slip and entered the number the teller had given me and returned to her cage. "Please write a cashier's check for this and then close our account."

The lady looked intently at me. "Is there something wrong sir?"

"I reckon you could say that. Your bank president can fill you in on the details."

"What are you doing?" Jim wanted to know.

"I'm closing our account. I don't intend to do anymore business with this bunch of bastards."

The teller handed me the cashier's check and we walked across Main Avenue to the First National Bank and opened a checking account. While there, I met several of the officers including the president, Bill Hurd who told me that he was delighted to have us as customers. I met young Mahlon "Butch" White, who was just out of college and learning the business. His father, Bill White, owned the bank plus several others in Colorado. I still do most of my banking with the First. It's been a great relationship, but back then I had no idea how we were going to survive and get our ranch built if we couldn't get a loan. I decided I'd come back and talk to these people, but first, I had better come up with a workable plan.

When Jim and I returned to the ranch and told our wives what happened, a great curtain of gloom descended.

"What are we going to do?" Twila asked me.

"Damned if I know. I need to call George and tell him about it." A period of silence followed while everyone sat starring at the floor. "I sure never expected this to happen. I guess I've got to see if the Groves will accept a second mortgage."

Jim blew air between pursed lips, "Not much chance of that happening. Don't ya think they're hoping we'll fold so they can take it all back?"

Again the room filled with silence. Twila, her big blue eyes shining with tears, lifted her gaze and looked at me. She understood the implications of what could happen. She cleared her throat and whispered, "You probably should have got Mr. Stallons to put it in writing."

I lowered my eyes to avoid her gaze. I could have replied a number of ways such as, I'm sorry I was so stupid. Sorry I didn't exercise sound judgement. Sorry I let you guys down. But all I said was, "Yeah, I know. I know. You're absolutely right."

On the phone with George, I repeated what Twila had said and admitted that I sure made big mistake. George told me to take it easy, that he was there too when we talked to Stalons and it was as much his fault as mine. But I knew I had screwed up big time and now we were going to pay for it. "No, Hap, I gotta take the rap for this one. I should have known better. But regardless, the sad fact is we need to figure out our next step 'cause we haven't got very much money left and we've got to put the roof on the lodge before winter. That's a must."

"You guys better think about getting some jobs pretty quick to bring in some money. I'd sure as hell like to help out but we haven't been able to sell our house yet and we've lowered the price. Jim wrote and told me that they're gonna be hiring for the Lemon Dam project pretty soon. If they do, you boys should be able to get some good paying jobs up there."

The conversation concluded the same way so many had in the past. Nothing was decided and it looked as though I would have to figure out a way to keep the outfit afloat.

I had a heart to heart talk with Jim Akin and his crew telling them exactly where we stood. I said we had enough money to cover wages for about one more week. I asked them to get the building closed in as much as possible with the materials on hand. They all worked like beavers that final week but neither the roof nor the front wall of the dining room was started. Being laid off was hard on those guys because work was scarce and they needed a weekly paycheck. I promised them we would get going again as soon as I could put some financing together.

Herb and Vern stayed on and finished most, but not all, of the rock work. Then Herb flew back to Ohio secure in the knowledge that someday he would be paid. He said he had a wonderful time and enjoyed every minute of it. Vern, on the other hand, was dying to get home to his wife. His phone calls to her were becoming more frequent, longer and definitely more explicit as to what he was going to do with her when he got back. I couldn't blame him. She was a beauty! Today they would describe her as "hot!"

We decided that I should go back with Vern in the binder and leave it with George to use when he was ready to come out. A few days later, Vern and I said our good-byes, and climbed into that damn old International for another exciting trip to Ohio. It's a wonder we got back at all, given the way he pushed that truck whenever he was driving, but we were lucky and completed the journey without a major breakdown. Amazing!

I was looking forward to seeing my family, Kent Vasko, my mare *Moab Cole* and some of my friends while I was in Ohio. I was looking forward to seeing my dad too, but I certainly wasn't looking forward to asking him for money. No. I was dreading that.

CHAPTER NINETEEN

Life is what it is.

Vern was driving during the last leg of the trip. By the time we were within an hour's drive of his home, he was getting really goofy, and driving that big International like it was a sports car. With his hormones at the boiling point, he was out of control and when we were within a hundred yards of his driveway, he started blowing the horn and yelling out the window. As we turned in the drive, his wife came busting out of the house and ran toward the truck. Vern, without setting the brake or turning off the engine, shoved the door open and ran into the welcoming arms of this wildly attractive lady. Vern had invited me to stay for dinner but I concluded that the last thing they were thinking about was dinner, so I took off and drove to Willoughby Hills.

Situated on six rolling acres was the home and business place of Mel and Jeannette Schaefer. Mel was a roofing contractor who owned the farm where Sonny Braman and I had kept our horses. In addition to the house and guesthouse, the farm had three beautiful barns. Mel had purchased the place not so much for the home in the country as for the barns in which he could store roofing materials for his business. Sonny and I had rented one of the barns for our horses before Mel bought the place and, after he moved in, he allowed us to continue renting it. We got him interested in riding and found a nice quarter mare for him by the name of Jo Betty. Over time, we became pretty good friends with both Mel and Jeannette, who was, and is, just the nicest, friendliest, kindest lady you can imagine.

I spent an hour or more telling Mel and Jeannette what we had accomplished so far in Colorado and I related the sad story about the Burns Bank refusing to give us the loan they had promised. In spite of the bad news, I still painted a very rosy picture for the future, suggesting that with an infusion of new money, we would get the ranch built and open for business.

Mel was about my age, but in spite of being relatively young, he was one heck of a shrewd businessman. His roofing company was one of the largest and busiest in northeast Ohio. At any given time, he was probably roofing a hundred houses or more in large-scale subdivisions.

Mel had helped us immensely when he purchased nine shares of our stock for $5,400 the previous February. He said he would buy more, but only on the condition that between himself, Horton and Dodson, they would own no less than 51% of the company. He wanted to make certain that if it came to a showdown they would control a majority of the votes. He told me that as long as I had the majority of stock I could, for all practical and legal purposes, do anything I wanted and the rest of the stockholders would be powerless to stop me. He had a point. However, I asked him if he truly believed that I would intentionaly do something that might damage the other stockholders who, after all, were my friends. He responded with exactly the right answer: Business partnerships are like marriages. You never know in the beginning of the relationship how it will turn out. A marriage can be great and go on forever or it can end in divorce. Mel understood how things worked in the real world and he never permitted emotion to color his business dealings with Colorado Trails Ranch or me. Benevolence in business was something Mel Schaefer shunned.

Eventually, I agreed that he could purchase enough shares so that when added to the equity of Horton and Dodson, they would control 51% of the company. What could I do? I knew it was a stupid business move on my part, but if we didn't get some serious money and get it soon, we would never get the place built and no doubt, lose most of our investment. We agreed to meet again before I went back to Durango.

I drove over to the Hortons' home. Donnie, George and the two boys seemed pleased to see me. We talked well into the night about everything that had happened since I had left Ohio, including Schaefer's deal. We discussed our prospects and I told them quite honestly that it looked like we might have to put everything on hold until we could find enough money to finish the lodge, build some cabins, find a good water source, and all the rest of it. I suggested that they should put the sale of their house on hold, although I didn't think they were trying very hard to sell it.

I left the International and George drove me to my parents' apartment in Shaker Heights. The following morning, my mother prepared breakfast and we sat at the dining room table chatting away like a couple of magpies. Observing the room and its décor, I couldn't help but make the comparison of her home to ours in Durango. One was definitely the antithesis of the other. She was keen to hear about her grandchildren and I obliged. Borrowing her car, I drove to my father's factory and scampered up the steps to his second floor office. He was sitting at his desk, chair tilted back, foot on the drawer, cigar in his mouth, just like always. We had a long talk, during which I found myself lapsing from time to time into the Weldon Delany dialect. Interestingly, my dad didn't seem to notice. We had the same discussion that we had many times about the short season, the lack of experience, the money thing and so on.

One new item of conversation arose when he stated

that he wouldn't loan me any money. He felt that loaning money to family members could bring about resentment and other problems and he didn't want to take the risk. He suggested that we might be pouring money down a black hole. Still, he wasn't about to let his son leave empty handed. To my great surprise, he offered to buy my shares of stock in his company for $10,000. He had given me the stock when I was a kid, so his offer was totally agreeable to me. In today's business world, that transaction would be referred to as a "no brainer." I would go back to Durango with that $10,000, another $5,400 from the sale of stock to my two brothers, plus a promise from Mel that since I agreed to his terms, he would make a substantial investment.

I visited Joan Seibert, the young girl who was keeping and showing my horse, *Moab Cole*. She was doing very well, winning numerous ribbons and trophies. I told Joan that I was giving her the mare as I couldn't afford to ship her to Durango. I had done quite well with *Moab Cole*, winning enough show ribbons to run a line of them around all four walls of my large recreation room in Chesterland. She was one fine filly!

While in Ohio, I decided to visit my friend Bill Olson at his saddle shop in Willoughby. Coming out of the shop, I turned to walk to my car when, to our mutual sur-prise, Sonja and I found ourselves face to face. After recovering from the initial impact of our chance meeting, we hugged, let go, then hugged again.

"My God, what a surprise!" she exclaimed. "You're about the last person I expected to see today or ever." Sonja laughed. It was actually more like a giggle. Then I laughed. We were nervous. Seeing her again and without warning was unsettling for me and, no doubt, the encounter was eliciting a similar response from her. "Where the heck have you been? You used to call me, even after Marye came back. Finally, I just gave up on you."

"God, Sonja, I am sorry." I looked around. People were passing by as we stood on the sidewalk talking. "C'mon, let's go over there and get some coffee, okay? I want to talk to you." We slipped into a café and took seats at a corner table. "First, let me say how wonderful you look and how much I have missed you." I gazed into those blue eyes, admired her perfect little nose and sucked in her sweet smell. She began to speak, but I held up my hand. "Wait. Please wait and let me say this. You don't know how many times I've thought about you and wondered if I made the right decision. You and me, we were just so good together. I mean the entire relationship was . . ."

"Perfect?"

"Yeah, perfect. I loved being with you but when I got out to California and saw the three kids I had to make a choice. I wanted you, honest to God, but I could not bring myself to abandon my kids. I just couldn't do it. Just the same, I have to admit that I still love you and maybe I always will." I paused momentarily and gazed at her intently. "Life is what it is. We don't always get to do what we want. It's part of life; its part of growing up and at my age, I reckon it's about time."

Sonja didn't speak. She rested her chin on clasped hands and looked at me. At length she said, "Well, maybe I'll always love you too but . . ." she paused and looked down, "that doesn't matter any more because in a month, I'm going to be married." She raised her eyes and in a brighter tone said, "He's a nice guy; you'd like him."

"I'm sure I would. I'm pleased that you found someone . . . really! I just hope he'll be the right one."

Sonja smiled, "*You* were the *right* one!"

I guess we talked for another hour. I wanted to hold her and kiss her and everything else but we didn't do any of those things.

Sonja had brought more than just another romantic interlude into my life at a time when I needed more than sex. Magically, it all came together and in spite of my marital status, I was perfectly at ease with it. The sex was marvelous, but even more was the intimacy that went with it. We talked and talked about everything, nothing held back. I had none of that at home. Marye and I communicated on different frequencies. Sonja and I were on the same wave length. So why didn't I have the guts, or decency, or wisdom or something to own up to the fact that our marriage was a mistake and should end? Was it the children? Was I afraid of the consequences? Or did convention, the untidiness of divorce as it was perceived then, keep us together. To this day, I can't answer those questions with any degree of conviction. All I know is, saying goodbye after that chance meeting with Sonja was very difficult; we both hated to let go.

CHAPTER TWENTY

From roofing to radio

I returned to Durango and, after paying the bills and mortgage, had enough money left over to keep us alive for awhile. During my absence, work on the lodge had stopped and the crew had scattered around La Plata County. Crew or no crew, we had to finish the roof, the east wall of the dining room and install the windows and doors before the winter snows arrived. I called Homer to see if he could help us out but he was working on another job. Swede, however, was not working and said he would give us a hand. I told him we would be unable to pay him but he said that he would trust us to pay him whenever we could. You don't find much of that anymore.

It was a perfect autumn, with deep blue, crystal-clear skies and comfortably warm temperatures. Fall colors were popping up on the hillsides. Oak brush and quaking aspen trees had begun their fall ritual, changing their green leaves to bright yellows and reds. Working with Swede on the east wall of the dining room early mornings, provided a lovely view of Shearer Creek valley and the aspen-laden high hills beyond. We laid our tools aside and stepped out on the porch to watch the sun sneak up, its rays first sparkling across the river then lighting the valley. What a sight!

The east wall of the lodge building was 50 feet long, consisting mostly of windows between 8 x 8 fir beams. Though Swede professed to "Know nothin' 'bout no funny papers," he read the blueprints well enough to help Jim and me get the wall built and the windows installed. He also hung the seven exterior doors. After working for almost two weeks, he left to take a paying job.

The roof decking had been laid by the carpenters over the bedrooms in the back part of the building and covered with fifteen pound felt (tar paper). We had enough 2 x 6 tongue and groove west coast fir on hand to deck the roof over the dining room. This decking would also serve as the finished dining room ceiling. What we didn't have on hand was a carpenter or roofer to do the work. Swede had given us rudimentary instruction on how to go about the job and now it was up to Jim and me to do it.

The pitch of the roof was what they call in the trade, a "ten in twelve," which is one hell of a steep roof. Real roofers find this pitch difficult, but Jim and I were not *real* roofers. The front of the lodge sat right close to the edge of the hill. The first time on the roof, Jim looked down and wondered what might happen if we slid off. I said that I was quite certain that we would have an arduous trip and our chances of survival would be about zero to none. Given our lack of experience, Jim didn't find that comment appropriate or funny.

Regardless of my negative musings and with disregard for the concomitant danger, Jim and I climbed the 6 x 6 purloins, set four feet apart, and laid the first twenty-foot length of 2 x 6 decking. That was scary, but as we continued nailing down additional boards, we were able to sit on the decking we had laid and nail down the next piece. We used twenty-penny nails and drove them in with heavy roofing axes. Talk about fitness training, you swing one of those axes all day long and I guarantee you'll come away with some serious muscles. I will say that we were mighty proud for having had the guts to work on that steep roof.

After covering the decking with twenty pound felt, the next and last thing we had to do was put on the aluminum roofing that we had purchased from Farmers Supply. We didn't have a clue about how to apply it. The Kroeger family owned Farmers Supply and young Freddy Kroeger arranged for a representative of the roofing manufacturer to get us started. With his help, we began laying the aluminum roofing over the bedrooms where the pitch was more like that of an ordinary house. We scampered around on that like a couple of pros. The roofing guy left after working with us for only half a day. Now, we were on our own. Picture Jim and me on the roof under a very intense Colorado sun, nailing down bright aluminum metal. We were instructed to just pound the nails right through the metal without pre-drilling a hole, which resulted in a ton of bent nails plus beating the crap out of our fingers.

After completing the roof above the bedrooms, we started on the steep part over the dining room. Our main concern was to avoid slipping off into oblivion. Even so, we had some heart stopping close calls. By the time we finished laying the aluminum roofing, a great metamorphous had taken place. If you think movie actor George Hamilton has a deep suntan, you should have seen us after we finished putting on that silver roofing. We worked on the roof in the sun for well over a week. We weren't sun tanned, we were baked black! Our backs were sore, our muscles ached, and our hands and fingers looked like hamburger, well-done hamburger. But, the roof was on, the lodge was dried in, and we were dog gone happy about it.

I wrote a letter to my parents telling them about what their grandchildren had been doing and other family news, concluding with:

I've been playing the dual roll of carpenter and office manager. Frankly, I prefer the former, but the latter is a necessary evil. Every time I have to spend time in the office, I keep wishing I could be out on the job in the sunshine pounding nails.

Herb finished the corner fireplace on the first floor and part of the south wall and chimney. Truly, I have never seen such beautiful stone work and everyone who comes up here raves about it. One thing is for sure, I'll never be ashamed to show our lodge building to anyone.

I read in the paper that we are going to have mail service out here starting next week. That will be a good thing. The next thing I hope they do is improve our phone service. We have a twelve party line, which is why you always get a busy signal when you try to call.

I really enjoyed seeing everyone when I was in Ohio, but seeing the mountains and breathing the pine scented air again made me realize even more than before, just how wonderful this country is.

By this time, we were out of money and I do mean *out.* Jim tried his best to find work but had no luck. Delany didn't get the foreman job at the Lemon Dam Project so that option fizzled out. I had been looking for work without success when, just for the hell of it, I stopped by radio station, KDGO to see if they needed a disc jockey or someone to write commercials or anything at all. I chatted briefly with Wayne Moorehead, the acting manager, filled out an application and left. I had little hope that they would hire me. I also applied at KIUP, the other local radio station.

Twila went to the Safeway store every few days asking for a box of bones for the dog (They gave away bones

back then.) which Marye would boil up with some vegetables from our little garden to make soup.

The situation was getting desperate. Between us, we
probably could not have come up with a ten-dollar bill.
We held a pow wow and decided that Jim would take a
bus back to Ohio, find a job and when he had enough
money, send for Twila and the boys. The only obstacle
was that we didn't have $35 for the bus ticket. We called
George and Donnie in Ohio and told them what we needed. George said he would line up a job for Jim and send
some money for bus fare, plus a little extra for groceries.
It was another one of those "No problem" conversations
and George truly was a hero that night.

It was just a couple of days after Jim left on a
Trailways bus that I was called into the house to answer
the phone. The voice on the line was that of George
Worley, the new station manager of KDGO Radio. He
asked me if I was still looking for work and I answered
that I was. He told me that his afternoon announcer had
suddenly quit and was I interested. I told him I definitely was interested. I also told him, when he asked about
my radio experience, that I knew something about radio
since I had been a radioman in the Navy during the war,
although I didn't elaborate on just what an Aviation
Radioman did.

I cleaned up, put on some fresh clothes and drove to
Durango. KDGO was located on North Main Avenue in a
little house. The gal who had given me the job application obviously didn't recognize me as being the same
person who had talked to her previously. I had since
worked on the roof and, as she told me later, she thought
I was black or as it was said back then, *colored*. She
introduced me to the manager, George Worley. He was a
tall, middle-aged man who I later learned had owned a
jewelry story in Texas. I assumed he had some experience in radio; otherwise, I reasoned, he would not have

been hired to manage a radio station. That proved to be an incorrect assumption.

During the interview, he again asked me about my radio experience. While I didn't come right out and say that I had never seen the inside of a radio station, I did say that I was unfamiliar with the engineering side of it, as all the Cleveland disc jockeys had engineers in the control booth. I didn't say I was a disc jockey in Cleveland or anywhere else, but I think Worley may have inferred that I was. I had listened to some of the best disc jockeys in the business, especially Big Wilson, a very glib and entertaining guy on one of Cleveland's network stations, so I thought I could handle the patter. I was a good reader, so I knew I could read the news. Furthermore, I really did know something about transmitters and receivers as a result of my Navy training. Having listened to both Durango radio stations, I knew it was pretty simple stuff that sounded more like the forties than the sixties.

Mr. Worley said there would be no engineer. The man on the mike had to do it all, but since I was a radioman, I would have no problem learning how to operate a Gates control board. Of course, I had no idea what he was talking about, but I was filled with confidence and told the man that I could do it. In fact, I recall using George Horton's favorite expression, "No problem."

I was told to come back around four that afternoon and commence my radio career. I returned at the requested time and George Worley took me into a little room he called the Control Room that I assumed had been the dining room. A disc jockey sat at a control panel and was working the afternoon program. The control room had some wooden shelves against a wall that contained several hundred LP (long play) record albums. These albums were arranged by type: instrumental, male vocal, female vocal, show tunes, novelty, etc. On the short wall was a large window that looked out into the studio, formerly the living room. Under the control room window on a U-shaped counter, was the Gates board. This unit contained the switches, dials and meters that controlled the signal to the transmitter and what went out over the air. In larger stations, the engineer would run the "board" while the disc jockey or news reporter would be at a microphone in an adjoining studio.

When the shift was over and the network news came on (KDGO was an ABC affiliate), Mr. Worley sat at the control board and pulling two records from their jackets, placed them on the right and left turntables, cueing them up so that there would not be any "dead air" (delay) when started. He wrote the time on the log sheet and when the news ended, toggled the mike switch and said in a very serious and somber tone, "This is radio station KDGO in Durango, Colorado. And now, it time for more music." He didn't sound anything at all like the upbeat jocks that worked the big city radio stations. His delivery was more like a network announcer from the nineteen thirties that projected about as much excitement as the last ten minutes of an hour-long class in anthropology.

I studiously watched the station manager work the first hour of a four-hour shift. When he "hit the ABC news" at the end of that hour, he instructed me to take his place at the board. The news program ended, I switched that line off, opened the mike switch and gave the station I.D. Then I flipped the left turntable switch and the record that Worley had already cued up began to play. The log called for a commercial message, so when the song was over, I read the typed message from the loose-leaf binder in front of me. However, I didn't turn off the turntable, so the next song began to play *while I was reading the commercial.* The manager reached over, flipped the switch and gave me a "look."

The manager watched and helped me for half an hour then said he had to go home for dinner. I couldn't believe it. He left! Left me alone without another sole in the whole damn building. What ensued thereafter was nothing less than mayhem. I got so gol darned mixed up I didn't know if I was afoot or horseback. There was so much "dead air" that night that by the time my shift was over, I seriously doubt that there was a single person listening when the Spanish language program began.

Worley wasn't discouraged. He was well aware that we had very few listeners at night after we went to the required low power signal of 250 watts. Rather quickly I learned all the engineering stuff and ran my program with very little "dead air."

About a week after I started, the station manager requested my presence in his office. He told me to have a seat and said in his overly somber, NBC quality radio voice, "I've been doing some checking up on you." Oh boy I thought, here it comes. "You didn't tell me about your business background and I understand that you have a degree in marketing. Is that correct?"

"Yes sir."

"Well, young man, it seems to me you are wasting your talents being an announcer [he never used the term, "disc jockey"] when you could make more money, and be of much greater service to the station, selling commercial time. You need to be out on the street doing something important and worthy of your education."

"I really like being a disc jockey. I'm starting to get into the swing of it and I'm running a pretty tight show and . . ."

"Never mind all that." Worley paused and glanced at the ceiling, then as if inspired continued, "But wait a minute, here's a thought; you know, you could do both if you want to. You could sell during the day and then take the four to seven board shift. That way you'd continue to make your hourly wage for your air time plus you'd get commissions on what you sell. How's that?"

I agreed that I would try it, though I knew that commissions would be slim as we only charged a couple dollars for a one minute commercial. In addition to selling air time, I had to write the message. It certainly wasn't a great job, but I enjoyed it. I wrote commercials and recorded them on tape using music backgrounds similar to what I had heard on the Cleveland stations. Then I would go to a business owner and play the tape on the station's portable tape recorder. When the owner asked, I would tell him, "That sir, is your radio commercial and with a ten time a day schedule, I think you'll see some very good results." That method of selling did quite well. I made up jingles and songs and did all kinds of things with commercials that neither KDGO nor KIUP had ever tried. I did so well with it that Worley announced one day that I was the new sales manager. He even had some cards printed with my name and title on them. So, I was the boss of the entire sales force, but it wasn't too hard for me to manage since, except for one old guy who worked part time and Worley himself, I was the entire sales force.

Eventually the owners of KDGO replaced Worley with Jim Doran, a crackerjack radio engineer. KDGO became the station with imaginative commercial writing, upbeat music, chatty disc jockeys, and very cool station promos. I opened the "Elder Affair" show with my theme song and then with music under, I said, "This is Dick Elder with my flat friends the records, going 'round and 'round with the kay dee go sound, the sound of music." In today's sophisticated world of high tech radio and T V, what we did back in the early sixties in the little cow town of Durango, Colorado sounds about as exciting as watching clothes dry. But we changed the sound of radio in the Four Corners area and it was exciting for me and the entire KDGO crew.

I was finally making a little money and enjoying the work so much that I was tempted to sell the ranch and make a career in radio. Really! I'll tell you how serious I was. I walked in to Joe Shober's office at Triple S Realty and asked him if he thought he could sell the ranch for $75,000. He said he would see what he could do. Fortunately for me, and the rest of this story, no one was the least bit interested.

CHAPTER TWENTY ONE

*There's a lot more to the hunting business
than just killing things.*

The cost of long distance telephone calls being prohibitive, I frequently wrote to my parents during 1961. Many of the letters contained graphic details and were three to four typewritten pages. From a biographical perspective, they provide a totally accurate account of events and circumstances during our first year in Colorado. Here are samples lifted from some of them:

I wrote:

Another week has gone by filled with comings and goings, progress and regression, work and play, contemplation and disappointment. I try to keep in mind a line from Thoreau, "Go confidently in the direction of your dreams. Live the life you have imagined." I'm sure as heck trying hard to do just that.

I was supposed to leave on a cattle drive at 5:30 this morning, but stayed to talk to an insurance man. He thought my presentation was excellent and drew up a 20 year, $50,000 loan package. However, the Co. turned us down saying it was too risky to loan to a guest ranch that wasn't even in business yet.

Yesterday Jim and I drove the logging roads to Missionary Ridge . . . and armed with a Gov't. Permit to cut 1000 feet of timber which we cut into lengths of 10 to 24 feet to use for porch supports. The poles were 8" in diameter and weighed about 200 pounds each. This would not have been so bad but at ten-thousand feet, it's hard to breathe.

Jim and I agree that if we can't find work around here, we'll go to Arizona to find work on a dude ranch providing they would offer work for the girls too.

On July 29th I wrote:

I hit on another idea, which if accepted, would mean we could get going right away. I offered Camp Silver Spruce a 33% ownership in this company in return for their $25,000 mortgage. If they agree, I'm sure I can borrow at least $25,000 and complete our buildings.

To offer a third of our company to the camp for $25,000 was incredibly stupid and dramatically demonstrates my willingness to do anything to get the ranch built, no matter how foolish or fiscally unsound. Fortunately, the camp turned my offer down.

We have been working on our hunting program with Willard McDaniel [no relation to lawyer Larry McDaniel], a kid who says he knows the high country around here. He and Jim and I saddled up and rode off toward Missionary Ridge in the San Juan National Forest. It was by far the most exhausting yet wonderful ride I ever was on. Altogether we were on horseback for over seven hours and covered some rough country. Some places were so steep we had to dismount, take hold of the horses' tails, and let the horse pull us up. My horse collapsed once from the effort, but we finally made it to the top. I think we could see for over a hundred miles. It was positively breathtaking. We rode the rim through the brush, over fallen trees, creeks, a million obstacles that would make a 'trail class' horse look silly. There are so many new and wonderful things to see around here that I'm sure I'll not see it all in the next forty years.

We did a show for the camp across the road a few nights ago. We taught them new songs, had community singing, sang folk and western songs to them and Mark and Nancy had a couple of cute bits they did. The camp kids and staff were a wonderfully receptive audience and it was lots of fun doing the show.

August 4th

I have this altruistic hope that we may provide a shred of happiness for some rut-bound people who might have gone through life firm in the belief that things are more important than people and money can buy happiness. But I'm sounding like a humbug. Enough to say that these concepts are very important to me and it is why I'm here and why I'll sacrifice until this thing we are trying to do is a reality. I don't care if it takes ten years, we'll get this show on the road and we'll give people a vacation they won't soon forget.

Mary and children went to LA last Monday. My mother in-law had to send the money for the bus fare which didn't make me particularly happy, but it was necessary as we are just about broke. Good thing a couple gals from one of my riding classes came out for a visit and paid us $50 each to take them riding, sightseeing and put them up for a week.

It pains me to admit that one of those twenty-year-old girls from Chesterland ended up in my bed. It was a sort of a flashback to my childhood days when our young maids would do the same. We were in my bedroom on the second floor of Coney Cove trying to be very quiet so that we would not awaken the other girl who was sleeping in the adjoining room and Jim and Twila whose bedroom was just below. In spite of our attempt at stealth, Twila heard us fooling around. The next morning she took me aside and gave me a fearful reaming out. She told me in no uncertain terms that she was, in her words,

very disappointed and extremely upset with me. I
assured her that we were "just messing around, nothing
serious," which was the truth, but I doubt that she
bought that story. I felt very guilty and contrite. I
respected Twila and loved her as a brother might love a
sister. She was an honest, good, completely reliable,
straight shooter and when she said she was "disappointed," that hurt. I certainly appreciated the fact that she
never again spoke to me, or, as far as I know, to anyone
else about the incident.

Back to the letters:

*The various suppliers have been very sympathetic
and have told us that we could pay when we could and
that they won't hound us [for money]. The gossip about
town is that the Groves over at the camp are hoping
we'll fold up so that they can take this land back but
we've got the suppliers on our side now since they see
we are earnest and are not trying to give them the
runaround. Groves wrote me a letter offering to buy
back some 90 acres for $4,500, the amount of our pay-
ment this December. I'd hate like hell to do it as it would
cut us off from our best entry to the National Forest and
create a lot of other difficulties. [Groves] says he wants
the land for grazing horses, but I know he has it in mind
to divide it into cabin sites.*

*Our contractor, Jim Akin, was out yesterday with the
last of his bills for material and labor. It came to about
$1,400. According to our contract we were to pay him
the last $1,000 of his fee upon completion or by not later
than Aug. 30 in case we didn't complete the building.
He told me that we had some $104 coming to us from a
discount he received on a lumber bill and that if we gave
him that to take care of removing his equipment, etc.,
from our job, he would forget about the $1,000 fee.*

*Regarding questions that mother asked about Coney
Cove, we have no living room, only the office which con-*

tains those two chairs we had by the fireplace, two used desks, a file cabinet and the piano. The room measures approx. 11X14 and is paneled with a drywall that has a simulated wood finish on it. It actually is the only decent looking room in the whole house. Regarding my vocation, you are right. This gives me the chance to be the ham that I am and a whole lot more.

I read those lines, written over forty years ago, and find it hard to believe we had indeed let ourselves get in such a fix. We were in debt up to our ears! It may be even harder to believe the generosity of our creditors, workers, and Jim Akin. This sort of behavior is the stuff of fairy tales. In today's world, what would be the probable outcome? Any one of those companies or individuals to whom we owned money could have ended our dreams by simply requiring payment, but they didn't and so the story continues.

Jim returned to Ohio a week before I wrote this letter on Aug. 23rd:

I still have plenty of work to do. I've got to prime coat all of the outside windows and doors and build some scaffold in front and nail down the roofing at the eves and get up in the valleys on the roof and caulk and screw them down so the snow can't work under it and build a pump house around our house well and insulate under the bathroom so the pipes won't freeze and I don't know what all. I guess that will keep me busy plus I have 20 head of horses to wrangle every day. Of course, I get a big kick out of that.

Have you seen Jim? If not, call up Hortons and invite him over for dinner. I'm sure you all would enjoy hearing what he has to say about this place and about things in general. You might give him a big steak as we have not had one since we moved out here and I know he would enjoy the hell out of it and could write and tell me how good it was. He's welcome to spend the winter in

Cleveland. I wouldn't trade with him if he had a $20,000 a year job. But, as I've been told on so many occasions, I'm NUTS!

September 10, 1961:
Today was the day that we were to peak on high radioactivity as a result of Mr. Kruschev's fireworks a few days ago and I couldn't help but think that the rain we are getting today was loaded with radioactivity. I wonder how it is going to affect us. With all this brink of war talk going on, I'm kind of glad to be living out here. We're thinking of taking our big septic tank [the one we built for the lodge], which has never been used and making a fallout shelter of it. It's a big concrete block structure with a concrete top and should do the job all right.

September 15:
Last Wednesday evening the station manager, George Worley, said he wanted to talk to me when I came off the air. I thought this odd in as much as he usually gabs with me while I'm on the air. Anyway, when I signed off at 7, he was still in his office waiting. He asked if I wanted to walk right into his job when he left and went to another station. My answer was brief. I told him no. I told him I came out to build a dude ranch and that's what I was going to do. If I wanted a regular job, I would have stayed where I was back in Ohio. I don't mind the selling too much, as I get to know about every business man in town and that's good for the ranch.

Rented two paint horses to the movies for a film they are making near here. Other than that, the horse business has been very quiet.

I was airing a "tight" and entertaining radio show. My commercial sales were increasing, and thus my earnings were a little better. We had to be careful with money, but could now afford to eat some decent food and from time to time treat ourselves to small luxuries like a movie or a restaurant meal. Although I tried to leave no stone unturned in my search for investors or long term-loans, I wasn't having any luck.

Big game hunting was to begin on the third Saturday in October, and I had booked some hunters for a five-day hunt at the start of the season. I walked into George Worley's office in early October and told him I would be gone for a couple of weeks to pack in hunters. He jumped up, put his hands on the desk, leaned way over so that his face was inches from mine and barked, "What? What are you talking about? You just can't up and leave like that!"

"I'm sorry George, but I have to do it and I am giving you time to prepare for my being away."

Worley sat down. "No, this just isn't going to work. We need you on the air and on the street. You can find someone I'm sure, to guide your hunters."

I told him I was committed to take the hunters and at one point he got so steamed that I thought he was going to fire me. So I suggested ways my show could be covered for the week and advised that it would be a slow sales time anyway with many of the store owners themselves out hunting, and in the end he reluctantly agreed to my hiatus. After that however, things were never quite the same between us. He held a grudge and when I returned after hunting, he hassled me whenever he could. I sure wasn't sorry to see Worley go when Jim Doran took over the radio station.

I must confess that I cannot recall many details of my first big game hunt in Colorado, but I do remember taking the State Guides and Outfitters test in order to get my Outfitters License. The local Wildlife Conservation Officer (WCO) was a great guy by the name of Gene Bassett and he came up to the ranch and gave me the test in the unfinished lodge dining room. It really wasn't a difficult test, mostly common sense answers were the correct ones and Gene helped me along with it. I passed and received license number 241. That number should give you an idea how few legal outfitters there were in Colorado in 1961. Shortly after receiving my Outfitters License, I joined the San Juan Basin Packers and Outfitters Association where, during pre-hunting season meetings, I had an opportunity to meet many of the local outfitters and, at least in my mind, become "one of the boys."

I went down to Gardenswartz Sporting Goods in Durango and good old Lester "Buss" Gardenswartz gave me credit so I could buy the camp equipment we needed. He sold me an old Marlin 30-30 lever action rifle that I still have. I picked out tents, sleeping bags and pack saddles with canvas panniers, lash ropes, lanterns, skinning knives, and other items and all on credit. Incidentally or maybe not so incidentally, during the following year when I was making regular calls to update his radio advertising for KDGO, Buss never once asked me when I was going to pay the $3,500 I owed him. When I finally did pay my bill several years later, he did not charge one cent of interest. That's the kind of a guy he was.

In the late 80s while working on the film, *City Slickers*, Billy Crystal and I were chatting about Durango and its inhabitants. He said he didn't think the people were very tolerant of Jews. That remark surprised me and I told Billy he might change his mind if he would take a look at the bronze plaque on the Ninth Street Bridge. It reads, *Gardenswartz Memorial Bridge*. Obviously, the people of Durango admired him and therefore chose to commemorate him.

We had six hunters booked for five days. They had written to the Durango Chamber of Commerce inquiring about hunting and horses to rent and we got the inquiry.

A week before the opening day, we packed all the supplies some five miles north of the ranch to our base camp on Shearer Creek in the San Juan Forest. It was a great spot. We built a pole corral to hold the "night horse," made a nice rock-lined fire pit, pulled up some logs around it for seating and placed the tents on flat grassy ground nearby. It took several trips with the packhorses to get the job done. Most of the packing wasn't very good and that lack of expertise contributed mightily to the resulting loss of items on the way up to our camp site. Many times we had to stop and repack the horses on the trail. At that time, I wasn't skilled in the ways of the "Squaw Hitch," the "Diamond Hitch" or any other hitch and Willard wasn't any better. We'd just take the lash cinch and start wrapping rope every which way hoping it would all hang together until we made camp. As time went on we got better at packing horses and actually got to the point where we could make the trip up to base camp without loosing half the stuff along the trail!

In 1961, the seasons were combined and every elk license allowed the hunter to take (the accepted euphemism for *kill*) one bull elk or if the hunter was lucky enough to have received a cow tag, one cow (female) elk. A deer license gave the hunter an either sex option. For an extra $5.00 you got an additional tag, which allowed you to take a second deer of either sex. A bear tag accompanied both elk and deer licenses. In theory, a hunter who purchased all the various licenses could legally take an elk, two deer and two bear.

Hunting was incredibly hard work, but we got through it and the hunters departed having each bagged at least one animal. One thing I promised myself was that I would get a much better sleeping bag before the next hunting season. Even with a pile of saddle blankets both under and over me, I froze my ass off every night.

I wrote a letter about hunting on October 30. Here's a paragraph from it:

Hunting season got off to a bang. I'll say that there's terrific money in it. I made net almost $500 in five days but I really had to work for it. Up every morning by 3:30, wrangle [the horses] then by the light of a Coleman lantern, groom and saddle, grab some grub

*then up on a horse by 5:00 or sooner and spend from 10
to 13 hours going up and down the hills and into the oak
brush to beat out game while getting all beat up by the
brush and trees. I had 6 hunters, which is all I could
handle with just myself and the kid Willard I told you
about. I'm going elk hunting myself on Sat. and if I hit,
I'll have meat to last all winter. This hunting thing has
been quite an experience.*

A couple days later I wrote this:

*The financial advisor of SBA said that he was going
to recommend that we be given the loan. However, the
committee still must pass on it and I still have heard
nothing from them. They liked my alternate plan which
is to pay off the camp and then loan us $50,000 and
they would have a first mortgage on the whole deal. If
SBA refuses the loan and I can't find people to put up
enough money to get us going, then I guess I'd have to
sell out, as I couldn't afford to hold it for another year
without income from it.*

*Had a pretty good snow, close to two feet. I had a fire
in the Pontiac and burned out all the wiring, the bat-
tery, the generator, and all the electrical parts.*

After the car fire, I remember remarking that if it was-
n't for bad luck, I wouldn't have any luck at all.

Nancy added a note to her grandmother:

*Gram, please draw out $10 from my account and
send it to me. I need it for clothes and also, Christmas is
coming.*

Obviously, ten dollars went a long way back then.

My next letter is dated November 25, 1961.

*We had a nice quiet Thanksgiving. I worked until five
then when I got home with our chief engineer, Jay
Bundy, we had a very nice dinner.*

*Howard called Thanksgiving while I was at work.
Worley has me working every holiday to pay me back*

for taking off during hunting season. Howard asked Marye if we wanted to ship a couple kids to Cleveland. We would let Nancy and Lorrie [sic] go but the thing that bothers me is the expense would be rather a lot and we're so pressed for money here it seems like so much damn foolishness to waste it on such a luxury. This concept may be hard for you people to understand, but when you live on less than $300 a month, you don't toss money around or you find you aren't eating the last week of the month. Now don't misunderstand, I'm not beefing. I wouldn't trade places with any of you. I enjoy where I'm living and what I'm doing and most of all, what we will be doing, so I got no gripe coming.

Marye just rang the dinner bell so I best sign off. Got to leave for work by four and tonight I work until sign off at 10 PM. Then I have to wait around town till midnight so I can take Nancy home from the dance.

Was I giving my parents the poor me routine? Was I trying to make my dad feel guilty for not stepping up and sending me the money I needed? Yes, I believe that is exactly what I was doing. He could easily have afforded to loan me $50,000 and make my financial troubles go away, at least for a time. Later he told me that he really didn't see how we could get the ranch built and even if we did, he didn't believe we would ever make any money. Shortly after mailing that letter, I regretted having made the point about our financial condition. My dad didn't require any schooling from me on poverty. He grew up on a farm at a time and in circumstances far dire than anything I was experiencing. Besides that, my dad was just a young kid when his father died which forced him and his brothers to rely upon themselves for whatever they needed. All of the Elder men and women were strong-willed individuals. They were able to plan their lives confidently in the sure knowledge that they would succeed in whatever they attempted. I have no doubt that some of that grit found its way into my genetic makeup.

CHAPTER TWENTY TWO

My Christmas Carol

The last letter I sent to my parents in 1961 was written on Christmas Eve. More than any other, this letter faithfully describes the impact of our move to Colorado and why I obviously was happy I had done it. It also exhibits my proclivity to "ham it up," as my mother would say. Admittedly, it was an attempt at prose but, amateurish and verbose. Afraid of boring you, I have whittled it down to about a third of the original length.

The Colorado Carol (abridged version)

NOW I SHALL TELL YOU a Christmas story; the story of our first Christmas in the mountains of southwestern Colorado, near the city of Durango AND of the events leading thereto.

CHRISTMAS EVE DAY BROKE BRIGHT with a full Sun shinning down from a deep blue sky. From the cabin window we witnessed its progress. First on the mountain top behind the mesa on the west side, then slowly downward till it glittered from the silver roof of the lodge and danced merrily on the powder snow on the hillsides until all the smooth white snow laying in the bottom land looked like millions of sparkling diamonds reflecting in the Sun. Just minutes ago it had been dark.

NOW WAS A MOST GLORIOUS TIME of day when animals, stiff from the chilling temperatures of the night, would move out into the warming rays of the sun and stretch cold limbs.

NOW WOULD HORSES lower heads, lay back ears and cocking a hind leg, stand content in the sun's soothing warmth.

AND SO IT WAS that while in the mountain valleys the animals of ranch and farm dosed and the creatures of the forest moved out from their beds under pine boughs in search of browse, did the people of the hills arise and welcome the day.

TO SAY that this was an unusually nice day would not be an accurate statement as we had been having beautiful days since the snowstorm last week. Friday night, after leaving the radio station with our engineer, Bundy, we had headed up the Florida Road in his old De Soto sedan. The moon was full...big and bright. The snow glistened on mountains that rose majestically in the shadows while deer bounded onto the road and stood motionless in the harsh glare of our lights.

NEXT MORNING after a hearty breakfast of pancakes and meat, we armed ourselves with the chainsaw as we could no where find axe or hatchet, then drove up the Texas Creek Road to show Bundy the sights and to look for a tree.

JAY BUNDY had never seen Vallecito Lake. How different from the summer time! No sound of outboard motors echoing from the hills, no gay laughter of young girls or of children racing through the street. Vallecito Resort sleeps. Beyond are all the lakes and little rivers of the San Juan Wilderness. How I long to see those remote places that so few have ever gazed upon. I thought of that time during hunting season when I rode my little mare over those high hog backs above Missionary Ridge, when it seemed that I was on the pinnacle of the world and could look out and see what few men had ever seen.

My day dream abruptly ended as Bradley screamed in glee. On the way back, we stopped at Helen's store to say "Howdy" and wish her a Merry Christmas.

Since we had failed to do so all morning, Bundy, Mark and I went out on the ranch to find just the right tree. With all of the spruce and pine we have, you would think that finding a Christmas tree would take a matter of minutes. This may be true, but finding the *right* tree is another matter.

I passed a big rock, one side naked in the sunlight while the shaded side was snow covered. I sat down while Bundy moved on ahead and Mark dropped down into a small draw below me. Basking in the hot Sun I let my eyes move slowly about. Below was a grove of pine trees their trunks deep in snow, their branches flocked with the white powder. My eyes followed Texas Creek Road up to Paradise Ranch. Smoke curling from the chimney meant that Ethel Endersby was baking bread or pies in her wood-burning oven. It was just a week ago that, after skating on their pond, we sat in her cozy kitchen drinking fresh-brewed coffee and eating thick slices of bread that had just come from the oven. We ate a whole loaf and then some. About a month before while the kids were at their 4-H meeting, the rest of us, Delany, Dempsey, Art Endersby and myself had sat around telling lies while devouring about all of the days production. Ethel didn't mind though, she said that's what she baked the stuff for, to be eaten. I got to thinking back on that night when ole Pat Dempsey had all of us near to rolling on the floor with laughter telling us about some of his experiences when he left home to go on the bum as a young kid of 17 during those hard depression times. Of course, Delany had his stories to tell, no way to shut him up once he gets going.

We had all gone ice skating that night too by the light of a bonfire and lanterns. After that, we roasted wieners and drank cowboy coffee. I played guitar and we had us a regular old sing-along. By Ned, I couldn't have had a better time for a hundred dollar bill. I thought of my Dad, who for years had frittered away his life on the weekends and during the afternoons at a card table. How different people are and how different their wants and pleasures.

MARK'S CALL put an end to my reflections. He had found the perfect tree. I cut off the top four feet then we descended the steep slope with the tree, its supple limbs bouncing easily behind.

"TEN TO TWENTY DEGREES below zero in the high mountain valleys and zero to ten below at the lower elevations. Expect a high tomorrow of forty degrees . . ." It was Reggie Chamberlin's voice coming over the little green radio that sat by the kitchen sink. The tree was up, all decorated and we could see its light twinkling from our seats at the kitchen table.

AFTER A FINE MEAL, we sat around the table talking and drinking coffee. Outside the cabin, the sun, having made its journey for the day, had gone over the mountain leaving our part of the world in darkness. Slowly the moon rose, looming large over the ridge on the other side of the river, then it traveled over the pines and then to the mountains behind us shedding its bright blue light upon the snow.

AND SO ON THIS NIGHT would the animals of farm and forest take their rest; just another night. Not so for the children who lay in beds, brains spinning, wakeful in anxious contemplation of what the morrow had in store. I felt the pleasant, even welcome sense of weariness mixed with warm contentment, for I had enjoyed an almost perfect day and how many of these do we have in a lifetime?

TOMORROW THE SUN will break over the ridge across the river lighting the mountain tops and it will be Christmas. But never mind tomorrow, I had today.

CHAPTER TWENTY THREE

We relied on unreliable information

The winter of '61/62 was a real wake up call for all of us. The problems we had with water pipes freezing, nails in the yard, rocks, mud and snow on the Florida Road, skunks nesting under the house, and propane heaters exploding, were added to the usual hardships brought about by very cold weather. At least I had wages of $2.00 an hour which allowed us to eat and pay for a no-frills life style. After I began selling radio time, we did a little better.

The school bus would stop to pick up Nancy, Mark and Laurie around seven in the morning. It could be very cold at that time of day. Zero to fifteen degrees below zero were fairly common early morning temperatures. Many a winter morning, after an overnight storm that may have dumped a couple feet of snow, I had to shovel a path so the kids could get to the road where the bus picked them up. I knew it was damn cold when the moisture in my nose formed ice crystals and I had to tie a bandana or scarf around my mouth and nose so my lungs wouldn't freeze.

Being in the mountains, we didn't get much sunshine early in the morning during the winter months. It was as late as nine o'clock before we saw the sun peak over Eagle Ridge and spread its warmth on Coney Cove. Once the sun rose high enough to clear the surrounding mountains and ridges, the temperature rose very rapidly and we had to start shedding coats. I have witnessed overnight lows of 30 below zero, yet daytime high temperatures could climb to 50 or 60 degrees. Except during snowstorms, which could be heavy, the cloudless sky was clear blue. If there was no moon, the pitch-black night sky was filled with stars. The Milky Way was seen directly overhead and in no other locale have I witnessed it so clearly. The light from a full or nearly full moon would reflect off of the glistening snow creating a blue-white light that was so intense you could drive a car at night without headlights.

There was no way I could get up to the lodge building after the first few storms. With snow up to my knees, walking up to the lodge was just too exhausting given the 8,000 foot elevation. Recognizing the need, Marye and the kids gave me a pair of used "Trailblazer" snowshoes for Christmas that they had purchased at Gardenswartz Sporting Goods store. They were made with wood frames and had rawhide leather webbing. The bindings consisted of a bunch of leather straps and buckles. These shoes were long and narrow with the front turned up sharply while the wood frame formed a long trailer behind.

"Buss" Gardenswartz was one of my regular radio accounts and shortly after Christmas he asked how I liked the snowshoes. He inquired if I knew how to walk in them and attach the bindings. I didn't have a clue. I never wore snowshoes in Ohio; I hadn't even seen a pair except in the movies or in magazines. In answer to his question I said of course I knew how to use snowshoes. I wasn't about to tell this shop keeper who knew more about hunting, fishing and the great outdoors than I would ever know, that I, the Great White Hunter, didn't know the first thing about how to strap on snowshoes. Never!

As a result of my inability to confess to Gardenswartz my total ignorance in the art (and believe me, it is an art) of snowshoeing, I did not fare very well in the snow. The darn things kept coming off my boots or my foot would slip through the hole in the webbing and get stuck. It took a while before I could shush along with any degree of skill.

On January 4, 1962 I sent a letter to my Mother and Dad in which I described conditions and events in a much more favorable light than reality required. Nowadays it would be said that I was "putting a spin on the story."

We are all fine and really enjoying the winter. The town has all but closed up so I've been spending time doing ranch work, getting quotations on materials and trying to interest people in investing with us. Trying to get those hard noses at the bank to give me a commitment for interim financing prior to a loan from SBA.

The past few Saturdays I've been working for Vern Woodworth doing a pointing job at St. Marks Church. My job is to knock out the old mortar with an electric hammer. The darn thing quit on me yesterday morning and we couldn't fix it, so I spent the rest of the day with a four pound sledge hammer and a hand chisel chipping out mortar. When the sun went down, it got colder than hell and by the time we left at 5:30 I was about half frozen.

Our New Year's Eve was spent at Paradise Ranch with one of our neighbors. I worked until 10:00 and then went out there. Marye and the kids were already there and had dinner. I ate, had one spiked eggnog and then we sat around and told lies like always 'till a little after twelve and then we went home. Must say that it was one of the more quiet New Year's Eves of my life, but don't feel as though I missed out on anything.

Three year old Bradley had a knack for causing us much consternation. One morning Mark, Nancy and Laurie were waiting for the school bus and Bradley was with them. A short while later, after the bus had picked the kids up, Marye looked around for Bradley but couldn't find him. We looked everywhere and no Bradley. I threw a saddle on a horse and rode the hills around the house yelling his name. Soon we had the neighbors involved in the search. We thought that perhaps he had crossed the road and had fallen into the Florida River, so we ran up and down the river bank. Frantic, we came back to the cabin and were just about to call the sheriff when the phone rang. Marye grabbed the phone and heard Nancy's little voice say, "Mom? Bradley's down here at school. Can someone come by and pick him up?"

Jim and Twila's little boy, Eric, did something similar that got us all crazy. He came up missing one morning and we went on a regular manhunt all over the place only to learn that he had wandered down the Florida Road to the Spear A Ranch. Mrs. Delany called us when she saw him playing around in her garden. She told Twila that the boy was just fine and she didn't mind him being down there but thought maybe Twila *might* want to know where he was.

Marye and the kids, Brad included, were ice-skating on the frozen Florida River. Bradley was playing around on the ice when he walked on a soft spot that gave way. Brad was in the water and quickly under the ice by the time Marye got to the hole. She saw Brad under a thin layer of ice. She instantly kicked in a hole with her skate and dragged the near-frozen little boy from what easily could have been his death.

It seemed like we spent an inordinate amount of time trying to find Brad when he was little. He would wander up to the lodge site and look over the edge of the basement where we were working. Not knowing he was there, the workers continued their usual banter flavored with an abundance of cuss words and little Bradley sucked in all their lively and colorful conversation. It was no wonder that some of Brad's first words started with F or S. One Sunday after church, Reverend David Bechtal, the

Presbyterian minister, braved the Florida Road and paid us a visit. We were sitting around the kitchen table politely sipping tea and nibbling Marye's luscious sugar cookies when Bradley walked in. He was chatting away with some imaginary friend using most, if not all, of his newfound vocabulary. That episode may have had nothing to do with it, but I don't recall the good reverend ever calling on us again.

Our market research suggested that the county roads would always be plowed in winter because, "the school bus had to get through." Sometimes the school bus didn't show up at all because the road had not been plowed. Looking back with the advantage of hindsight, I can see how our brand of market research got us into so much trouble. I told you in a previous chapter about how we chose Durango instead of Pagosa Springs. That was a good move, albeit dumb luck. But most everything else we did was based on folklore, hearsay, local commentary and the like. We could have gone to the Chamber of Commerce, they had one back then, or the Board of Education, or Fort Lewis College or any number of reliable sources for valuable and useful information. But we didn't and that is why we got ourselves into a pickle so often. We relied on unreliable information.

CHAPTER TWENTY FOUR

A recalcitrant juvenile

Flat tires became a certainty during 1961 and 1962 caused by rocks on the Florida Road and nails behind Coney Cove. Years before, the roof over the main part of the building had caved in during an unusually heavy storm. Rather than make repairs, the Groves decided to tear down everything except for the undamaged part where we now lived. Apparently, there was no attempt to pick up the nails that fell on the ground during the demolition process. These were square nails made in the early 1900's and quite rare, except behind Coney Cove, where they were plentiful.

Had you been there, you would have laughed to see us walking around with heads down, picking up nails and collecting them in Mason jars. I can't remember how many quarts of those damn nails we had, but I know we had a bunch. In spite of a concerted effort to rid the area of nails, we kept getting flat tires.

That winter and spring, I had to drive the Jimmy, rather than the Pontiac to town, as conditions mandated the four-wheel drive to get through the snow and mud. The Florida Road, when it was dry, was so dusty that if you were behind another car, you would have to pull over to the side of the road and let the dust settle so you could see where you were going. The county didn't send the road graders out to plow snow right after a storm either. They only had a few graders so it could be several days before the road was plowed. In the winter the sun is very intense in Southwest Colorado and the unplowed roads would very quickly turn into a muddy mush. In spite of the problems, I nearly always made it to work in that old Jimmy.

Meanwhile, I kept trying to line up financing for the ranch, but without success. In early January 1962, while calling on the First National Bank to pitch a new radio advertising campaign, Butch White suggested that I talk to Ed, a new guy they had just hired. Ed Searle, I was told, had spent a number of years working for the Small Business Administration before coming to Durango.

We walked over to Ed Searles' desk and, after introductions, Butch asked Ed to help me with an SBA loan. I related the history of my dealings with SBA and Ed advised that he would see what he could do.

I had been down so many blind alleys in the past, especially with SBA, that I had about given up on the prospects of getting a loan from them but, after our conversation, I was encouraged and came away with a very good feeling that perhaps this time something positive might happen. It was obvious that Ed Searle understood how things were done at SBA having worked there for many years. I figured that he, more than anyone I had talked to so far, would know how to navigate through its bureaucratic waters.

With a light-hearted bounce in my step, I strolled down Main Avenue thinking that perhaps this time we had a shot at getting a loan. I looked at my watch and realized that I still had a couple hours before my show, so I stopped at the Diamond Belle Saloon where several cowboys I knew were tossing back shots to see who would be the first to either pass out or puke. (Cowboys used to do that sort of thing.) Foolishly, I ordered an Ancient Age tempered with ginger ale. I had replaced Old

Forester for the less expensive brand. I spent some time swapping lies with the boys, watching them play their goofy game and probably had too much to drink because the scantily-clad cocktail waitress was looking even better than usual.

At the radio station, I stopped to talk to the office gal, who I'll call Penny. Penny, I guessed, was in her mid-thirties, had dark brown hair, green eyes and her twenty to thirty pounds of overweight manifested itself mostly in her chest.

Sitting on the edge of her desk, I noticed that her shirt was unbuttoned to the middle of her abundant cleavage. "Listen Penny," I said, while I unabashedly stared at her chest, "you know, you've been bothering me for a long time. You know that?"

"Bothering you? What do you mean? I haven't bothered you."

"No no. I don't mean it like that. I mean, you've been sort of, you know, ah, looking like someone I'd like to get to know better."

"What are you talking about? We've known each other for, what is it, six months or . . ." She suddenly looked intently at me. "Say, have you been drinking?"

"Drinking? What? Ah, no . . . well, yeah I had a couple down at the Belle but . . ." Dave's closing theme came over the monitor in the office and the big wall clock read five minutes to four and I hadn't even pulled my music yet. I hopped off her desk. "Oh hell, I gotta get in there. Are you gonna be around a little longer?"

"I'll probably leave at four thirty like always. Why?"

"Come in the control room before you leave. I need to talk to you. Okay?"

"Sure." She turned back to the log sheet she had been typing.

In the control room, I frantically pulled albums from the rack paying little attention to titles. "Hey Dave, how ya doin?"

Dave swiveled his chair around. "I got your theme cued on two."

"Thanks. Sorry, I'm running late." Dave toggled the mike, announced the station ID then spun the network pot (volume control) as I took his place at the board. The network news ended, I opened the mike, flipped on the number two turntable with my opening theme and began my show. "Afternoon everyone. It's time for the Elder Affair. This is Dick Elder with my flat friends the records . . . etc, etc."

Dave and I shot the breeze during the first song and then he left. A little later I walked over to the bathroom to *tear* the news. In addition to the normal fixtures, this bathroom housed the Associated Press Teletype. The news was printed on a continuous sheet of paper that fell into the bathtub as it exited the machine. We called it "tearing the news" because we would tear the long sheet into smaller sections. Isn't that interesting?

Penny saw me coming out of the bathroom and followed me into the control room. While a record was playing, I said to her, "Here's what I was trying to tell ya before. I was wondering if you might want to come back here later on and ah, you know, maybe have a little fun."

"Fun meaning what?" She cocked her head to one side and put her hands on her hips. A smile spread across her face as she said in a slow and seductive voice, "You want to get into my pants? Is that the kind of fun you're talking about?"

At that moment the music ended so I flipped the turntable switch and over the monitor we heard *Baby Elephant Walk*. "Now what was it you said?"

Penny smiled. "You know damn well what I said. You want to screw me don't you?" She came close to my chair, leaned over, cupped my face with her hands and kissed me on the mouth. Still holding my face she moved back and then kissed me again. I felt her tongue inside my mouth. With her lips close to my ear, she whispered,

"What do you think the answer is? I gotta go home and feed my family but how 'bout I meet you back here after Don signs off?"

The *Baby Elephant Walk* cut ended and segued into the next cut. Not good radio, but who cares when a young lass has taken your hand and placed it on her abundant breast? Certainly not I. During the following twenty minutes there was more teasing and fooling around and my "tight" little radio show went plumb to hell. After receiving mutual commitments to meet when the station was closed for the night, Penny took off.

Don Stickle was a young schoolteacher at the Southern Ute Indian Tribe's school in Ignacio. He and I had become good friends and enjoyed the sport of trying to make the guy on the open mike crack up (laugh or loose his place while doing the news). One time while I was doing the news, Don set fire to some paper in a wastebasket and pushed it under my chair. Another trick was to reach over the DJ's shoulder and start flipping dials and switches to totally confuse the guy at the board.

After selecting his music, Don pulled up a chair next to mine and said, "What the hell kind of show you running anyway? I was listening to you on my way over here and you were letting records run into the next cut or two. Your newscast hardly made any sense. What's a matter with you? Are you sick? Your face is kinda red."

I swung my chair around to face him and with a look of surprise I said, "Ya know, I think something is wrong with me. I was feeling a little dizzy during the news and was having trouble reading it. Besides, a lot of it came over the wire pretty garbled and I had to make some of it up."

Don laughed. I think he smelled my liquor-laden breath. "Okay, okay. I see how it is. You better drink some coffee before you head home, know what I mean?"

I left the station and went down to the Western Steak House for some of Woody Wong's chop suey. Don would be leaving the station after sign off at ten and the place would be deserted when Penny and I returned.

A few minutes past ten, I cruised by the little house on north Main and saw Don Stickle get in his car and drive off. I didn't park in front but drove around to the back of the house, parked the car and entered through the back door. I sat in the dark for ten or fifteen minutes then Penny arrived and knocked lightly on the door. I opened it and we were in each other's arms. I took her hand and led her down the stairs to the basement apartment that had been fixed up to house a former engineer. We more or less fell on the couch and did some heavy kissing and feeling and eventually got to it. I was very much sober by this time and when it was over, and it was over in less than half an hour, I wondered why in hell we had done it. I guess it was pretty exciting but not all that great. Maybe Penny felt the same way, although I really don't know because we never did it again, and this is weird, we never once talked about it. It was as if we both had dreamed it. After forty years, I'm somewhat surprised I even remembered that incident. Maybe it did make an impression after all. The mind is a funny thing!

I would like to report that the episode with Penny was my only extramarital transgression during those early years in Durango. I would *like* to report that, but I'm afraid it would be a monstrous lie. The truth is, there were others and in that regard, I was no better at practicing fidelity in Durango than I had been back in Ohio. It wasn't and never has been so much the sex, although, as my friend Chuck Johnson once put it, "the worst I ever had was wonderful." No, it was more about the excitement, the adventure and the perceived need to have a romantic interlude that propelled me into these lapses of acceptable social and moral behavior.

You may ask, why? Why was I so afraid of cultivating a loving relationship with my wife? Was the "Fearless Cowboy" afraid of intimacy? No, I don't think so. It is just that I was not comfortable with my wife, nor did I think, and I emphasize, *think*, was intimacy comfortable for her.

Though it pains me, I must admit to this flaw in my otherwise impeccable character. Although I've tried to act like an adult, I was, in this regard, a recalcitrant juvenile bent on playing games and seeking erotic adventure. There are times when you just can't come up with a good explanation for doing something seemingly contrary to logic, especially if you're a man. Some guys just do this stuff with little consideration of the consequences.

CHAPTER TWENTY FIVE

*Some cracks are difficult, if not
impossible, to repair.*

The euphoria I felt after talking to Ed Searle dissipated as weeks passed with no further word. The prospect of getting a loan from the SBA and the vague and elusive dream that somehow we would get Colorado Trails built, had always remained in the back of my mind. Now, I began to lose the ardor I once had, particularly since I had a steady job that was easy when compared to the rigors and worries associated with building the ranch. My family had settled into a slightly more comfortable lifestyle, the kids were happy, Marye got involved with the church, and I was enjoying my job.

My parents celebrated their forty-first anniversary on May 5 and I wrote a letter of congratulations and continued with news of current events. I painted a somewhat different picture than that which I portrayed previously. My center of focus at this point seems to have shifted away from the ranch to the activities of my family. I told my folks that:

April was a real good month for me at KDGO. I made as much money as I was making back in 1955. Now, that's what I call progress???

Had a nice letter from Larry [a friend from Ohio] who said that he wished he could have guts enough to break away from the rat race. As I explained it to him, it doesn't take guts. It's all in your mind. You decide what in life is important and then you try to take the road that will give you those things you really want. If it's things you want then you're stuck in a world of things and the frantic race for dollars to satisfy the craving.

Mrs. Groves from the camp offered Marye the job of supervising their kitchen. She would plan menus, do the buying, keep records, etc. and be in the kitchen to supervise and do some cooking, too. She offered to do the job for $75 a week. They told her they couldn't pay more than $60. I wouldn't let her take it. It's a long rough seven day a week job and for $60 it flat isn't worth it.

Was the assumption that $75 *would* be worth taking the job?

On May 26, I wrote about these events:

Had a really good week. Amongst other things, sold the new shopping center called the Town Plaza, an all day remote broadcast and was our competition mad!

The Durango Motel Association had election of officers at their monthly meeting and much to my surprise, I was elected Vice President. I turned down the Presidency of the Riverview School PTA. I don't want to get involved in a lot of things that I haven't the time to handle. I did take a 4-H riding instructor's job, but it will only last till Fair time this Sept. and you know how I enjoy working with horses.

In May, I received a contract from Mel Schaefer in which I agreed to sell him some of my stock and notes in an amount equal to a simple majority of one share when combined with the holdings of all other stock holders except those related to me. I did not give up any right to purchase additional shares in order to maintain my position nor were my preemptive rights set aside. He agreed to complete his purchase by December, 1962.

The Mel Schaefer deal certainly gave me a lift and got me back on track. The terms required that I take money from the sale of my shares and put it back in the company in the form of promissory notes. The good news was that Mel was now substantially involved. My hope was that, in addition to his money, we would have the use of his considerable talent as a solid entrepreneur and proven money maker. Admittedly, it was a gamble. Only time would tell if I had been wise to give up my majority equity position in order to get Mel fully involved.

All the stockholders except Twila and my two brothers came to Durango for a meeting. I have no recollection of the occasion, but I do have the minutes. A part of what was recorded follows:

The president discussed the past, present, and future building program and the financial status of the ranch. He suggested that many obstacles had to be overcome, but that in view of the recent developments, primarily the purchase of stock by Mr. Mel Schaefer, it appeared as though the June 15 deadline of 1963 to be ready for guests would be met. The president also discussed the importance of individual responsibility to the company with particular emphasis on the relationship of personal problems and corporate matters. The president also suggested that in his opinion no additional work could be contemplated at this time, until satisfactory financial arrangements had been made to cover the balance of construction work and until Mr. Horton was able to move permanently to Durango.

Mr. Horton suggested that we get up a pilot model cabin. Mr. Woodworth said he could pour piers for one of the cabins and perhaps do some more work on the lodge building. Mr. Schaefer was also in favor of putting up one cabin during the summer or early fall of 1962 and Mrs. Elder agreed.

Mrs. Horton, commenting on another phase of the president's report, stressed the importance of working as a single unit, placing honesty with each other as well as with one's self as an essential ingredient to the general well being.

It seems clear that Donna Horton and some of the rest of us were concerned that the close relationship amongst the three families was beginning to unravel. The uncertainty of our ability to obtain financing and the emotional strain that was the product of that uncertainty was manifesting itself in a number of ways. Had the money been available to move the project along, I don't think these cracks would have developed but as it was, I was feeling some hostility from my friends.

CHAPTER TWENTY SIX

"Deek, I got a little trouble, man."

The fall season brought another spectacular change of colors with glorious weather and crystal-clear blue skies. Fall also brought another hunting season, which began the middle of October and continued until early November.

Somewhere along the way, I had met a cowboy by the name of Dave Sanchez. He was something else! I visited his home one time and had dinner with him and his wife who served up a most delicious meal. The modest house was spotlessly clean and tidy and his wife made sure that Dave's Levis were pressed and starched. I swear you could cut bread with the crease in Dave's pants. Dave could do things with a rope that left you with your mouth open wondering how the hell he did it. I hadn't seen anything like it since watching the amazing rope tricks Will Rogers performed back in the thirties. Dave was a Cracker Jack packer who could throw a diamond hitch on a packhorse quicker than you could say the word and you didn't have to worry about it coming loose. When it came to hunting and outfitting, Sanchez was the best. I hired him to help us set up camp and guide hunters. He was to provide his own horse, "Sonny," whom he referred to as, "That crop-eared son-of-a-bitch." Sonny had the tips of his ears frozen one winter and they either fell off or had to be cut off. In any case, his ears appeared to have been cropped.

George had lined up a group of hunters and he took time off from his job at Thompson Products to help with the hunt. This hunt wasn't as successful as the one in 1961. It rained a lot the first few days and on the third day we had a huge wet snow that collapsed the tents, turned the trails into a muddy mush, made the horses irritable and caused George and me to wonder what the hell we were doing up there. As if conditions weren't bad enough, one of the hunters gave Dave Sanchez a "fifth" of bourbon without asking George or me if it was okay. Dave went off somewhere that night and commenced to drink without stopping until he had finished the entire bottle. For the next two days "Dave wasn't worth a shit," as one of the hunters put it.

I can't remember what the success ratio was for that hunt, but I think most of the hunters filled their deer licenses and we probably bagged a couple elk. The whole experience was something I wanted to forget as quickly as possible. The only good thing that came out of it was that George and I had a chance to spend time talking about the future of Colorado Trails Ranch.

You have to wonder what the hell they were thinking about, but the hunters gave Dave Sanchez a half gallon jug of Old Charter hundred-proof bonded bourbon as a parting gift. I was there when they made the presentation and immediately grabbed the jug and told them I would "protect it" until Dave was safely home.

In the car, with the jug locked up in the trunk and his pay check of six hundred dollars in my pocket, Dave said to me, "Dick" (He pronounced it Deek, as in peek.), "Limme have the bottle man. I just gonna take one sip . . . that's all. C'mon."

"No."

We drove down Main Avenue in Durango heading for Hesperus where Dave lived, when he whined, "Listen Deek, why you don't let me out here. This'll be fine. You don't have to go all the way to my house then. Okay?"

"No! I'm taking you home. You can do whatever the hell you want to after that, but I'm not leaving you here in town. You got that? No estoy bromeando." (I'm not kidding.)

"Shit man. C'mon. I earned that money. Gimme the check and lemme off here. You can keep that shittin' bottle, I don't care. C'mon."

I didn't answer him but drove fast enough so that I knew he wouldn't be tempted to jump out. Dave sat there sullen and all bent out of shape until we stopped at the little café in Hesperus where his wife worked. She was behind the counter when I walked in and asked if I should leave Dave at the café or take him home. She said to bring him in. I went back to the car and told Dave to get out, then opened the trunk and gave him his bedroll and beat him to the jug of Old Charter which I carried into the building.

I walked up to the counter and handed the jug of whiskey to Dave's wife saying that it was a gift from the hunters. She took the jug from me, "Well, that was very nice of them." So saying, she whipped off the cork, walked to the sink and poured the entire contents down the drain. Dave was immobilized as he watched in utter disbelief. I swear I thought he was going to cry. Dave's wife threw the empty jug in a wastebasket then returned to where I was standing and asked, "Did you give Dave his pay yet?"

I reached in my pocket and handed her the folded check. "No, here it is. I thought I better hand it directly to you so it didn't get drunk up in town." I knew that if I had given Dave his check and let him off in Durango, there would not be one cent of it left by morning.

"I sure do appreciate your bringing Dave out and holding on to his money," said Dave's wife as she carefully placed the check in her shirt pocket. "We need the money right here a lot more than them damn fools down at the Sportsman. Those boys ain't nothin' but drunks and free loaders but Dave here just loves ta hang out with 'em. Dios los cria, y ellos se juntan, no?"

I smiled, "Birds of a feather, right?" She nodded.

Dave sat on a stool with his head in his hands. He glanced at his wife then said to me, "Es una vibora venenosa!"

Dave's wife marched up to him and with righteous indignation said, "I'm a snake? Well, what are you then? You have no good sense when you drink, you become stupid."

Dave looked up and in a whisper replied, "Dejame en paz!"

"You know I'm right," she told him, "It's always the same. Si te digo que la burra es parda, es porque tengo los pelos en la mana!"

I think what she said roughly translated to, *if I tell you the donkey is brown, it's because I have the hairs in my hand.* The English equivalent would be, *I know what I'm talking about.* She sure as hell knew what she was talking about.

I drank the cup of coffee she offered, then leaving a totally shattered Dave Sanchez, got in the car and drove back to the ranch. In his mind, he probably figured that all his hard work had netted him nothing except one great night up in the forest when he had a whole bottle of good whiskey that he could call his very own.

Here is one more little story about old Dave. You may get a kick out it. One winter morning, just after sun up, I heard a knock on the front door of Coney Cove. I slipped out of bed into the freezing room, jumped into a pair of Levis and a flannel shirt and ran down stairs to answer the door. There stood Dave! "Hola, Deek. Como estas hombre?"

"Get in here. It must be below zero out there. What the hell ya doin' here?"

"Deek. I got a leetle trouble man. I gonna need some help with the car and my amigo down there."

"What car? Where?" We were in the kitchen now and I was boiling up some water for coffee. "What the hell you talkin' 'bout?"

"The shittin' car slid over the side and hit that big pine last night. It killed my amigo."

Apparently, Dave and some guy he had just met, were at a bar at Vallecito Lake. I guess they were pretty darn drunk by the time the bar closed and Dave told his companion to drive. They headed for Durango on the snow packed Florida Road, which was hazardous enough when dry and the driver is sober. They were rounding the sharp curve just past Coney Cove when, for whatever reason, the car slid off the road, rolled down a steep bank and hit a large pine tree. The driver's head smashed into the windshield so hard it cracked the glass. (Seat belts had not yet been invented.) Whether the blow killed him immediately or he died later is unknown. Dave was in the back seat sleeping when the accident occurred so he was vague about the details. He did say he was thrown to the floor and when he got up, he saw that the driver was dead, or so he concluded. Deciding that there was nothing to be done, Dave got his bedroll from the trunk, crawled into the back seat and went to sleep.

After hearing Dave recount this story, I didn't believe a word of it. I figured he dreamt the whole thing. Nevertheless, I put on a coat and overshoes and we walked down the icy road and saw the skid marks which we followed to a steep bank on the south side. Looking down, I saw Dave's wrecked car against a tree. We slid down the bank and looked in the windows but they were frosted over. I couldn't get either of the front doors open, however, I was able to get a back door open and there behind the wheel was a dead man, sure enough.

In spite of all the disappointments, frustrations and problems we had, I must confess that although we lived on the Upper Florida River Road in an old log cabin with a minimum of comforts, we frequently found ourselves in the middle of some exciting and memorable incidents. Meeting and interacting with interesting off-beat people like Dave Sanchez made the entire experience that much richer. He and dozens of other characters filled our daily lives as we struggled to build the ranch. It was wonderful!

CHAPTER TWENTY SEVEN

Shane and snow on Wolf Creek Pass.

In January, 1963, Ed Searle called and told Marye that he wanted to see me. Driving to town, I was prepared to learn that the SBA had turned me down again. Ed smiled when I entered his office, which I took as a good sign because Ed, being an ex-SBA employee, didn't do a lot of smiling. I listened intently as Ed explained that the reason it had taken so long to get approval was the concern the agency had with the first mortgage held by Camp Silver Spruce. However, SBA agreed to a second mortgage which was something they normally did not do.

I had originally asked for a loan of $10,000 but in the interim I had changed that request to $30,000 when it became apparent to SBA, the bank and me that $10,000 wouldn't begin to cut it. The interest rate would be 5½ percent, the term, 10 years with annual payments of around $5,000. I told Ed that it sounded good to me and asked him to please pursue it.

Government agencies do not move at the speed of light and the SBA was no exception. My Uncle Harry once told me, "They'll cover you over with paper work and after you've fooled around with them for a hell of a long time, they'll turn you down." Harry's admonition not withstanding, several weeks later I received a call from Ed Searle who told me that SBA had approved the loan and the funds were now available.

With $30,000 in our checking account, life was looking good for a certain young disc jockey who suddenly found himself back in the construction business with enhanced prospects of becoming a dude rancher. At that moment, I was convinced that once we opened for business, we would have no trouble paying both the first and second mortgage payments. Wrong!

We had a total of $33,000 with which to build the cabins, complete the lodge, buy furnishings, equipment, and all the other things we would need. In spite of real-world realities, we plunged ahead because we felt that with our renewed ability to finish the construction phase, we could count on Mel Schaefer to invest more money.

There is an entry in our stock ledger that shows that I transferred 22 shares for which I had paid $2,200, to Schaefer Roofing Company on April 18, 1963. I retained the notes that I had purchased with those shares and Mel was required to purchase notes with a face value of $11,000 to comply with our stock sales requirements. The $11,000 we received from Mel combined with the loan proceeds would enable us to do most of the things we needed to do prior to opening if, and it was a big if, we were very careful in prioritizing our spending. I told everyone that if it wasn't absolutely necessary, we wouldn't buy it, build it or do it.

After receiving word that our loan had been approved, I called the Hortons and Dodsons and told them the good news. It was a great moment. We were back in business after all. During that conversation, George told me that he thought he would be able to return to the ranch in March.

Less than a month later, Jim and Vern "Woody" Woodworth arrived in the old International truck, packed with the Horton family's possessions. Hitched behind was a used house trailer that would serve as the Horton home. George, Donnie and their two boys arrived in their station wagon. Twila and her boys Eric and Brian had remained in Ohio at the Horton home and would come out later.

Upon their return, we got real busy real fast. Woody came up with a low cost solution for guest housing. He drew up plans for A-frame style cabins, which we later named Alpine Cabins. An A-frame structure is very simple to build. The roof rafters are set at a very steep pitch resembling the letter A and become the side walls as well as the roof. The two ends are regular stud wall construction.

The A-Frames went up fast and they were cheap to build. After building the first cabin for about $1,200 in materials (the four of us supplied all of the labor), we decided that the bedrooms needed to be a little larger. We remedied the problem by adding two feet to the length of the cabin and changed the bathroom layout. By the time we built the third cabin, we were able to get the floor joists laid and blocked, the end walls framed and erected and the roof rafters and ridge beam up in less than a day. Altogether, we framed six of these cabins and finished four in time to use that summer.

Mel Schaefer had given us sufficient aluminum roofing shingles to do five cabins because he found that this type of roofing was too labor intensive to use on low-end houses. After putting these shingles on the first cabin, we came to the same conclusion, that it took too much time to install them and so we devised a much faster method of application. We called Mel to tell him about it and he cautioned us about deviating from the recommended method of application. We roofed the cabins our way in spite of Mel's warning. Over the years we had to replace the shingles that were applied using our "improved method," but the shingles we put on cabin #1 using the proscribed method will probably last forever. Mel, as usual, knew what he was talking about.

I went to Coast to Coast Hardware in Durango and made a deal for a dozen lavs (bathroom sinks), toilets and enameled steel shower stalls. The showers were terrible. The stream of water from the showerhead beating against the thin steel walls made a hell of a racket, but it was the cheapest way to go and cheap was what we required. The bedrooms had wood floors and the bathroom floors were covered with linoleum. The bathroom walls were of sheetrock (plaster board) that was taped, plastered and painted by our wives. Donnie Horton was especially good at the taping, plastering and painting trades. George did all of the electrical wiring and all three of us worked on the plumbing.

We also continued to work on the interior of the lodge. Vern had designed and built the lodge septic tank out of cement block during his first stint with us. The leach field, which is necessary to take the affluent from the septic tank and allow it to be absorbed into the ground, was something we bypassed altogether. We just dug a large hole and piped the discharge from the tank into it. As for the cabin sewer systems, they were at least as good as any built in 1800. We used no septic tank at all, just a hole in the ground and covered it with three-inch thick wooden planks. We didn't know about any requirements for septic system inspections, so as far as we were concerned, they didn't exist. Nobody seemed to care anyway.

Meanwhile, we had to have water. Bill Groves finally admitted that they had tried several times to drill for water, but never were able to get it. Now, wouldn't you think we would have determined in advance of practically anything else, if safe drinking water was available and in what quantities? Remember, we were getting water for Coney Cove from that goofy little so-called well across the road, but that wouldn't do us any good for the lodge and cabins.

Once again, it was Woody (we never called him Vern) who provided the solution by suggesting that we try building a "dug well" somewhere close to Shearer Creek. From the dug well he theorized we would pump the water in plastic pipe up the hill to a storage tank and from that tank, pump it wherever we needed it. Using a backhoe, we dug an 8X8 foot hole near the creek. When we got down to about twenty feet or so, we hit shale and found that water was trickling into the hole. We rented a jackhammer and large compressor in town and beavered away at the shale until we had whickered out a hole about four feet in diameter and a couple feet deep. Using the shale as a base, Woody laid cement block and built what looked like a huge pickle barrel. He left the vertical joints open in the first course of block so that water could seep into the well.

I remember being in the hole operating the jack hammer when suddenly everything seemed to be spinning around and I passed out. I had experienced the onset of tick fever. Several days before, I had a tick stuck in my leg that I pulled out without taking the necessary precautions. I didn't know it at the time, but you never should pull an imbedded tick out of your skin as the head may pull off and cause an infection. I was out of action for quite a few weeks. While I lay in bed not knowing what was going on, the boys and gals kept working away. For years thereafter, I would have sudden attacks that made me dizzy and I would get the chills and sweats all over again. I was told that there are very few cases of Rocky Mountain Spotted Tick Fever in Colorado. I guess I was just lucky.

The annual meeting of the stockholders was held on June 5, 1963. The Hortons, Elders and Dodsons were present. The meeting began at 10:00 PM and adjourned at midnight. The late hour for the meeting was necessary because after dinner we frequently would use flood lights and keep working away. Eighteen-hour days were the norm.

The most important part of that meeting was recorded as follows:

The treasurer's report was read and a balance sheet as of the closing of the fiscal year was submitted. The

current financial picture was discussed by the stockhold-
ers as well as the status of the construction program. It
seems there would be approximately a $7,000 shortage
when anticipated plans were completed. Various meth-
ods for handling this situation were discussed.

Pat Howley, the owner the Town House Restaurant,
helped me put together a shopping list of things we needed in our kitchen and referred me to a company in
Colorado Springs that sold used kitchen equipment. I
called, told them what we needed and made a date to
drive up there. George suggested that I take Shane with
me and we left before dawn in the infamous
International. Shane was a teen-age kid who simply
showed up one day and asked for a job. He was a weird
kid, but we hired him because he agreed to work for just
room and board. If you are old enough, you may recall
that Shane was a movie character in a popular western
and my young traveling companion, for some unknown
reason, embraced the name.

The trip to the Springs was uneventful and when we
arrived at the restaurant supply warehouse, I looked over
their huge inventory and selected a used Garland range
with six top burners, a large oven with broiler and a nice
griddle. I also bought a used deck oven that could be
used for baking and roasting, a Wolf griddle, a Wolf deep
fat fryer, an old maple top butcher table and a maple top
chef's table with pot rack. With a salesman in tow who
gave me guidance about what he *thought* we might need,
and Pat Howley's shopping list, I hurried through the
store making selections. In the span of an hour or so, I
purchased silverware, dishes, glasses, serving items, pots
and pans plus all the other items I thought we needed.
Interestingly, I actually stayed within the budget.

It was late in the afternoon when Shane and I left
Colorado Springs with a truckload of kitchen equipment
and supplies. We sailed south down I-25 to Walsenburg
then headed west on 160 to South Fork where we

stopped for some dinner. It was plumb dark as we began to climb the east-side of Wolf Creek Pass when, without warning, as it had been a clear evening, little flakes of snow began falling. The thing I dreaded most was happening all over again. Snow on Wolf Creek Pass!

A mile or so from the summit we saw big rigs parked as drivers struggled with snow chains. A number of cars and a few semis had skidded off the road and were stuck in ditches. We too were barely able to maintain traction and frequently the rear of the truck threatened to slide off toward the ditch. Fortunately, we made it to the top and there I stopped for a cigarette and a breather. It was like a replay of the time that Jim, George and I found ourselves on Wolf Creek Pass in the same kind of fix.

Shane took a deep breath and sighed, "Sure glad that's over."

I smiled, "Hell boy, that was the easy part. Getting down this son-of-a-bitch is what's gonna be scary. Let me tell ya, once we get ta goin' and hitting them sharp turns, it's gonna be a bastard trying to keep from skidding off this damn mountain."

Wide eyed, Shane looked at me and exclaimed, "Really?"

I cranked down the window and flipped my cigarette. "Really!"

It was snowing hard as we made our decent, but I kept the speed down to under ten miles an hour by using the gears and very little brake. We came around a corner and I saw lights blinking in the distance. Here, road had leveled off somewhat and I slowed to where we were barely moving. Ahead I could now see a big semi rig that appeared to be stopped smack dab in the center of the two lane road. When we got to about a hundred feet behind the stalled truck, I tried to stop but the back end of the truck began to slide toward the ditch.

I was sweating now. "Listen Shane, I can't get this outfit stopped so I'm gonna try ta get around that guy but it's gonna be pretty tricky. You open your door right now and hold it open. If I say jump, you jump out. Understand?" You don't wait a Goddamn second. You get your ass outta here. Got it?

I didn't take my eyes off the road ahead, but I heard the door handle click as Shane opened the door a crack. "What do I do after I jump?" Shane wanted to know.

"You'll think of something." We were getting close to the semi and I could see there was just enough room to squeeze by but it was going to be tight. I also saw headlights coming toward us and I couldn't tell how far away they were. "Hold your door open, slide over and get your feet on the running board. Go ahead. Do it!"

Moving at no more than a couple miles an hour, I eased the truck into the left lane, shifted up a gear and applied a little gas. The approaching headlights seemed to be getting mighty close. Trying to keep our truck from sliding off the road and down the steep embankment, I jockeyed the old binder very close to the semi. I remember thinking that if we go over the side, all of the kitchen equipment will be wrecked and we'll be screwed. Just past the semi, I eased back to the right lane and saw that the headlights belonged to a car that had stopped. Seeing our truck coming right at him probably had scared the crap out of him.

I nodded toward the car, "Damn good thing that guy stopped or we'd a had a hell of a wreck. Ya know, I think our outside dual [rear tire] was actually hanging off the road when we went by that son-of-a-bitch."

"Okay to close the door now?"

"I sure as hell hope so.

We pulled into the yard and parked the outfit by the barn about the time the sun was coming up. I guess George heard the truck as we drove by his trailer and he came out to greet us. "Geeze, we've been worried about you. Where the hell you been?"

Marye and Nancy, 1948

Coney Cove—winter, 1961

Yard next to cabin—camp in background, 1961

Barn and horse pens, 1962

Lauren, Bradley, and Dick, 1962

"Hap" and Donnie Horton atop Eagle Ridge, 1963.

The Lodge shortly after completion, 1963

Jim and Twila Dodson, 1964

Alpine Cabin (A-frame), 1964

Shearer Creek Valley looking north toward San Juan Forest

Mark, Nancy, Marye, Dick, Lauren, and Bradley in front, 1963

Jim (Ponhoss) Dodson

Flipping buttermilk pancakes

Sing-a-long after dinner

Dick and Buck, 1962

Dick and the old "Binder"

Shorty Mars— "Coffee as strong as Mary's breath"

Hilton Fix, 1964

Dave Sanchez in hunting camp

The first X-Wing cabin

The Lodge dining room in 1964

Bob Bellmain being goofy in staff show

James "Shorty" Mars

Dick on Flicka with pack string—hunting, 1961

Trail ride viewed from the Lodge porch

Tony Burch and Hap Horton with elk taken during hunting season. Note pack horses in background

Ray Duncan—Purgatory lodge in background

Dick, Dolly, Don Stickle at our wedding, 1966

Bruce, Geneva, and George Begley

Jeanette and Mel Schaefer

Trading post, Mercantile, and Office

"Ran into some snow on Wolf Creek. I'll tell ya all about it after I get some sleep. I'm bushed."

Shane, on the other hand, was all fired up and as I walked toward Coney Cove, I could hear him bending George's ear, babbling on about the death defying adventure he had just come through.

Marye was in the kitchen when I entered the cabin. "Want something to eat? I'm making omelets with bacon for the kids."

I shook my head, "No. I'm going to bed. Wake me up in a couple of hours will ya?"

Marye asked, "How was the trip?"

Bradley ambled in and I gave him a hug, "The trip? Oh, fine. Ran into some snow on the pass, kinda held us up. I'm sure Shane will tell ya all about it."

Shane sure did, in fact, that's about all he could talk about for a week and with each telling, the tale grew to such proportions that even I got excited listening to it.

In spite of the hazards of the road, the kitchen equipment got to the ranch safely and that was all I cared about. As with everything we did, we unloaded the truck the hard way with muscle and sweat and a lot of cussing. When at last all the equipment was in place and hooked up to the gas line, Marye was delighted with the way the range, oven and other pieces fit in the allocated space. At least, I got that right.

Twila regularly visited the Durango Chamber of Commerce and read every inquiry. Any inquiry that asked about things to do in the Durango area got a response from us in the form of our brochure. This brochure was a little booklet that described our program and facilities (such as they were). It had only three photographs, the lodge, an Alpine cabin and a view of Coney Cove. We also used some drawings by Sky Spaulding to depict other elements of the ranch. As I look at that advertising piece today, I'm appalled that we had the nerve to use it. The copy isn't bad and the format was decent, but I can't help but wonder what people thought when they saw it. Even the cover had nothing more than a drawing and our name on it. The back cover had a little picture of Coney Cove, a place for the recipient's address and our return address. The rates were listed in the brochure itself which wasn't very smart, because if we wanted to change the rates, we had to scrap the brochure. Later, we used rate sheets inserted in the brochure.

A full week, seven nights, Sunday-to-Sunday rate for adults was $99.50. The family rate for two adults and two children was $355.00 and included, in addition to a room with private bath, horseback riding twice a day, archery, riflery, trap shooting, water skiing on Vallecito Lake and other sports. Evening programs included hayride, square dance, staff show, campfire sing a long and a chuck wagon dinner. Our guests would be given three full meals a day, a round-trip ride on the narrow gauge train to Silverton with dinner afterward at the Town House Restaurant in Durango. Oh, did I mention free transportation to and from the airport or bus terminal? Yeah, that too! You may well ask, how did you arrive at these rates? I don't remember although I am sure I tried to figure costs. Maybe $99.00 sounded like a good number so I went with it. You may also ask, how could you make any money providing all of that for only ninety-nine dollars a week? The answer is, WE *DIDN'T*!

CHAPTER TWENTY EIGHT

The red dust should have been an omen.

It was another one of those beautiful blue-sky mornings in May when Sam Carson arrived with a load of horses. Woody, Jim, George and I were building the third A-Frame cabin when we spied Carson getting out of the stake bed truck. George and I dropped our nail aprons and drove down to Coney Cove.

"Hey Sam," George yelled. "Watcha got on the truck?"

"Looks ta me like they be horses, but ya never kin tell." Sam laughed. "Hows 'bout I jest back on up ta that chute and we'll jest ease these boys off."

We guided Sam to the ramp, pulled off the gate and the horses scampered into the corral. Sam said that he needed to build a little fire. Figuring that maybe he wanted to boil up a pot of coffee after his trip up from New Mexico (cowboys do stuff like that), we helped him gather some sticks which he stacked in the middle of the yard. Sam pulled a small can of coal oil (kerosene) from the cab of his truck, sprinkled the fuel on the wood and lit it off. With his cowboy hat, he fanned the flames until there was a good bed of hot coals. Reaching behind the seat of the truck, Carson pulled out a couple of long-handled branding irons and placed the business ends on the hot coals. Now we understood why he needed a fire. He was going to brand the horses! As the kids today might say, 'Duhhhh.'

With a couple of Johnson rope halters, Sam ambled into the corral and haltered two horses. Handing a lead rope to each of us, he said, "Whyn't ya take 'em over yonder next ta the side of the loadin' chute an' set 'em up sos they can't move away whenever I hit 'em with the heat."

George obediently led his horse over to the side of the chute and turned him sideways against the rails. Sam pulled the two red-hot irons out of the fire, walked over to the left front shoulder of the horse and bam! The old horse let out a hell of a squeal and leaped forward, almost taking George down.

Sam let go with a giant guffaw that darn near caused him to swallow his chew of tobacco. "Ya might jest wanna not be standin' in front of the horse. Better if ya kinda stand ta the side, eh?" Sam turned to me, "Let's have that one over here."

I maneuvered the horse against the rails and Sam did the deed, getting about the same reaction. George returned his horse to the corral and haltered another while Sam went to the fire to reheat the two branding irons. The procedure was repeated until all of the horses carried his quarter circle, S bar C brand. I noticed that his was not the only brand some of those ponies were packing but, not wanting to pry into his personal business, said nothing.

"I'll be back late this evenin' with 'nother load. You'll want to be checkin' them brands in a day or two make sure none of 'em fester up. I'll bring some stuff up with me whenever I come back to put on 'case ya have any that's not pealing right."

Sam got in his truck, fired it up and was about to leave when he had an afterthought. "Say, I was jest a-thinkin'. I seen that big ole truck ya got there," he pointed in the direction of our International parked by the barn. "Ya reckon you could rig it to haul some horses? See, if ya could, I'd pay you boys to run on down to Sunnyside and gather the horses I got winterin' down there."

"Where the hell is Sunnyside?" I asked.

"Ya jes go south down the highway like ya wuz goin' ta Farmington. I reckon it's maybe 'bout twenty mile from that Eagle Block place."

"What have you got down there?" I asked.

"Well, theys the bunch that I was afixin' to bring up here fer yer string. Ya savvy what I'm a getting' at?"

Sam pulled a beat up package of Beech Nut chewing tobacco from the back pocket of his Levis as I replied, "Yeah, I think so. You want me and Hap here to go down to Sunnyside and gather up your horses. That about the size of it?"

Moving the chew to the other side of his mouth, Sam said, "Kee-rect. You bring 'em on up here and I'll give ya a discount off the rent of say, ten bucks a head. That sound fair to ya?"

George asked, "How many ya got down there?"

"Hell fire, I'm not just exactly sure, maybe . . . I dunno, less see." He pushed back his hat with a finger, spit a stream of brown juice and rubbed the gray stubble on his chin. We could tell that he was thinking real hard. "I'm gonna say 35 head, give or take."

George popped up with, "That be a good five or six loads. They just running loose down there?"

"Well hell yes. 'Course they be runnin' loose. They be turned out all winter long for Christ's sake." Then he quickly added, "But don't you worry none. Ain't gonna be no job 'tall fer ya. They be gentle as dead pigs."

"They packin' yer brand?" I asked.

"Naw, they're slick. [No brand.] Well, maybe theys a few got a mark or two on 'em."

Here's the wrap on that conversation. Sam had a bunch of unbranded horses running loose on the east side of the Animas River down in an area south of Durango known as Sunnyside. He didn't say who owned the land, but he did say and repeated it several times, that all the horses we found on the east side of the river were his and they should be brought up to the ranch. He told us there were no pens or corrals down there, but we could build a rope corral to hold the horses as we gathered them. Since there was no loading ramp, he told us that there were plenty of little "hilly places" and we could back the truck up to a cut bank and load the horses that way. We agreed on a $15 credit for each horse we hauled to Colorado Trails.

George and I had a pow wow and decided that we should do it. If we couldn't get the horses gathered, then we would just call Sam and tell him to come and get them himself. I don't think either of us had the slightest clue as to the real reason Sam was willing to up the ante to insure that we gathered those horses.

THERE WAS A STRONG SOUTH WIND BLOWING, CARRYING particles of dust that gave the sky a weird red hue that we had not seen before. It should have been an omen, but regardless of the wind and the dust, we decided to take a run down to Sunnyside to look the situation over. We drove south on Highway 550 out of Durango some twenty miles to the area known as Sunnyside. Sam had told us to be on the lookout for a red barn with white batts. (These batts were not the little flying critters, but strips of wood as in board and batten siding.)

We saw the barn and turned onto the dirt road that went steeply down to a grassy bottomland adjacent to the river. The strip of land was about a quarter mile wide and miles long. We saw horses grazing on both sides of the river. A couple of sorrel horses were nearby, but ran off when they saw us. We got close enough to a gray mare and a couple of bays to check for brands, but didn't see any. Most of these horses were still wearing winter hair. My vet training told me that much of that long coarse hair was probably due to parasite infestation. The feet on most of that bunch were in terrible shape. It's a cinch that they hadn't been trimmed in a long, long time.

I sat down on a rock, reached in my shirt pocket and pinched a Camel from the pack. George already had one in his mouth and was putting fire to it. He held the match for me and said, "Boy, I don't know about this deal. I got an idea this bunch is gonna be a booger to catch and load and even if we do get 'em caught up, ya think we're gonna be able to use 'em?"

I didn't answer but that thought had crossed my mind. How in the world could we put green riders on horses like these? We sat for a while smoking, enjoying the moment, the sound of the river, the serene setting of grazing horses. "Pretty down here ain't it? Lots of grass, good water. You'd think Carson would have put out some salt blocks. You seen any?"

"Nope." George got up, brushed off the seat of his Levis, and walked over to the truck. On the way back to the ranch, we talked about how we would go about gathering the horses and by the time we got back home, we had convinced ourselves that we could do it.

The red dust that had blown up from New Mexico lay everywhere including the interior of Coney Cove, not the tightest home in the valley. All the furniture, dishes, clothes, everything inside the house had the red grit on it. I remember Twila saying that she could even feel the grit in her mouth.

We hadn't used the International for a while, but it fired right up with just a little coaxing from the gas pedal and generous use of the choke. To provide safer footing, we nailed wood strips to the wood floor of the cargo box. For ventilation, we removed one of the doors and filled the opening with a wooden gate

The red dust still filled the sky when we took off the next morning to gather horses. Looking east as the sun came up, we saw a spectacle of color that was both beautiful and foreboding. We almost turned back, thinking that maybe this wasn't the best day to start this job, but we drove on to Sunnyside anyway and jumped out our two wrangling horses. After getting all our stuff assembled and building a fairly large rope corral, we bridled our horses and set off. We were able to get the first load of seven horses gathered up fairly quickly. Most of them moved right along and into the corral without much trouble. By noon, we were able to lead them, one at a time, into the truck. That was the hardest part because horses are naturally afraid of confined areas, especially dark ones, but they couldn't resist the reward of oats we used to bribe them.

After unloading at the ranch, we headed right back. There was a group of horses right close to the river about a mile or so down stream from our rope corral. We got behind this band and slowly moved them toward the corral, but one old mustang horse changed his mind and broke to the right. George took off after him and tried to head him but that snuffy son-of-a gun pivoted right around, headed for the river, ran down the bank, through the water and up the other side where he stopped and thumbed his nose at us. Meanwhile, the horses I was holding, got all fired up and broke away. Fortunately, they ran toward our corral which we had built between two little hills. Unfortunately, after running in, they bolted right out. We tried our best to gather another load but it was getting dark and our horses were tired so we quit for the day.

After feeding and watering our saddle horses, we laid out our beds (sleeping bags), built a fire and fixed a dinner of pork chops, canned baked beans and stewed tomatoes. Later on, while drinking strong coffee and smoking cigarettes, we talked about what we were doing and why we were doing it. Horton seemed to be feeling very relaxed and happy, so I said, "Well, Hap, here we are. If this ain't cowboyin' I sure as hell don't know what is." George smiled. He didn't need to say a thing. He was flat out loving it. We decided that this was the life. The cowboy life. It was, after all, the fulfillment of my childhood dreams.

THREE DAYS LATER WE HAD MOST OF THE HORSES BACK AT THE ranch and without any major injuries. Early the next morning, my sleep was interrupted by heavy pounding on the door. Slipping into my Levi's and boots, I wondered if Dave Sanchez had another dead man in his car.

I opened the door slowly and was confronted by an Indian fella and a large ruddy-faced man wearing a small badge. "You the man that owns the horses out in that pen?"

"What? Who are you?" I replied, trying to read the words on his badge.

"I'm the brand inspector and this here is Billy Bagay. Now, what I want to know is, do you own those horses out there in that pen?"

"No, I don't own them. They belong to Sam Carson . . . he owns the trading post down in Aztec . . ."

"Yeah, I know who he is. What we want to know is why those horses are in your pen. How'd they get here anyways?"

I was starting to get the picture. "You boys come on in, I'll make us some coffee and I'll tell ya what it's all about."

The two men took seats at the round table in the kitchen and I put some water on to boil for coffee. Jim walked in scratching his head wanting to know what was going on. I brought him up to speed, then told the brand inspector that Sam Carson had hired us to gather up his horses wintering down at Sunnyside and that he said he owned everything on the east side of the river.

Billy broke in, "Some of them horses in da pen back dare has got my brand. You dint see it?"

"Carson said most of 'em was slick, but that some might be branded from former owners. Hell, we just took a job. We don't know that guy too well. But we sure never took nothin' from the other side of the river. You sayin' that we may have gathered up some of your horses?"

The brand inspector held up his cup while I poured the coffee. "What I'm saying mister is, there's some purdy strict laws in this state about rustlin' livestock, ya follow me? Looks like to me, you've stolen some of this here man's stock and transported them on up here and that ain't legal no ways. I'm gonna have ta call the sheriff and have you and your partner locked up and if anybody else was in on this, they're gonna join you."

"Look boys, I'm plumb sorry about this. Shit, I had no idea Carson didn't own them horses. You just show me the ones that are yours and we'll load 'em right on up and haul 'em on back."

"Damn straight you will," said the man with the badge. "But it's up to Billy here. If he wants me to call the sheriff I sure as hell will. So, what say, Billy? If he brings your horses back, you still wanna press charges on 'em?"

"Naw, maybe this feller make mistake. I know that damn Sam Carson. Traded at his store plenty. He would steal a man's horse fer sure if he think he get away with it."

"That's true enough. He's a slippery bastard." The inspector pushed his chair back and stood up. "Okay. That's how we'll leave it. You get them horses back and don't be takin' no week to do it!"

"Yes sir. We'll start haulin' 'em today."

After all that work, we had to take back about half of the horses we had worked so hard to gather. It taught us several lessons. One: Marye was right from the start about Sam. Two: Sam was not the kind of guy you could trust. Three: Sam would look you right in the eye and lie. Four: Sam would and did rustle horses.

When we talked to Sam about the incident, we told him he was going to pay us $30 a head for each horse that made the round trip. He didn't argue. He said that some of the Indian horses must have crossed the river and got mixed in with his bunch. We didn't buy that. He said he was plumb sorry about it and did we want to go gather some horses he had near Pagosa Springs. We declined.

We did use Carson's horses though we had our doubts about his method of acquiring them. In spite of everything, I enjoyed being around the guy. He was so damn colorful, so ornery, so totally a renegade kind of cowboy/horse trader, I just couldn't help but be fascinated by him. When it came to story telling, be it truth, half-truth or pure D bullshit, no one was better at it, not even Weldon Delany.

Some years later, it was said that Sam hired a Mexican kid to set fire to a bar and liquor store he owned down in Aztec, in order to collect the insurance. But when the fire investigators were sifting through the rubble and ashes, they found a book of matches with the imprint on the cover that read, *Carson's Trading Post, Aztec, New Mexico.* Sam got wind that the law was looking for him so he took off to Arizona and hid out in the Superstition Mountains. Sam's brother Bob was the only one who knew where Sam was hiding. One day Bob called me up and said he had a note from Sam saying that he would sell us all of the horses we were using along with the saddles and tack for $150 each. As much as I liked some of his horses, I just didn't want to take the chance of being hung . . . for a horse thief!

CHAPTER TWENTY NINE

Job description? What the hell is that?

Although there were not many, every time we received an inquiry in response to our "advertising campaign," we immediately initiated correspondence with the inquiring party. While we did book a few families and some couples, most of our correspondence went unanswered. Actually, what we were looking for demographically were single young men and women. We had thought to pattern our program and the composition of our guests after the Jack and Jill and Silver Spur ranches I had visited in the fifties. With that in mind, we designed the cabins to accommodate up to four people per room by furnishing each bedroom with two sets of bunk beds.

We had a reality check on the validity and wisdom of our marketing decision when we discovered that most inquiries came from families with children. Had we done some intelligent and thoughtful market research, we would have realized that both Jack and Jill located in Rothbury, Michigan and Silver Spur near Gresham, Wisconsin, were within reasonable driving distances of major metropolitan areas such as Detroit, Chicago and Cleveland. And Durango is near where? You get the picture? In the sixties, it was a solid ten-hour drive from Denver to Durango over several difficult mountain passes.

Additionally, Denverites could go to any number of established dude ranches in Colorado and Wyoming that were much closer and easier to get to. Los Angeles is 1,000 miles and Phoenix is 450 miles from Durango and at the time, Albuquerque, a four-hour drive, was not a large city and it never has been a good dude ranch market. Therefore, the idea that we could fill the place with young singles was ridiculous. All of the obvious information was overlooked and we remained somewhat oblivious to the mistake until we opened for business. It didn't occur to me back then, but in today's litigious climate, I would give serious thought to initiating a lawsuit against The Ohio State University, naming the college and all of my marketing instructors as co-defendants for failing to provide me with the necessary wisdom to operate in the real world.

The Durango Chamber of Commerce provided names of college kids looking for summer jobs and we wrote to them offering positions with *incredible* benefits. For example: The pay would be $50 to as much as $65 a month, plus tips, room and board. We didn't state it in correspondence, but the room would be shared by up to six others of the same gender. The work week was *only* seven days, with maybe a half day off, once in a while. Seriously, the best incentive we offered was working in the prettiest part of Colorado. Most kids were under the impression that a job on a dude ranch would be nothing but fun, fun, fun!

At the time we didn't think much about it, and I reckon neither did those kids, but looking back and remembering with clarity what young college men and women wanted in a summer job compared to what they require now, boggles my mind. Sixty hours or more a week was fairly standard for a female dude ranch employee whose job description, if we would have had one, might read: "Rise at six in the morning, go over to the lodge and set up for breakfast. Help the cook with whatever she needs, squeeze oranges for juice (no instant), make coffee (no instant), set the tables, take orders from the guests as they come in, serve breakfast, clean up the tables and sweep the dining room floor, then wash the dishes, pots and pans by hand (no dishwashing machine). If you have time, grab something to eat, set the tables for lunch then go down to the cabins, clean the rooms and the bathrooms, make the beds, change towels if they seem too dirty to use again, if not, fold and hang them up. After finishing all those chores, lie around the pool and work on your suntan. Oh sorry, we don't have a pool; besides, you won't have time to lie around anyway."

That was just the morning routine. Then there was lunch and dinner to serve, after previously doing all the required preparation with cleanup afterward. When the typical staff girl had finished with the evening meal chores, she was frequently needed to assist with the evening activity, as were the rest of the staff.

The boys working with horses (no girls ever worked as wranglers back then) enjoyed an easy seventy-hour week. Their job description: "Rise at five, saddle your wrangling horse, ride out and gather (round up) the remuda, turned out to graze on some 600 acres of mostly wooded land with lots of places for horses to hide. When the grass gets short in late summer, the horses may wander up Shearer Creek and into the National Forest, north of us, or they might find a place on our east boundary where the fence is in terrible shape and slip through to a neighboring ranch. Honestly, you will never know in advance exactly where the hell you might find these critters. There will be times when, in spite of your best efforts, some of the horses will not be found. Don't worry about it, they'll show up eventually."

"After you locate some horses, drive them down to the corral, then go back out and find some more until all the horses are in. Tie up your horse (don't forget to loosen the cinch and give him some water) then get busy grooming the horses you've gathered, give them some grain, then saddle and tie them using a halter. When all the horses are groomed, saddled and tied, all the wranglers can ride up to the lodge for breakfast. Your breakfast will be served in the dining room around seven and you need to be out of there before the guests arrive at seven thirty. If you didn't find the horses in time, you will miss your regular breakfast altogether because the first ride goes out around eight. When this happens, the head wrangler, Hap Horton, will try to get you something to eat from the kitchen. Wranglers (we called them "trail guides") will lead rides in the morning up to around noon. Before going to lunch, be sure to loosen cinches, water, remove bridles and hang halters on all the horses. You will be sitting at tables with guests and we want you to interact with them. If your clothes are smelly, change out of your horse-clothes before coming into the dining room for lunch. After lunch, return to the corrals and water the horses, tighten cinches, bridle and mount up the guests as they arrive for trail rides starting around two. After the last ride, unsaddle the horses and turn out to graze. This process repeats all over again the next morning."

The good news was, there was no riding on Sundays as the guests left in the morning and the new ones didn't arrive until afternoon. The bad news was, the staff didn't have Sunday off because that was a day that could be used for fence repairs, painting, maintenance jobs, clearing trails, building new trails or for finding horses that hadn't been located during the week.

In spite of what you have just learned about jobs at Colorado Trails Ranch, we were able to hire a crew of eight kids who, along with the three families, worked their asses off all summer. I have heard from many of these staff people over the years, and interestingly, most of them tell me the same thing: "That summer at CTR was one of the best in my entire life." Go figure!

The first two staff girls arrived mid May. They were friends who attended Kansas State University majoring in education. They had just finished their junior year, so I reckon they must have been about twenty years old when they joined our band of merry workers. I picked them up at the Trailways bus station down town and while traveling on the infamous Florida Road, about which you've already heard more than enough, I talked about the good stuff they would be doing during the summer. These two very likable gals were full of enthusiasm and said that they were looking forward to a great summer.

After a forty-minute bumpy ride, we pulled into the ranch. At this point in time, we hadn't done a blessed thing to the entrance area and admittedly it was a pretty sorry sight. The girls looked around and saw nothing but dirt and weeds, beat up pole corrals, the old barn and Coney Cove. Not a vestige of landscaping was in view unless you count the little vegetable garden surrounded by chicken wire next to Coney Cove. Seeing their obvious dismay (Or was it shock?), I quickly explained that all of this, meaning our entrance, would be fixed up real soon and look much more appealing. The girls didn't say anything. Not wanting to dwell on it, I continued along to the top of the drive. I think the girl's spirits rose slightly when the new lodge building popped into view. I parked behind the lodge and led them in via the kitchen door. After showing the girls around the lodge, that "better feeling" quickly evaporated. We were still nailing up spruce paneling in the dining room, the kitchen hadn't been painted, the basement area was filled with materials and junk of all kinds and the front part, destined to become the game room, still had a dirt floor and unpainted cement block walls. The four bedrooms and bathroom on the second floor above the kitchen had bare wood floors and very little furniture. Donnie and Twila had painted the rooms a few days before and the acrid smell of fresh paint filled the air.

I introduced the girls to everyone working in the building, retrieved their suitcases from the car and escorted them to their room, the large one on the north end. There were three sets of bunk beds to accommodate six staff girls in that room. Donnie had made up the beds and left a couple towels on the chest of drawers that was next to each set of bunks. These were five-drawer chests, so each girl had two-and-a-half drawers plus about a foot of hanging space in the closet. The cowboy rooms on the second floor of the old Strater Hotel were better. I told the girls to relax and to feel free to look around until we rang the dinner bell. I can just imagine the conversation between those poor Kansans after I left.

Those two young gals worked just as hard as the rest of us, struggling to complete the work on the lodge and four cabins. They were just great! A couple weeks later, more staff, both male and female, arrived and they too pitched right in. Believe it or not, but by now I'm sure you believe it, we were actually still in the building process throughout the summer and any time a staff member had nothing else to do, they were assigned to some job that related to construction. During the summer, a number of guests also helped with various jobs. They thought it was fun! Regardless, we didn't complete much of the work that should have been finished before we opened.

Carson's horses weren't all that bad for riders with experience, but for green or first time riders, it was pretty hairy at times. When I recall some of the rides, especially those long rides into the San Juan Forest, on horses that were not well trained for dudes, I'm frankly amazed that some guest didn't get badly hurt or killed. As it was, we had folks come off, but fortunately, there were no serious injuries.

It should be noted, and this is important, that in the 60's and 70's there where not nearly as many lawyers as there are now and lawyers did not take frivolous or ridiculous cases to court because Colorado juries had little tolerance for such cases. If a guest fell off his horse and broke a leg, even if the horse had bucked him off, chances are we would have taken the injured party to the hospital where he would have paid his own way and that would have been the end of it. We would have said that we were very sorry and the guest would probably have said something like, "Oh, don't worry about it. It was probably my own fault." We never had a law suit brought against us as a result of a horse-related injury. The foregoing not withstanding, we learned that spending time training the horses before the season began was something we absolutely had to do if we were going to live up to our declaration that we would *provide safe and enjoyable horseback riding.*

George was in charge of the riding program and the wranglers. Being the handy guy he was, his services were always in demand for a host of jobs and that left him little time for getting the horses ready and the crew trained. Still he didn't complain. He'd be asked to do something and he'd just say, "No problem." But just between you and me, I think he did resent being pulled away from his primary job as head wrangler and this got him upset a lot more than he let on. Woody would have been a big help but he needed to make some money. Reluctantly, he left to seek work as a masonry contractor.

Whenever time permitted, Jim and I helped George by working with the horses, guiding rides and giving riding lessons. We also supervised the rifle, trap and archery ranges. All three of us would be involved with evening programs in one way or another, although the burden of those programs fell mostly on me.

Our wives had their areas of work as planned during those early meetings in Ohio. Marye was the cook, but she had help from Donnie, Twila and my oldest daughter, Nancy. Twila took care of the office duties but she did all sorts of other things as did Donnie, whose main job was that of head housekeeper. It must be said that Donnie made sure those cabins were scrupulously clean in spite of the masses of dirt that the guests brought in or the wind blew in. Marye did a great job in the kitchen. That gal could cook and bake! No two ways about it, albeit she was something of a "health nut" and decried the way most of us ate. Marye served up meals that were delicious and actually good for you. The older children were given jobs, too. Everyone made a huge effort to get ready for the first guests of 1963.

Our first bit of business was a big barbeque in early June. Freddie Kroeger of Farmers Supply lined us up with a DeMolay group of five hundred boys and their adult leaders. The lunch went well although we had some behind-the-scenes problems. I tried to light the deck oven and it wouldn't fire up. I kept fooling with it, knowing full well from my experiences with the little heater in the Coney Cove bathroom, that propane gas, unlike natural gas, is heavier than air and doesn't evaporate. I finally got the burner to ignite and it did so with a bang that could be heard a mile away as I was blown plumb across the kitchen and into the opposite wall. People came running from every direction and found me sprawled out on the kitchen floor with all the hair gone from my eyebrows and arms. Luckily, I was wearing a cowboy hat so I didn't loose very much hair off of my head. Explosion notwithstanding, the oven was lit. Someone suggested that there should be an easier way to light the oven and I said that I sure planned to find out before I tried to light it again.

Something happened with the water. Actually the water was fine, it was just that none of it was coming out of the taps. Freddie Kroeger, who had sold us the pumps and other well equipment, came to the rescue and figured out what was wrong and eventually we had water again. The three toilets in the lodge got a lot of use, as you can imagine but, before the event was over, all three were plugged with sewage backing up from both the toilets and floor drains. It was a smelly mess. With the bathroom facilities out of order, the trees around the area got peed on a lot.

We received $750 for that barbecue, pretty damn good we thought. We charged $1.50 per person and I think it would be safe to say they sure as hell got their money's worth.

Our first honest-to-God dude ranch guests arrived the last Sunday of June. Were we ready for them? Hardly, and I'm afraid they knew it.

CHAPTER THIRTY

Do you folks have something against marriage?

We had two families of four and a couple reserved for our opening week. We were excited yet nervous because there was so much more work to do and the guests would be arriving before we were anywhere close to being ready.

Opening day was on the last Sunday of June, 1963. Dressed in our best western attire, we waited for the guests to arrive. In the early afternoon a car with Arizona license plates drove in and stopped behind Coney Cove. Just as we had rehearsed it, George rode up to the car on a good looking bay to greet our very first guests and in his version of a western drawl said, "Howdy folks and welcome to Colorado Trails Ranch. If you'll just follow me, I'll take you on up to your cabin." With that, he urged his horse into a smart trot and headed up the drive past the lodge and down the trail to *Twin Pines*, the first cabin on the right. I followed on foot. The new arrivals parked their car in front of the cabin and a boy and a girl jumped out and ran toward the cabin door.

The driver was Dick Bridges, a good-looking guy I judged to be in his mid thirties. His wife was a tall, attractive blonde gal who extended a hand and said, "I'm June Bridges. Pleased to meet you."

George dismounted and tied his horse to a tree branch with one rein. "I'm Hap Horton."

I introduced myself and we escorted the couple into the cabin where, much to my consternation, the kids were jumping up and down on the bunk beds with their shoes on! "We want the top beds," they screamed at their parents. Dick Bridges tried to settle the kids down so he could hear what George was telling them about their room. The Bridges listened half-heartedly until George mentioned that there would be another family in the adjoining room. The Bridges looked at each other then asked us if they could possibly have a room with something other than bunk beds or, better still, a cabin with two rooms.

Explaining that all of the rooms were furnished with bunk beds like the one we were standing in, George and I left. Outside, George walked over to his horse, grabbed the rein, pulled loose the slip knot, checked the cinch then turned to me and said, "I don't think they were any too happy with the bunk beds. What do you think?"

I took a Camel from my shirt pocket, lit it with a stick match, and took a long drag, exhaling the smoke slowly. "No, don't think so. Probably wasn't the set up they were expectin' to get. Guess they want another room with a regular bed, that's fer sure." George led his horse as we walked back down the cabin road. I looked back toward the car. "They haven't taken their stuff out of the car yet. I don't know. We'll just have to wait and see."

George mounted his horse and picked up the reins. "I'd better get on down below and wait for the next ones ta show up." He tapped his pony with a heel and trotted off.

The gals in the lodge wanted to know how it went and I said fine and that they would have a chance to meet the Bridges at dinner. At that point however, I wasn't all that sure we would see them at dinner or anywhere else. I walked through the dining room, which looked real nice all set up for dinner, then went out on the porch. I pulled up a chair so I could see the road below and watch George on his horse down by Coney Cove.

About ten minutes later, I heard footsteps on the dining room floor. Turning, I saw Dick Bridges heading for the porch door. He stopped for a few seconds to admire the view then took a seat next to mine. "Mind if we have a little talk?"

"No, not at all. What's on your mind?" (As if I didn't know!)

"I was just wondering. Do you folks have something against marriage?"

"Not sure I follow you pard. Whaddaya mean?"

"The bunk beds. You don't want married folks to sleep together at your ranch?" He paused then added, "Or is it something else . . ." Dick's voice trailed off.

"No. No, no, no. Ya see, we were mostly expecting single folks. Young men and woman who would share a room and that way it'd be pretty inexpensive for them." Dick's eyebrows shot up. "I don't mean they'd be in the same room, the men and women. They'd be in separate cabins. And the other thing is, we wanted to create, you know, the real ranch feeling, like you were a ranch hand in a regular bunk house, that sort of thing."

Dick thought a moment, "I see. But you have no problem with men and women sleeping together . . . ah, married folks, I mean."

I laughed out loud. "Damn Dick, I got four kids. I reckon me and the wife must a done it at least four times."

Bridges laughed. "I'm sorry; it just seemed kinda peculiar to June and me that's all. But it's okay. I've got the picture now. It'll be fine."

In my best Western drawl, I said, "Yeah, I reckon it would strike folks that way if they didn't know what we was tryin' t'get across . . . I mean the *Western* thing." Dick Bridges nodded his head and it appeared to me that maybe he was coming around. "Want a cup a coffee? I'll gettcha one. Wait here. By the way, wait 'till you taste my wife's cookin' tonight and ride around this beautiful country tomorrow, you won't be givin' your cabin another thought. Besides, when the kids are off on a ride or something, two people can get into one of them bunk beds if they put their minds to it." Bridges laughed.

I brought a couple mugs of coffee and Dick and I sat there chatting away getting to know each other a little. He was with the phone company in Phoenix. He told me his wife was a teacher and their kids, Mikelyn was 13 and Scott was 12. A little later he said he had better go back to the cabin and help June unpack. I was so relieved that he had decided to stay that I remember strolling into the kitchen singing, *It's a most unusual day.*

The other family of four and the couple arrived by car later on that afternoon and George escorted them to their cabins in much the same manner. The newcomers' reactions to the accommodations were similar to that of the Bridges, but they didn't turn right around and leave, as did some others during that first summer.

We had a great dinner with home cooking such as these folks had probably never had before. They raved about the meal, particularly the homemade breads and pie. The ten guests must have thought it strange to be the only ones sitting in a two thousand square foot dining room, large enough to accommodate a hundred people.

After the desert dishes had been cleared, I pulled out my Gretch guitar, got up in front of the room and invited the guests and staff to sing along with me. They seemed to enjoy it every bit as much as we had when we sang at the Jack and Jill Ranch. One of the songs we sang was the then popular theme of the Negro anti-segregation movement, *We shall overcome.* Honestly, I had no idea what the song was all about; somehow its implications escaped me. For me, it was just a great tune that I had heard Pete Seeger sing and I learned to play it. From my perspective, it was another good folk tune. That, my friend, should tell you how isolated we were from the *real* world.

We had no television and I paid little attention to the news even when I read it while working for KDGO radio. While I'm sure we were aware of Martin Luther King and his marches in the south, I don't think the impact of the movement was relevant for us. So I blithely went through the summer singing, *We shall overcome*. When we had guests from the Deep South, those areas affected most by segregation, I would get strange looks from some of the southerners when we sang the song. Finally, some guy asked me, "Why the hell are you singing that damn song?" I asked him what he meant and he told me in no uncertain terms that he hated that song and everything it represented. When I told him I had no idea what the song was all about, he gave me a questioning look as if to say, What are you . . . a moron? He then proceeded to explain the civil rights movement, albeit from the perspective of a prejudiced white man and said that it was an insult to play that song in front of southerners. I couldn't afford to take a chance on that family leaving before their week was over, so I didn't play the song again that week or whenever I knew we had southern folks on the ranch. My conscience, of which I had very little, would remind me that I was a chicken shit to cop out by not singing the song, but my brain, which I did engage on occasion, insisted that we needed the money to survive. The brain always won that argument.

Here's another example of the degree of our isolation in terms of world events. Some years later on a Sunday, I sat down to dinner with five guests and during the course of conversation one of the fellows said to me, "Well, what do you think about the war?"

I assumed the guy was fixing to tell me a joke, so I replied, "I give up. What war?"

The man gave me a strange look, "The war between the Arabs and the Jews."

I still thought he was embarking on a joke so I said, "Yeah, what about it?"

Now, everyone at the table is giving me a strange look. "You don't have any idea what I'm talking about, do you?" I shook my head. "The war between the Arabs and Israel that started about a week ago?"

"This isn't a joke, right? Okay, I really don't know what you're talking about. So, how's it going?"

They all laughed. "It's not going. It's over! It was over in six days. The Jews beat the hell out of them. It's over!

The "Six Day War" was a major international event and not one of us working at Colorado Trails knew a damn thing about it.

Let's see. Where was I? I was going to tell you about that first Monday of our opening week. Monday morning after breakfast, the guests came down to the corral and George got them lined out with horses. After I gave them a riding lesson, they went off on a trail ride. The six adults rode in one group and the four children in another. Each section had a guide in both front and back. The horses were well behaved and the guests came back a couple hours later bubbling with enthusiasm.

Our children's counselor kept the kids busy between rides so their parents never heard the children say, "I'm bored." That is something that vacationing parents really appreciate and they said so. We had no swimming pool but we did have a large pond that was used for swimming, although the water was colder than a well digger's ass. We didn't have any formal game courts, but we did have a flat area where we put up a volley ball net. We played softball, had a target for archery, shooting stalls for riflery and a clay pigeon thrower for trap shooting. Among the shooting sports, archery was the most difficult because the arrows that missed the target (that would be most of them) ended up in tall grass and were very difficult to find. We spent a lot more time looking for arrows than we did shooting them.

It was all very primitive and about as minimal as it could be. What we did have however, was a comprehensive riding program with lessons. Teaching riding and training horses was my forte and I don't mind saying that I was damn good at it. Riding lessons continued throughout the week both in the confines of the arena and on the trail. Everyone loved that. When it came to teaching riding and training horses for pleasure riding, we definitely were innovators and remained so for almost forty years.

Our guests had something to do all day and every evening as well. Trips on the narrow gauge train and water skiing at Vallecito Lake, fishing trips and picnics at interesting and picturesque venues added both variety and quality to the vacation experience. This full program concept with two and, later, three separate children's programs, was something of a departure from that which most western dude ranches offered at the time. Admittedly, I stole some ideas from the Jack and Jill and Silver Spur ranches, particularly in the entertainment area, but I have always been very up front about that, claiming that I don't care where I get my original ideas.

Providing a friendly atmosphere, excellent food, spotless (albeit Spartan) rooms, beautiful country in which to ride, horses that didn't pitch you off, plus a staff of attractive, clean-cut kids, was our stock in trade. That mix seemed to work and the guests overcame their initial disappointment with the accommodations, our minimalist sports facilities, and the sorry way things looked generally. What we lacked in facilities we made up for in program content and in that regard, we were able to meet and exceed their expectations of what a dude ranch vacation should be. Many guests from that first summer, returned the following year and for years thereafter. The Dick Bridges family was one of those. Mikelyn Bridges worked for us during her college vacations and Scott Bridges moved to Durango many years ago building a home on the Florida Road just seven miles from

Colorado Trails. Dick and June divorced. Dick remarried, and when he retired, he built a home in the Animas Valley just north of Durango.

I was chatting with Scott about those early visits to our ranch and he recalled that kids loved the A-frame cabins. He told me that his family had a fabulous time and loved every minute of their vacations with us. He reminded me that during their second visit in 1964, I tried to talk his dad into buying stock in the ranch. Dick seriously considered my offer but eventually declined. Scott said that his dad regrets that decision to this day.

It was during that first summer that we began to use the phrases, *Just for the Fun of it and Colorado's friendliest* in our advertising. But the truth is, there were times when I wasn't all that friendly. The pressure of being in charge, the resentment I was feeling from my partners, whether real or imagined, the perpetual money shortage and my failing marriage sure as hell didn't contribute to being one of "Colorado's friendliest." I recall a guest saying to me that she thought I was, at times, "less than pleasant."

I would get upset and cranky with the staff, my wife and kids. For example, I wanted everything to be as perfect as we could get it. Whatever the guest wanted, I tried to accommodate. Frequently I repeated our credo to staff members who had forgotten it. "Your job at CTR is to make certain that our guests have the best vacation they ever had." I would be trying to create a certain mood among the guests during our final campfire sing-along and the mood would be broken by one of the kids, usually Bradley, fooling around and Marye did nothing to quiet him. Then I would get depressed and want to escape. Sometimes I did, just walk out on some activity in which I was participating, leaving the staff and guests wondering what the hell had happened.

One evening late in the summer, after walking away from a Saturday night chuck wagon dinner, I got into our little VW and began driving. I headed out toward Bayfield then turned east on highway 160. I began driving faster and faster, the gas pedal pressed to the floor. My head was spinning. Unexpectedly, I decided to run head on into the first big rig that came along, just end it right then and there. I thought, *The hell with it! It's just too much. I can't deal with it.* I saw a semi coming down the two-lane road and I decided that, *This will be quick and easy. I'll just slip into the oncoming lane in front of that truck and that's that.*

When the semi was about thirty seconds away, I had a sudden flash, *What about the truck driver? What's going to happen to him? Will he be killed too? Maybe he's happy with his life and doesn't want it to end.* My foot relaxed on the gas pedal and I remained on my side of the road as the semi whizzed by. I pulled off the highway onto a dirt road, stopped, shut down the engine and let go of the wheel. I laid my head back and closed my eyes. I had a headache, spots were dancing in front of my eyes and my entire body started to shake uncontrollably. I felt very cold. With teeth chattering, I spoke, "What's going on here? What am I doing? Is this what I've worked all these years for . . . to end up like this? Am I going to let every little thing that isn't perfect throw me for a loop?"

The violent shaking subsided, my head cleared and I opened my eyes. I got out of the car and walked down the dusty road. I saw mountains to the east and north and fields of freshly cut hay in precise windrows. I slipped through the fence, picked up a hand-full of the curing green hay and held it to my face letting its wonderful aroma wash over me. Steers were grazing unconcerned behind a barbed wire fence while above, puffy white clouds floated in a dazzling blue sky. The early evening sun was warm on my face and I thought, *This is what is real. This is what it's all about. I'm out west in Colorado where I belong.*

I turned to the steers and shouted, "I can do this. I *will* do this! I don't give a shit what happens or what anybody says or how long it may take. I *will* build the best Goddamn dude ranch in the state. I *will* do it!" Taking a deep breath, I walked back to the car muttering aloud, "Now just relax. You're gonna be okay."

When I returned to the ranch, I felt calm. I had experienced an epiphany and I knew it. Now, I was sure that I was mentally ready for whatever lay ahead.

When I got into bed, Marye whispered, "You stormed out so abruptly. We've been worried. Where have you been?"

"Nowhere special. Just out for a drive. Blow off some steam."

"Well, what's the matter?"

I lay there in the darkened room. A smile spread across my face. She turned toward me. "Tell me, what *is* the problem?"

I turned my head and whispered, "Nothing. No problem."

"Oh, don't tell me that. That's what George always says."

"Well, I'm sayin' it now."

CHAPTER THIRTY ONE

"That bullet missed me by a hair!"

After a few weeks of operation, the staff became more adept at their jobs and settled into the daily routine. The guests were the big problem. We just didn't have enough of them. The best census for the entire summer was probably no more than 20 people. During the slack weeks, and that was most of them, we continued to work at various projects. It was cheap labor but still more than we could afford. I had some one-page fliers printed which we took to the train station each afternoon and distributed them to disembarking passengers. We booked a few guests from that effort and from the Chamber of Commerce, but the pickins were mighty slim.

In August, Bill Groves from Camp Silver Spruce stopped by with an offer to buy seventy acres for $4,100.00. Can you believe it? We had paid $77 an acre and now they were offering to buy back at $58. As much as we could have used the money, we turned down their offer. *That* was one of our smarter decisions.

By Labor Day most of the staff had left, leaving us to take care of the few guests booked for September. On closing day, after bidding good bye to our last guests, I sat on the lodge porch with a cup of coffee, lit a cigarette and propped my feet up on the railing. The oak brush on the opposite hillside, the cottonwood trees along Shearer Creek and the groves of quaking aspen that dotted the hillside above the Florida River were beginning to don their fall dress. I was feeling both sad and happy. I was sad the season was over and the guests were gone, as I enjoyed their company and loved performing for them. Concurrently, I was happy the season was over because we were exhausted and needed rest.

In spite of the huge effort we had put into the previous three months, we were actually deeper in debt than we were in June. The gross income from summer operations was only $12,300 and that didn't come close to what we needed. As for the three families, we ended up working all summer for no more than room and board. Even our poorly paid staff fared better. Some hunters had reserved for October, but hunting income would not amount to much and the profit, if any, would be negligible.

I smoked, drank coffee, and pondered the same question that had dogged me for years . . . how to avoid the inevitable? The same worn out answers played again. We had to sell more stock or borrow more money. Neither seemed very promising.

Details of the hunting season that began around mid-October have long since been forgotten except for one incident. Two hunters had gone back to the ranch with George to take a hot shower and spend a night in a warm cabin. George guided them back to camp early the next morning but by the time they arrived, we had all left to hunt. George told his men to move up the canyon to a little open meadow and tie their horses to the only two trees in the clearing. George then left to ride the ridge to the east above them and try to move game in their direction. He had no sooner made it to the top of the ridge when he heard gunfire and yelling coming from the valley below. He quickly rode back to the place where he had left his hunters and saw our roan mare laying on the ground with the two men standing near her.

I was north of them working the same high ridge and heard the shot and the yelling. Sound travels far in those canyons. Wondering what the hell was going on, I rode down as fast as I could and found the three of them in the little clearing. The excited hunters blurted out this story: After tying their horses to the two trees and loosening their cinches, they proceeded to remove their rifles from their saddle scabbards. One hunter said that he was standing by the neck of his horse, the red roan, pulling out his rifle when he heard a shot, felt something whiz by his face and in the next instant, his horse fell to the ground. The man was white as snow and shaking badly. I thought he was going to faint as he exclaimed, "My God! I could have been killed. That bullet missed me by a hair!" Upon hearing the shot, the other hunter had looked up toward the ridge from whence the sound had come and saw a man with a rifle running off.

The wounded horse was alive and within a few minutes got to her feet. We looked her over and saw the entry hole in her neck about six inches below her head. I palpated her neck trying to locate the bullet and thought I found it about ten inches below the entry hole between the jugular vein and the wind pipe. Using the long narrow blade of my Buck knife, I cut a hole where I hoped to find the bullet but it was not there. I cut another hole at a likely location and no bullet. Then another and another until I was below the base of the neck in her chest and that is where I located the slug. What was so amazing was that the bullet, traveling as it did, between the wind pipe and jugular vein, did not sever one or both of them. I got a bottle of Scarlet Oil from my saddlebags and poured some in the top hole but most of it ran out the other holes so George plugged the holes with his fingers. After a few hours, I led the wounded mare and the two men back to the ranch. The hunters decided that they had had enough and left. The red roan mare had an uneventful recovery and we continued to use her for many years thereafter. How much fun you ask, is guiding and outfitting hunters? Not that much!

Hunting season was over and we winterized the buildings. What winterizing entailed will be explained in a subsequent chapter. Jim left to join Twila and their kids in Ohio, the Hortons moved their house trailer to the Island Cove trailer park in Durango, George got a job as a dispatcher with the Highway Patrol and I tried to get back on with KDGO. I was told that my services were no longer needed. It seems that my annual hiatus to work at CTR was no longer acceptable to the management. Besides, they had hired someone to take my place and were not about to fire him. The contemporary expression is, "I was bummed." I had played a significant part in creating the *Kay Dee Go Sound*. Additionally, I was their number one salesman of air time. I have to say that I felt betrayed, although I couldn't blame them. Had I been running the station, I wouldn't have hired me either.

CHAPTER THIRTY TWO

Don't go anywhere, I'm coming over.

After being inundated by summer tourists, after Labor Day Durango became something of a ghost town. Consequently, most of the restaurants and some businesses closed. Most of the bars, however, remained open all winter. The Full House, owned by Bob Cosgrove and Chuck Johnson, was one of them. I met these two actors at the Diamond Circle Theater while attending the melodrama with our guests. The Full House was near the train station at the lower end of Main Avenue and patronized by locals and Fort Lewis College students. Some of them were serious drunks. It was in this highly charged venue that I found myself after hunting season.

Shortly after I had been rejected by KDGO, I saw Bob Cosgrove and when asked, I told him I was looking for work over the winter. He hired me on the spot to take his place tending bar and assisting Chuck with the entertainment on Friday and Saturday nights. Bob was going to winter in Hawaii.

When we first started working together, most of the comedy was ad lib stuff, but after a while, the patter became rapid and funny. I played the piano, guitar, and sang harmony.

Home was a house we rented for the winter on north Main Avenue. Living in town made it possible for Marye to get a job at Community Hospital. The kids loved living in town as they were able to participate in all sorts of things that living in the country precluded.

The time I spent at The Full House was a time that I sure don't regret. I learned many things about people while working there. Mostly I learned that people who spend a lot of time in bars are a sorry lot. To this day, I rarely visit a bar. I may have had my faults, but being a damn barfly wasn't one of them.

It was not difficult for me to say goodbye to The Full House and its patrons. I had my fill of working nights, listening to the mindless chatter of drunks and was eager to move back to the ranch although I'm not so sure that my kids were all that eager to leave town. They loved the many opportunities living in Durango afforded them. Marye wasn't all that excited about returning to the ranch either, as she was enjoying her job at the hospital and the comfort of living in a house that wasn't plagued with the problems of Coney Cove.

Like it or not, we gave up the house and moved back to the ranch. Coney Cove was a mess! Over the winter the pack rats had moved in, the skunks had taken up residence under the house again, some of the water pipes had burst in spite of my best winterizing efforts, and I had a hell of a time getting the water going. You can well imagine that after all of the wonderful pleasures of city living, my family was not too pleased with conditions at Coney Cove. Regardless, we cleaned the place up, rid the cabin of most of the rodents, and went to work on ranch projects.

In the early spring, I packed up our little blue VW beetle and went on a marketing trip. I wrote to my partners on April 22, 1964.

I took two promotional trips so far this year. The first one covered some 4,300 miles and took close to three weeks and the total cost was $300.00. I traveled into Kansas, Western Missouri, Oklahoma and Texas. I tried to see as many guests from last year as possible. One of the reasons that the trip cost so little was the fact that most of our guests had me stay for meals and put me up for the night, so that most of the cost went for gas and auto expense. In cities where we had several guests, I would stay one night with one and another night with another and so on. Without exception, all the guests I visited expressed a desire to return and claimed that they had a wonderful time. I was shown movies and slides of the ranch in I don't know how many households. The people took brochures to give to friends and associates at work, some of them even threw parties and invited a group of friends in to hear about the ranch. Many of these people went very much out of their way to be helpful.

During the trip I contacted some square dance groups, called on travel agents and other groups that people told me about.

The second trip took me to Phoenix and Los Angeles. I talked to various members of the Phoenix Industrial Recreation Council, left them with supplies of brochures, plus I had 5,000 one-page bulletin board notices printed which will be displayed at all the member companies. I am trying to determine what pays off. The only way to know for sure is to try it.

Without a doubt, the most important contact I made during the Phoenix trip was with an executive secretary at AiResearch. Here's how that came about.

One day I saw Frank Bostock and his wife at a restaurant and they asked me to join them for lunch. I mentioned that I would soon be leaving for Phoenix to sell vacations. Frank's wife told me that she had a very good friend who worked for AirResearch Corp. in Phoenix. She thought that her friend could help me with the people who ran the employee's tour program. The name she gave me was Mary Ann Davis.

After arriving in Phoenix and checking into a cheap motel, I called Mary Ann and told her who I was. She had heard about me from her friend in Durango and said that she would be glad to do what she could to help me. As it turned out, she was the AirResearch representative for the Industrial Recreation Council (IRC), so she knew quite a bit about how that organization functioned. This was a great lead and I thought it could have huge possibilities. I suggested that we get together for dinner that evening so we could talk it over in detail. She agreed. After all, I was a friend of a friend and this was in no way to be considered as any kind of a *date*. It was to be a business dinner and a time for discussion.

I arrived at the Davis home at the agreed upon time and rang the bell. The door opened and there stood a trim, very attractive lady. She was 5'4", had black hair, brown eyes and a lovely smile. Over dinner, I learned that she grew up in the little town of Mesa near Phoenix and that her Sicilian parents still lived there. She told me that she was 30 years old, had a boy and a girl and that she was recently divorced. Over a nice meal at a restaurant in Scottsdale, she explained how the Industrial Recreational Council worked and how I might use it to promote vacations.

I picked at my food as we talked. This was exciting! The more Mary Ann told me about the program, the more I liked it. I also realized that the lady had charm and wit and carried on a very intelligent conversation. After a few hours with her, I was aware that there seemed to be a physical attraction that I found disconcerting. I kept telling myself to stay focused, that this was a business meeting and a damned important one at that.

After dinner, at her suggestion, we went to a club for a drink. There were several couples on the small dance floor, and after watching them for a while I asked Mary Ann if she would like to dance. It quickly became obvious to both of us that something was happening. There was some energy or vibes or whatever you want to call it, but as we continued dancing through the next song and the next and the next, we began holding each other very close. My lips were touching her ear, just barely brushing the lobe. I whispered, "This feels very good. *You* feel very good."

She whispered back, "Yes. Yes it does."

We hardly spoke a word as I drove her home. At her door, she told me she had a wonderful time and repeated that she would be happy to help me with the IRC. We looked at each other for a long time then, not saying anything but feeling everything, we kissed, first lightly then long and deeply. It was a marvelous kiss. Holding both of her hands in mine, I told her the name and location of the motel where I was staying. I asked if she worked on Saturday and she told me she didn't so I inquired if she would want to join me for breakfast. She said she wasn't sure. Nothing was decided one way or the other. I invited her to join me for dinner again and she replied that I should call her in the afternoon.

The ringing phone woke me. I looked at my watch. It was a little after seven. I lifted the receiver and mumbled a hello. Mary Ann said, "Don't go anywhere. I'm coming over."

We went out again that evening. On Sunday, she invited me to dinner at her parent's house in Mesa. I met the family and it went well. They called her *Dolly*, explaining that as a baby, she was like a little doll.

I remember vividly our conversation the night before I left Phoenix. We were sitting on the couch in her living room. I told her that I cared for her . . . a lot. She told me that she was glad that I had come into her life. She said she hated being alone, "Alone is lonely."

I agreed. Then I said, "I have to tell you something."

Her eyes widened and she stared at me intently. "You're not going to tell me you're married? You're not going to tell me *that* are you?" Her voice was quivering and her eyes filled with tears. It was as if a bomb had suddenly exploded. "Don't tell me that . . . please don't tell me that." I tried to say something but she went on, "I knew it was too good to be true. I knew it, I knew it. Why? Why didn't you tell me right from the start? Why did you let me love you?" Her tone became angry and I thought she might even take a poke at me. "Why aren't you wearing a wedding ring? What's the matter with you?"

I told her that I had never worn a wedding band and that Marye and I were separated and that we were going to get divorced, which was true. That was the reason why I had not told her I was married. I blurted out, "I'm in love with you that's why I'm telling you this now. If I didn't love you, I wouldn't have said anything, but because I do love you I had to tell you. Can't you understand that? Please try to understand, I didn't mean for any of this to happen. It just did. I'm sorry."

Mary Ann sat there glaring at me through tear filled eyes. She heard and understood everything I had just said but she didn't want any part of it. Without another word, she jumped up from the couch and went straight to the door, opened it and told me to get out and never come back. I tried to talk to her but she was adamant. Pushing me toward the door, she screamed, "Don't call, don't ever, ever try to see me or contact me in any way again . . . EVER!" I pleaded with her to let me explain but she propelled me out the door, slammed it shut, and that was that.

That episode was devastating. I tried to talk to her many times, but she would not speak to me and eventually I stopped trying. But I never stopped thinking about her. I felt sure that I was in love with her and that this was the real thing. I had never been with anyone, including Sonja, who got to me so completely as did Mary Ann. I just knew that somehow I would have to find a way to get her back in my life.

What I now had to do was get a divorce and then make the ranch a success. I was sure the divorce would be finalized soon, but the ranch part might take some time, perhaps a lot of time.

CHAPTER THIRTY THREE

Pouring money into a black hole

I returned from my trip on my thirty-seventh birthday. Although she was very angry with me, Mary Ann didn't do anything to sabotage my connection with the IRC. I spoke with a number of people who worked for large companies employing thousands and most were very receptive to the dude ranch vacation concept. Durango was only an eight hour drive from Phoenix or just a couple hours by air, much closer than most of the Colorado ranches. And Durango was a lot easier to get to from LA than the northern Colorado ranches or those in Wyoming and Montana. I played that mileage card both in Phoenix and Los Angeles. I thought I did a little better job with the travel agents and airline tour desks in L.A than I had the previous year.

The brochure that I had put together over the winter certainly helped our marketing effort. This new piece had pictures of the lodge, a better picture of a cabin, plus scenes of folks having fun on trial rides, at meals, around campfires and so on. I was satisfied that the time and money we spent on the new brochure and my trip would pay off.

Of course, I didn't mention Mary Ann to anyone except to say that she had been very helpful. My good friend Don Stickle from KDGO was one exception. I told him all about her and what had happened. He empathized with me, but other than being a good listener, there wasn't much he could do to help.

Meanwhile, time was marching on and we had a hell of a lot of work to do before opening for the summer. We attempted to improve the look of the ranch and attend to a number of unfinished items that we didn't get to the previous year. On May 24, 1964 we had a directors meeting followed by a stockholders meeting. It wasn't the big encounter we had in December and it was concluded in an hour. George, Donnie and I were the only participants as Marye was in California. I gave an account of what had been accomplished since the December meeting: We had rewritten the brochure, we had purchased the eight double beds proving once and for all we were not in favor of what many guests called the "Marriage Penalty." We now had eight rooms with a double bed and a set of bunks in each, and when cabin six was completed, four rooms with two sets of bunk beds in each. We bought a used hay wagon. We installed lighting in the snack bar. We finally completed the permanent wiring and lighting in the laundry area and re-wired our main electrical panel to code (more or less). The gray cement block walls of the game room and snack bar received a coat of white paint, but the plain concrete floor remained.

During the previous summer, the guests had been worried that a bear or some wild animal would attack as they walked back to their cabins in the dark. To improve that situation, we cut a couple of poles and placed one about a third of the way down the cabin road and the other a hundred or so yards beyond then hung a light on each of them. The two lights provided some physiological relief but really didn't help all that much. To turn them on, we had to run down to each light pole and throw the switch. When the guests were back in their cabins after the evening program, someone had to run back down to turn the lights off as we didn't want to waste electricity. As a reader of this history, I know you must be thinking, "Do I really need to know about a couple of lousy lights? What's the big deal?" That's exactly my point. It was a big deal. Every little so-called improvement we made those first few years was a big deal to us and, not so incidentally to the guests, especially the returning guests.

At the insistence of the ditch rider, we installed a head gate and a metering box. A ditch rider is the guy who checks on the amount of water being used to make sure that it is no more than the adjudicated amount, that is, the quantity of water you are *legally* entitled to. (This water information may be considered optional reading.) A head gate is a large valve used to regulate the amount of irrigation water flowing in a ditch and through a Parshall Flume, a simple device that measures the amount of water flowing in the ditch. Isn't that interesting? Of course it is, because we had to put those devices in or risk having all of our irrigation water turned off. Yes, they can do that and they *will* do that. In Colorado, water is a very touchy subject.

Probably the biggest job we completed that spring was cutting and "planting" two hundred and forty fence posts and stretching four wires of barbed on them. That was a rough job, especially with Hilton Fix to contend with. How do I know it was 240 posts? It says so in the minutes. Who is Hilton Fix? Be patient and I'll tell you about him.

The May 24 minutes also state that there was still some important work to be completed before we opened for the summer. We wanted to build a decent outdoor cooking structure, plus tables and benches at the cookout area adjacent to Shearer Creek. The cookout area was in a beautiful place, but the facilities were minimal. In fact, there were no facilities to speak of. We just had some rocks forming up a little fire pit and we did our cooking about the same way we did in hunting camp. In spite of the Spartan facilities, we still served delicious homemade buttermilk pancakes, wonderful T-bone steaks and other foods over which the guests oooed and ahhhed. They thought the rustic appearance, the complete lack of amenities to be truthful about it, was totally in character with a western ranch.

We still had to finish the electrical wiring and plumbing of cabin six including sewer lines and a septic tank. We needed to backfill around the pump house and water storage tank before some kid fell in and got hurt. There were innumerable issues crying for attention that I insisted had to be completed before guests arrived. It was May 24 and yet the minutes reveal that we hadn't even begun getting the cabins and lodge ready.

Camp Silver Spruce rejected our offer to allow their campers to use our riding trails for a fee of $200 for the entire summer. They felt that $200 was, and this is hard to believe, much too expensive. There was however, one bright note in my report, the approval of a supplemental loan of $10,000 from SBA. Quoting from the minutes,

The SBA insisted on dispersing the proceeds of the loan directly to our creditors. Mr. Elder advised the he had purchased [an additional] $7,500 worth of stock, proceeds of which have been used for paying creditors other than those paid by SBA and [for paying] operating expenses.

Again I was pouring money into a black hole, but by this time I was determined to do whatever it took to keep the outfit afloat or go down with the ship. The minutes state that with regard to unpaid salaries, the Hortons wanted promissory notes while I agreed to take stock. I am sure that the Hortons opted for notes instead of stock because they didn't have any real confidence that the stock would ever be worth anything. As for me, taking stock for back wages turned out to be a good decision.

I reported that the SCS would not provide any money for land improvement but I had arranged for the state forester to mark mature trees that would be suitable for cutting.

The forester has advised that the ranch has approximately one million board feet for cutting and the value should be approximately $8,000.

Wow! We were talking about some important money and that did not include the hundreds of great looking spruce, pine, and fir trees that we could cut for Christmas trees and sell for perhaps as much as a buck or two each. The final paragraph of the minutes reads,

There has been one man on the payroll since May 1st and another started May 14th. Additional members of the staff will start from June 1st and the rest will start the last week in June.

From that information, it appears that we didn't have very many guests booked for June.

The stockholder meeting began at 1:25 and was adjourned ten minutes later. Here's what happened:

The President advised the stock holders that reservations were well ahead of the number that were in at this time last year, however we still had a long way to go to insure a successful summer. He further advised that the hunting program had not yet been decided upon, but that he was thinking on joining up with James Mars of Bayfield from whom we are renting horses this summer in order to make more effective hunting programs with perhaps Mr. Mars handling the high camps.

Who is James Mars? Stay with me and you'll soon learn more about this Texas cowboy that everyone called *Shorty*. But first, as promised, let's take a look at a character by the name of Hilton Fix.

CHAPTER THIRTY FOUR

Hilton Fix

Marye and the kids had returned from California and although there was nothing overt to suggest that we were on the cusp of a break up, we both knew the marriage had to end. At the risk of oversimplifying a complex problem, I reckon our relationship can be summed up with one very familiar word, incompatibility.

But, let's get on with it. I promised to tell you the story of a very interesting character who came into our lives quite unexpectedly. I'll introduce him by conjuring up a scene that took place many years ago. While I have no recorded account of the exact conversations that took place, I do have excellent recall of the man, the words he used, his style of talking and his mannerisms.

One afternoon in the spring of '64, Marye answered a knock on the door of Coney Cove. Opening it, she found a grizzled old man standing there, hat in hand. He told her that he had been looking for ranch work in the Durango area for several days and that a man at the Phillips 66 station suggested that he contact us. It was a warm day and the old waddie looked hot and tired, so Marye invited him in for a cold drink. He carefully wiped his dusty boots on a piece of carpeting before entering. She asked the man his name and he told her it was Hilton Fix. She gave him some ice tea then, since she hadn't seen or heard a vehicle, asked where he had parked his car.

"Don't have no machine, ma'am. I reckon I come up on shank's mare." Hilton smiled, revealing a cavity devoid of teeth. While sitting in the kitchen with the man, Marye observed that his dress was that of an old-time cowboy; Levis turned up at the cuff, high heel boots, colorful bandana wrapped around his neck and a faded red shirt with pearl snaps. His denim jacket, frayed at the cuffs and buttonholes, had copper buttons embossed with the word "LEE." Hilton placed his wide brimmed hat under the chair, crown down.

"Are you saying that you walked all the way up here from town?"

"Reckon so," Hilton answered. "Purdy fair piece, that's fer dang sure. Reckon I didn't know what I was gettin' in ta whenever I started out. Feller down there at the fillin' station said he didn't think it'd be too fer ta go." Hilton cracked a smile, "It be a fair walk 'cept it was mostly uphill. How high up is yer outfit anyways?"

Marye, somewhat amazed, said, "Well, it's seven-thousand-five hundred feet here, about a thousand feet higher than Durango and I think it must be more than twenty miles from that gas station. So, yes, I'm quite sure you did have a rather tedious journey." (Marye talked like that.)

"Don't suppose you folks got any work fer an ole hand like me would ya? I kin do jest 'bout anythin' y'all need, 'cept I'm a little too stove up t'be doin' much fancy riding. Oh, I kin still ride, but what I mean is, I ain't much fer breakin' no young stock . . . such as that."

"I'm afraid you will have to discuss that with my husband when he returns. Meanwhile, I'll give you some more tea and you can take it outside and sit under that big cottonwood tree near the corral. Would you care to do that? Feel free to look around if you like. He shouldn't be very long."

Actually, Marye was, as she told me that evening, quite anxious to get old Hilton out of the house because he stunk like a dead horse in the sun. She didn't say it like that of course. She probably said that his body odor was a bit overpowering. However, when I got back a short time later and got a whiff of him, the dead horse thing came to mind straight off. In his defense I would have to say that it was a long, hard, dusty, uphill walk that probably took him half a day, so I think he was entitled to a bit of sweat and the smell that goes with it.

Hilton told me that he had run away from home when he was just a kid and ended up on some cow outfit eventually becoming a pretty good hand, or so he said. He claimed he was 54 years old but had been "rode hard over the years" and so he was "a little broke down but still plenty able to do a day's work." I guessed his age to be closer to 64.

"Tell ya what, Hilt" (He said that I should call him Hilt.), "why don't you clean up a mite then come back to the house about six for dinner." He said that sounded just fine. I told him he could bunk up in the barn loft if he wanted to and tomorrow we'd try to do some fencing to see how we got along. I told him that if it worked out, I'd give him room and board but would not be able to pay him anything until our summer season was underway. Without asking what the pay would be, he said that it sounded "like a fair bargain." I got him a towel and some Lifebuoy soap (an old time deodorant soap) and showed him where he could wash up.

That night Marye had prepared a treat for me and the kids. Artichokes! I guess they were selling them cheap down at the Safeway so Marye got a half a dozen nice ones and gave everyone a whole artichoke, except Bradley who was too young to eat them. We all commenced to ripping off leaves and dipping them in the big bowl of melted butter that was strategically placed in the center of the round table. We were about half way through our 'chokes when I noticed that Hilton had hardly eaten any of his. I asked him if he didn't like artichokes and he said he reckoned he liked them fine but was having a hard time chewing them up. He was trying to eat the whole leaf instead of just the pulpy part at the base of the leaf. The problem, of course, was that he had no teeth. Plus, he informed us that he had never so much as seen one of "these durn things" before. Marye was embarrassed and kept apologizing but Hilton said it was fine and that next time he would dig out his store-bought teeth. He managed to gum down the rest of the meal, thanked Marye "fer a first class feed," as he put it, then excused himself and went out the door. I followed. We stood silently for a while, and then Hilt pulled out a tin of Bugler pipe tobacco and deftly rolled some of it with Top cigarette paper. "Is there a Catholic Church anywheres near here?" Hilton wanted to know. I told him there were several in Durango. He smoked a bit then said that he always went to church on Sundays if he possibly could. "I don't mind working ever' day if need be but if I kin jest git a little time off ta make it to the early Mass . . ."

I interrupted, "Sure. That be no problem. Fact is we don't usually work on Sundays if we can avoid it. After we get guests coming in, well, that'll be a different story and we'll have to work every day. But for now, you can plan on goin' to church on Sundays. I'll be happy to take you to town sos you don't have to hoof it like ya did today."

"Thank ya. I sure would appreciate that. Well, reckon I'd best bed down now so good night then." He pinched off the lit end of his cigarette with his thumb and finger and put the butt in the breast pocket of his Lee jacket. I watched as he walked over to the barn. Hilton showing up was a Godsend for sure, since there was so much work to do around the place.

Hilton was up before the cock crowed next morning and ready to go to work. We had a hardy breakfast (mostly soft foods as I remember) and got at it by seven, "at it" being building fence. I had cut a bunch of scrub oak for fence posts and now all we had to do was plant 'em. When Hilton saw those posts he asked if that was what I intended to use. When I said yes, he gave me a droll look, which told me straight off that he didn't much approve, but he said nothing.

Hilton had the big iron bar and I was on the business end of a posthole digger. After we had a hole dug and the post tamped in, we'd change over and he would run the digger. At one point, he suggested that the next time I buy fence posts, I should, "go ahead and get 'em with the holes." I had heard that old joke many times before but laughed anyway and replied, "That's a damn good idea however, I don't have no money to buy fence posts with or without the holes so we'll just have to keep plantin' these scrub oak posts."

It only took a few hours for me to learn the true nature of the man. We came across a huge rock right where we wanted to put a post so I suggested we move over a bit to avoid it. He shook his head. "I don't believe ya ought ta do that."

"What?"

"I reckon if these here posts is gonna be on ten foot centers then that's the way they should be, on ten foot centers not ten foot somethin.'"

I took off my hat and wiped the sweat from my forehead with my sleeve. "What the hell difference is it gonna make if we're off here and there?"

"Well, fer one thing, what are folks gonna say when they see the posts ain't even spaced or if the line ain't plumb straight? What's that gonna make us look like?" He answered his own question. "Gonna make us look like a couple of green horns, that's what. My daddy always said, do the job right or don't be doin' it a'tall."

During that first day with Hilton Fix, I learned several very good lessons and I learned a lot about the character of this old cowboy who told me, "When I was jest 12 year old, me and daddy was in his ole Essex machine [car] drivin' some place or 'nother an' he said, 'Hilt, take the wheel.' An I switched places with 'em and by golly, I drove that machine jest like that. An' you know how come I was able ta do that right off? 'Cause I'd been a watching him real close fer a long time sos when it come the time fer me to do the job, I could do it. Ya see what I'm a getting' at? 'Nother words, if a man'll jest pay close attention ta the particulars of a job, any job, he can learn how ta do it his own self. When I was a greenhorn kid ridin' with the wagon fetchin' water and splitting wood fer Cookie, I kep a keen eye on them wranglers and cowboys . . . the boss too whenever he come 'round . . ." Hilt paused for a moment and looked up at the sky for inspiration, "What was his name? Dang me if I kin remember it. Anyways, like I was sayin', I watched 'em how they roped and dallied, how they heated the irons and how long they held 'em on the calf, how they rode the broncs that first ride and, well, all of it, ya understand? And when the old boss . . . what the heck was his name?" Hilt tried hard to remember but gave up shaking his head in dismay then continued, "Anyway, when he said fer me ta do it, by golly I jest went ahead an' did it."

We built a straight fence with the posts right on ten-foot centers and Hilton stayed on and was a huge help. After he'd been on the job for a while and we had gathered up a crew, Hilton Fix always referred to me as "The Boss." Sometimes, if he didn't agree with the way I wanted a certain job done, he would refer to me by another name. If one of the hands asked, "Hey Hilt, why are you doing it that way?" Hilt would reply, "Ah, that's the way The Brain said fer me t'do it." So, as I found out later, most of the hands that summer were calling me, "The Brain." I don't think they meant it as any kind of a compliment.

CHAPTER THIRTY FIVE

Thinking with the wrong organ

The first guests of 1964 arrived in late June. The Dick Bridges family was among those early arrivals and we were delighted to see them again. When they saw the new double bed in their room, they were overjoyed. Having achieved the status of "Old Timers" (repeat guests), we affixed a brass nail to their name badges as a mark of distinction.

We had some great young men and women on our staff during our second season. Bob Bellmaine had been our ski boat driver the previous summer and I was so impressed with his upbeat personality that I hired him. This guy was terrific! Everybody loved him, especially the staff because he was the only one with a car. Bob was a hard worker and talented as hell. He performed hilarious impressions of Jonathan Winters, played guitar, drums and piano, had a good voice and knew a hundred songs. Besides teaching water skiing, he guided rides, taught archery and riflery and was my right-hand man. His buoyant personality, his intense work ethic and his honest character invigorated the rest of the staff. Our 1964 staff show was mostly his creation.

As long as I've mentioned it, perhaps a few words about our staff show would be appropriate. As the name implied, it was a variety show consisting of singing, comedy and short skits. Aside from the entertainment value our show provided, there were several other and perhaps more important consequences. Firstly, the show allowed staff members who normally were not directly involved in guest activities to be introduced in a unique way. Secondly, the guests had an opportunity to observe sports staff, children's counselors and wranglers in a totally different setting. Thirdly, the show allowed our crew to work as a creative team. Today we call that "bonding." The staff show embodied my fundamental concept of the dude ranch experience: We of the staff were not "working" for the guests, but joining with them as friends sharing a common experience.

ONE OF MY RIDING STUDENTS FROM OHIO (I'LL CALL HER AMY) joined our staff that summer. Amy was a good rider, had a sparkling personality and was always ready to pitch in anywhere she was needed. One morning, prior to our season opening, I took her riding to show her some of the trails that she would be using when she guided rides. We had been riding for an hour or more when we came to a place on an old game trail that led into some bushes. Ducking low in the saddle, I worked my way through and came into a little grassy clearing that was surrounded with thick vegetation. I had not seen the place before and we both commented on what a delightful and secluded place we had found. Tying our horses to tree branches, we sat down in the soft lush grass under an old pine and reminisced about the old days in Geauga County five years before when she was a riding student. She told me that she had a crush on me back then and that she always looked forward to her riding lessons. I said that I had admired her determination to become a competent rider and was very pleased with how well she rode now. I added that I thought that she had become a very attractive young lady and was delighted that she was working with us. I can't recall the precise circumstances, but before long we were kissing and it got to the point where clothes were being unbuttoned. Suddenly I said, "Wait. Hold it a minute. Let's think about this okay? I mean, how far do you want this to go?"

"I don't know." Long pause as she buttoned her shirt. "I never have done it, you know, gone all the way before so . . ."

"So maybe you should think about this and maybe we should just cool off, get back on our horses and pretend none of this ever happened. Don't ya think that'd be a good plan?" I stood up and put on my hat. "C'mon. Let's take our time and we'll see what happens . . . if anything."

Amy, on her feet and adjusting her clothes said, "Would you want to make love with me even though I don't know anything? Maybe you wouldn't like it or . . . I don't know." ("Make love" was the way a girl in the sixties would have said, "have sex.")

"Sure I would Amy, it's not that. Listen, this is something you need to think about real hard. It's a big step for a young girl. You're what, twenty one?"

"I'll be twenty-three in August."

We mounted up and rode back to the corrals. It was tempting, but that was the end of it. I think it would have been a traumatic experience for Amy although she claimed otherwise. She was, after all, not much different than the maids of my childhood who were curious and felt that I was a safe first-time partner. Although that incident occurred nearly forty years ago, I remember it with absolute clarity. The mind is a funny thing!

During the early part of the summer, we had a thirty-year-old single girl stay at the ranch, I'll call her Jane. She was not the prettiest girl you ever saw, but pleasant enough with a bubbly kind of personality. About midweek, returning from a trail ride, the boys and I did the usual noon routine of pulling off bridles, loosening cinches, watering the horses and giving them some hay.

Jane, who had been on my ride, didn't walk back to her cabin as did the other guests, but sat on the corral fence watching us work.

When the chores were completed, we mounted our horses to ride to lunch. Back then, all the wranglers rode their horses to lunch and tied them up just north of the lodge in a stand of oak brush. As I was riding out of the corral I yelled over to Jane, "Better get on up the hill. They're gonna be ringin' the bell for lunch real soon."

"How 'bout giving me a ride up to my cabin," Jane yelled back.

"You boys go ahead on up," I said to the waiting wranglers, I'll give the gal a ride." The boys took off and I turned *Flicka* toward the fence where the girl was siting. Pulling up along side of her, I said, "Okay, just ease yourself on over behind me and try ta keep your legs from bangin' on her flanks or we just might have us a little wreck."

She did as directed and got her butt firmly behind the saddle and put her arms around my waist. "How did I do?" Jane inquired.

"Just fine, but ya don't need to hold on quite so tight. I need to breathe some ya know." We rode out of the corral and up a trail just south of cabin #6. The trail was pretty steep and Jane had me in a strangle hold with both arms tight around my middle with her face pressed up against my back . . . not the worst thing that ever happened to a cowboy. When we topped out, she relaxed her grip a little but then one hand slid down to my crotch and she commenced to fool around.

Twisting my head around, I said, "Whoa. What's going on here?" Flicka stopped with a jerk when she heard the word *whoa*. Good horse.

Jane blinked her eyes, "You don't want me to do this? You *really* want me to stop? I'll stop if you want me to but it's something I've been wanting to do since I met you Sunday night."

In front of her cabin I said, "I didn't say I don't like it, now did I? It's just that we're gonna be serving lunch in a few minutes and we need to get on up to the dining room."

You know how something you have heard in the past, some phrase or song or whatever, seems to stick in your mind forever? Well, what Jane said next is something I remember word for word. She slid off the horse, looked up at me and said, "I *am* planning on having lunch. I was planning on eating you!"

I am by no means suggesting that this sort of activity happened on a daily basis, but it did happen several times during the summer. I reckon these women were just bored and wanted to try something different. But why me? Hell, I don't know what they thought; maybe it was mostly because of my status. I was the "Boss." Was the guy up front playing the guitar and singing or the perceived romantic cowboy on his horse. Quite honestly, I was the *star of the show*. When I see how women go nuts over celebrities, I can understand why some girls might have been attracted to me. On the other hand, this theory may be nothing more than a load of crap. Maybe they were just horny and I was available.

I did get caught one night! That was a bummer. Picture this; it's the #6 cabin, the east side room we called *Mountain View*. A wildly attractive lady, I'll call her Velma, had vacationed at the ranch with her family the previous summer. On this particular night, she was alone since her husband had stayed home and her two boys were on an overnight camp out. Velma suggested that I pay her a visit after the evening program. I agreed and while we were in the midst of some fine love making, the door suddenly opened, the light was switched on and there was Marye with some people standing behind her. She was bringing a couple of late arrivals to a room she *thought* was vacant. Marye let out a shriek which she immediately stifled, quickly hit the light switch and pulled the door closed. That event never would have happened had I fixed the broken door lock. Yes, she saw me in the bed and no, she didn't say one word when I came back to our room.

There was some heavy tension going down the next day, but I said nothing and neither did Marye. The following day we had the discussion we should have had years before with the bottom line being that we would proceed with the divorce. I was thankful that we had finally decided to do what we had been threatening ever since our days in Ohio. Obviously, I was not sorry about this turn of events, but I am sorry that I didn't at least tell her, *I'm sorry.*

When the summer season ended and the last guest had departed, Marye loaded the kids and some clothes in the little blue VW and took off to take up residence once again with her parents. This time, it was a one-way ticket.

I guess you could say that our second year of dude ranching was better than the first in some respects. I guess you could also say that by any standard, I was a complete failure as a husband and father. From a moralistic standpoint, it is abundantly clear that I was a total failure as a considerate and responsible human being when it came to heading up a family.

I know it must seem odd that an intelligent, talented, educated guy like me could get so caught up in what had to be a destructive lifestyle. I would like to be able to give you some sort of rational explanation, but I can't, except to admit the obvious; that time and again I was thinking with the wrong organ.

CHAPTER THIRTY SIX

Weldon Delany and the Christmas tree caper

The summer of 1964 was not at all what we had hoped for although we had a first-rate staff, and the program was well received with many guests telling us that they had a wonderful time and would be back. It was the same problem as the year before; not enough guests.

Total income for the year was a meager $21,148 and although that was $7,000 better than the previous year, the bottom line showed a loss of $7,400. We had a long soul-searching meeting with the Hortons and by telephone, with the Dodsons and Mel Schaefer. We had mortgage payments due to both SBA and Camp Silver Spruce and nowhere near enough money to pay them. Nothing of substance came from that meeting, so I called for a stockholder's meeting on May 1, 1965. No one actually showed up but, since I held all the proxies, I just made up the minutes and let it go at that. The relevant portions follow:

The President advised that since the Horton family was moving back to Ohio, it would be impossible to conduct Directors meetings since a minimum of three directors is required for a quorum. He asked the stockholders to give him broader powers. The following resolution was passed. "BE IT RESOLVED that the president

251 ❖ Dick Elder

be empowered to act on all matters here-to-fore reserved to the will of the Board of Directors, that in his sole discretion he may enter into any contracts he may deem necessary, including acquire assets, trade or sell assets other than land, borrow money, make improvements and direct all operations without limitation."

Elder advised that he had not received any salary for the past year but had not requested a note covering the amount as he did not want to raise the loss figures for the year just ended.

The President advised that Mr. and Mrs. Edward V. Cory had made a firm offer to buy up to 10 acres of land at $200 per acre. He further reported that he had discussed this matter with Mr. Schaefer and Schaefer indicated that he would not be in favor of selling any land at this time. Since Elder was acting as Schaefer's proxy, he was bound to vote against the sale. The question was tabled.

It's clear that none of the others seemed to be interested in the affairs of the company, so I had no choice but to take complete control. It was a bloodless takeover, perfectly legal and by the book since I had all of the proxies. In retrospect, Mel Schaefer did Colorado Trails a great service when he advised against selling ten acres for $2,000. Within a dozen years, that land would be worth ten times as much.

My five-page report to the stockholders included information about what we had done or planned to do, nothing too exciting except for a paragraph near the end of the report:

It is my intention to move to the Los Angeles area this coming fall and go to work out there. Since I have to work in the winter, I may as well make some money doing it and you can take my word for it, you can't make any money in the winter in Durango. This idea of working for $1.50 or $2.00 an hour is getting kind of *old and I just can't get by on it any longer particularly with Nancy going to College this fall. I might add that a winter in the Los Angeles area should give me plenty of opportunity to work up prospects for the following summer since L.A. is our number 1 town for getting guests.*

In September, Shorty Mars, his son Cecil, Bob Bellmaine and I drove the horses to Shorty's ranch near Bayfield. Since there was very little traffic back then and the roads were all dirt, driving horses, sheep and cattle from one place to another was quite common. As a matter of fact, they still drive cattle and sheep on roads out in that country. I talked with Shorty about working with me during hunting season, but then decided not to take any hunters because it was too much effort with too little profit.

It took me a week to close down the six cabins for the winter. That process of winterizing was more than just closing the doors and windows and turning off the lights. After turning off the water to each cabin, I had to drain the water heaters. Some folks call them "hot water heaters" but that's silly, if you think about it. Actually, they are *cold* water heaters. Sorry, I just had to say it. I blew out all the water lines with compressed air, removed shower heads and squirted anti-freeze in to the pipes, removed the sink faucets and gave those pipes a shot of antifreeze and the toilet bowl and tank, after being drained, got more antifreeze. All the bedding had to be removed and rat poison and moth balls spread about liberally to keep the pack rats and other rodents from nesting. Each cabin took a whole day or more to do and the reason we were so darn careful about doing it thoroughly was because the first fall we didn't do all the aforementioned procedures and as a result, we had busted water pipes in every cabin. To make matters worse, which we seemed to be very good at, when we made repairs to the copper lines using flux, solder and a blow torch, the approved method for "sweating" (soldering) copper pipe joints, we would sometimes set the place on fire. Having gone through all of that hassle, we learned to be extremely careful and very thorough in our winterizing procedures.

I was sitting in the lodge kitchen by myself, as Marye and the kids had left for California, trying to decide the best way to winterize the lodge, when that damn cat skinner from down at the Spear A Ranch, Weldon Delany, came busting in.

"Hey Hoss, how ya gittin' 'long? Got a great idear fer you an' me ta make some money with. Wanna hear 'bout it?"

I sat there looking at Weldon as he took a seat across from me. I was about to answer his question when he answered it for me.

"'Course ya do. I'm tellin' ya this is jest what you been a-lookin' fer. Gimme one of them hump-backs." I handed him my pack of Camels and a book of matches. He lit up, blew some smoke in my direction and continued, "Look, you boys got all that timber up here that needs cuttin' right? Least wise, that's what yer partner tole me, that you was a-thinkin' 'bout getting' some outfit in here to timber it off." I nodded. "Now, them timber fellers is gonna need to be building roads up inta the places they be wantin' ta cut sos they kin skid them logs out. Am I right?" I nodded again. "Them roads is the key ta my idear."

I had to laugh. "And you want to be the one to build the roads with your eight." I was referring to his D-8 bulldozer.

"Sheet no. I ain't got that son a beech no more."

"You don't?"

"Naw, them fuckers come an' got it. I wasn't there when they come fer it or I'd a flat killed them sons-a-beeches. I tole Emmy Lou, why the fuck dint ya grab a fuckin' shotgun an' run them bastards off? By God, that's what I'd a done. Anyway, it don' matter none now, 'sides, building roads ain't what I'm a thinkin' 'bout. No, by God, here's what I'm a sayin' we should be doin'. Once them loggers got them roads in, finish up with their loggin' an' clear out, we get on up there and cut us a shit pot full a Christmas trees . . . Huh?" Delany raised his eyebrows and gave me a conspiratorial look like he had just let me in on the theory of relativity. "So? That's some great idear, right?"

"We've talked about cutting Christmas trees, but I don't reckon we gave a hell of a lot of thought to how we were going to get them out. So, yeah, that's a good idea you got there. But it all depends on how fast we can get a logger in here. We would need to have them trees cut and on the way to Phoenix or Albuquerque or someplace by say no later than what, early November?"

Weldon tapped the pack and slid out another cigarette. "It'd be better if them trees was shipped outa here sooner. Say, you still got that ole binder truck?" I nodded. "Well, didja ever make a flat bed outta it?"

"No, it's still got the box on it."

"Well, we kin still use it. I'll take me a run on down ta Albeekirk [Albuquerque], maybe go on ta Phoenix whilse I'm at it and see if'n I kin line us up some outlets fer them trees."

I located a logger who came in and cut all the trees on the west ridge north of the lodge that had been marked by Dick Berkholtz, the Colorado State forester. There was a hell of a lot of mature trees on that part of the ranch and even after cutting a bunch, you couldn't hardly tell that any logging had been done. Besides the money we received, there was another plus to the logging operation. The new roads and skid trails let us get to the Christmas trees and created a number of good trails for horseback riding.

Delany located a wholesaler in Phoenix who bought our trees. I can't say for sure how many trees we cut, but it was at least a thousand and I doubt that we received more than a couple of dollars per tree some of which went to Delany. I know it sounds like we went in there and savaged the forest and turned the hillsides into a wasteland, but in truth, we didn't do all that much damage. Most of the trees were cut from the tops of large spruce and fir trees. That meant that there was a good sized tree still standing, albeit with the top six to ten feet removed. Interestingly, those topped trees did not die as you might suspect, but continued to grow. After a couple of years, you couldn't tell which trees we had topped. Another point to keep in mind is this: We had trees all over the ranch and in the area where we logged and cut Christmas trees, the spruce, pine and fir were as thick as the hair on the back of a dog. So we made some much needed money, although not as much as we needed, and opened up some new areas for trail riding without doing any permanent damage to our woodlands. Today you would call that a win/win situation.

With the lodge and cabins winterized and the trees shipped, I went about the perennial task of trying to find work. I picked up some plumbing jobs. Someone heard that I knew something about installing aluminum roofing and hired me to put a roof on a cabin. I worked with Vern Woodward on a masonry job at Saint Marks Church, worked with Pat Howley, who owned the Town House Restaurant, on some catering jobs, broke and trained a couple horses for a guy, did some 'cowboying' for a several ranchers and anything else that came along. Jobs were scarce in La Plata County once the tourist season was over and I was living a hand-to-mouth existence, but never did I consider asking for unemployment compensation. Does that make up for flaws in my character?

Thinking that we would be "killed" by the SBA for not making our December mortgage payment, I was becoming somewhat frantic, convinced that after making the payment to Groves, I might be back to begging bones for the dog at Safeway.

Shorty Mars called and said he got a job hauling a horse to Phoenix and asked if I wanted to go. He suggested that while we were there we could talk to some dude ranches about renting horses and maybe dig up jobs for the winter. It sounded good to me and the next thing you know Shorty, his wife Faye and I were in his Dodge pickup heading south with a big old sorrel horse standing in the bed wearing goggles to protect his eyes from the wind. It was a fairly comical sight. Shorty and I took turns driving. Faye could drive the pick up just fine, but Shorty never let her take the wheel. When Shorty was driving, I'd pull out the tin of Prince Albert and roll cigarettes for the two of us. He'd do the same for me when I was at the wheel. There was so much smoke constantly swirling around inside the cab that poor old Faye didn't need a cigarette. All she had to do was breath to get the same unhealthy result.

Before I tell you about that trip and what happened afterward, I think now is a good time to tell you about Shorty, Faye and Cecil Mars. They were important players in my life.

CHAPTER THIRTY SEVEN

Shorty Mars

One afternoon, during our first year at the ranch, Jim and I made the twenty-minute drive to Bayfield to see what the town looked like. Bayfield was a village of perhaps a couple hundred people. The main street held a few shops that were supported by the surrounding ranching community, although most of the area's residents did their principal shopping in Durango.

Jim noticed a sign in the window of a café that read, *Home Made Pie.* Not able to resist the temptation, he pulled into the graveled parking lot. "Hey, this is just like back in Ohio. C'mon, let's get us some pie and coffee."

A middle-aged lady stood behind the small counter. She was a good-sized woman, but certainly not overweight, about five-feet-eight inches tall, her hair a reddish brown and she wore glasses that made her blue eyes appear larger than they were. She definitely had the look of a country gal.

Walking over to us, she said, "Howdy boys. Got several pies just come outta the oven and still purdy hot." I detected a Texas accent, but it could have been just country.

We introduced ourselves and she said her name was Faye Mars and did we know her husband Shorty who ran a dude string (horses for hire) up at Vallecito Lake. We told her we hadn't met her husband, but we sure would like to. Jim wanted to know what varieties of pie she was offering. Faye rattled off about eight different kinds she had made that day, advising that cherry and apple had just come out of the oven. Jim ordered apple and coffee and I had a slice of cherry pie and a glass of milk. We consumed the generous slices with the gusto of a hound dog then ordered a fresh peach and a coconut cream. My God! It was fantastic! The crust was so flaky and tender, the coconut cream was so smooth and delicious. You get the idea.

I said to Faye, "By golly, I reckon you can tell we're enjoying the hell out of this stuff." Jim's mouth was full, but he nodded in agreement and said something that sounded like, *bluerblob oo.*

Faye asked if we were the ones building the new dude outfit on the Upper Florida Road across from the boy's camp. She said she had seen our sign when she drove to Durango. The sign read: "Colorado Trails Ranch, the *New Look* in guest ranching." Below those words were, "Under Construction." The phrase *New Look* was in vogue at that time and referred to an over-hyped women's clothing style that featured longer length hemlines. Many companies jumped on the bandwagon and incorporated the phrase in their advertising. I felt we should not be left out of this marketing phenomenon and decided to use it. You do remember that I was a marketing major in college, don't you? You see how that degree was paying off?

The long and short of that visit with Faye Mars was that she invited our families to a Sunday dinner. The following Sunday, the Dodsons and Elders showed up at the little old ranch house of Shorty and Faye Mars. The place was located about five miles from Bayfield on an unpaved county road. After everybody had been introduced, including our kids and the Mars kids, Jim and Cecil (a third son, Bill, wasn't there), Shorty took Jim and me on a tour of his outfit. Walking out to the barn with Shorty, I sized him at no more than 5'4" inches tall. His slightly bowed legs were encased in jeans with creases that were every bit as sharp as those worn by Dave Sanchez. You could tell that Faye was particular about how her man and boys were dressed. She obviously was a gal who believed in the liberal use of starch and an iron. Shorty wore a colorful western shirt. A good quality Resistal silver belly (light gray) cowboy hat sat at a jaunty angle on his head, and for footwear, stout, not particularly fancy, high heel boots. Shorty wore glasses that perched on what some might call a fairly large nose.

Shorty had a way of speaking that was both colorful and totally in character for a Texas cowboy. He used a lot of comparatives in his sentences. For example, if he wanted to explain how strong the coffee was he might say, "The coffee was as strong as Mary's breath." That phrase will make no sense to you unless you know that "Mary" was a name the cowboys frequently gave to the camp cook who was in fact, a man. (*Cocinero*, Spanish word for cook, Slick, Cookie, Ole Slick and Greasy are other handles given to round-up cooks.) If Shorty wanted to let you know just how steep a certain trail was he might say, "It was steep as a cow's face." Commenting on one of the hands fancied up to go to town, he would remark, "You're dressed up like a sore toe." If a tool got the job done easily, he'd say, "Why, that's as handy as a pocket on a shirt." Ask Shorty how windy was it and his answer might be, "It was so windy, it blew the bit outa my horse's mouth." Anyway, that's what I mean when I say he used comparatives in his sentence structure.

In addition to the house, we saw a few sheds and a barn on the place. There were horses out in a pasture while others were in pens nearby. We could tell straight off that the man had some pretty fair looking horses and they appeared to be in good flesh. As he told us about this one and that one, it was obvious that he knew his stock and took pride in his string.

James Clinton Mars was a sure 'nuff cowboy. He looked like one, talked like one and the first time I saw him ride, I could tell he had spent a lifetime in the saddle. He told Jim and me a little about himself, how he had been wrangling horses for several large cow outfits in Texas while Faye worked as a cook. His boys, Jim who was about sixteen and Cecil around fourteen, were turning into first rate hands and were a big help to him both at the home ranch and with the dude string up at the lake. I don't recall what he said, if anything, about Bill.

Back in the house, Faye served us a chicken dinner that was, as we say now, to die for. The sausage cream gravy and mashed potatoes along with green beans with bacon were top of the line. My personal favorite that afternoon was the baking powder biscuits. They were the best I'd ever had. Faye offered us both pie and cake for desert served with milk for the kids and strong coffee for us adults. When I say "strong," what I mean is, you could bend a spoon stirring it.

Cecil Mars came to work for us when he was only fifteen-years-old but he could do the job of any man. He was a big, strong, good looking, even- tempered kid with bright blue eyes and light blond hair. His quick smile and frequent bursts of hearty laughter were infectious. I reckon he must have been over 6' tall and weighed in at close to 190 pounds. He could rope, he could sure enough ride anything with hair on it and he knew what to do around stock. His brother Jim was a savvy kid too and became a cattle rancher and eventually, head of the local Cattlemen's Association. Jim never did work for us. He preferred working regular cow outfits. Cecil however, loved working with dudes and the guests sure loved him.

So most of the Mars family came to work at Colorado Trails. Shorty leased horses to us and the following year signed on as our head wrangler. Faye was our cook and baker and Cecil worked as a riding guide. Cecil and Bob Bellmaine hit it off right from the get go and became great buddies. Bob pronounced his name with an English dialect, *Sessil,* and called him Sessil B. DeMars, a take off on the famous movie director, Cecil B. DeMill.

Faye, Shorty and I were now hauling a horse down to Phoenix in Shorty's Dodge pick up. After dropping off the horse, we got lined out with a cheap motel where, in order to save money, we three shared a room with two beds. The next morning, Shorty and I drove to Saguaro Lake Ranch east of Phoenix as I had heard they might be looking for a new manager. We had it in mind that if I got on as manager, I would hire Shorty to wrangle and Faye to cook. Shorty might also be able to lease some horses to the ranch.

We arrived at the ranch, drove through the gate, parked the truck and not seeing anyone, walked around. Signs of neglect were everywhere, almost as if the place had been abandoned. The ranch was not due to open for a month, but it sure looked like they had a hell of a lot of repair and maintenance work to do before the place would be ready to receive guests. We eventually came across an old broken down whiskey-breath hand who volunteered to show us around. We asked him, "Where's the boss?'

"Danged if I know," was his reply. We continued walking around looking at the facilities which, if you can believe it, were a lot worse than what we had at Colorado Trails.

"This here's the bunk house," our guide told us. We looked at what appeared to be a huge shipping crate with a door in it.

"The hands live here, in this outfit?" I asked. "Don't it get pretty hot in there? I don't see no windows."

"They's a big ole opening in the back with a fan in it, but it gets right nippy in the winter down these parts sos the big problem is keepin' warm at night. You fellers want ta go on up to the big house. They might be one of 'em up there, ya never kin tell."

Shorty gave me a questioning look."No. No thanks," I replied, we'll come on back again. Sure do appreciate you showin' us 'round."

"All right then," the man said and walked off.

Shorty and I walked back to the pick up. He removed his hat and wiped his forehead with his shirtsleeve. "Pretty dang hot down here and dry as a tank full o' dust."

"Well," I said, "what do ya think?"

Shorty was rolling a cigarette and was intent on getting it just right before answering. Sliding the paper edge across his tongue and completing the seal, he pinched one end and lit the perfectly prepared cigarette. Inhaling the smoke deeply, he shook his head from side to side. I watched this ritual impatiently and asked again, "So tell me, what does it look like to you?"

"It looks like a lot o' work and not much else, that's what it looks like."

By the time we drove through the gate, we had decided that Saguaro Lake Ranch was not for us. However, as long as we were in Arizona, we checked around to see if one of the many other dude outfits or resorts needed horses and a couple a hands for the winter season. Armed with the yellow pages ripped from a phone book, we commenced to make the rounds. We called on a number of places including the Camelback Inn, Jocake Ranch, and a little outfit whose name escapes me. I'll call it the Circle W and they were receptive to our proposal and I think they would have put us and the horses to work but while we were seriously considering the Circle W deal, something else came along. Actually, two other things.

CHAPTER THIRTY EIGHT

Purgatory . . . A Hell of a Place to Ski.

S horty and I were in the lodge discussing whether to sign on with Circle W or wait for one of the better outfits when the telephone rang. The caller was the owner of the Mill Creek Lodge located some 30 miles north of Durango at the south end of Coal Bank Pass. He told me that he was looking for someone to manage his place over the winter and suggested that I come up for a chat. I told him I'd be happy to visit with him and we set a date.

I told Shorty about the offer and he thought it might be a good deal, especially if I hired him and Faye. Shorty took off and I was in the process of peeling the lid off of a can of Spam (I actually like the stuff) when the phone rang again. This time it was Ray Duncan. He wanted to know if I remembered him. He told me that we had met when Vern Woodworth had brought him up to look at our stone work. I said that I recalled the occasion. "But," he continued, "what I'm calling you about is the possibility of your coming to work for me at the Purgatory Ski Area. Have you heard about it?"

"Oh, sure. I've been reading about it in the *Herald*. It's the biggest thing to hit Durango in a long time. So, what kind of job do you have in mind?"

Duncan went on to say that he needed someone to look out for his interests with the contractors building the day lodge. He told me that Jim Akin was working on the building and since I had worked with him before, that maybe I would be the right person for the job.

I told Ray Duncan that I was definitely interested and we agreed to meet after my visit with the folks at Mill Creek Lodge.

The owners of Mill Creek wanted me to lease the place for the winter and pay them either a fixed monthly rent or a percentage of the gross. They told me that they would be gone most of the winter and I could run the place as if it were my own. It was a nice deal except at that time, no one knew for sure what sort of economic impact the new Purgatory ski area would have on Durango and nearby properties. Still, the Mill Creek offer was the only offer I'd had except for the Circle W Resort which by then had lost some of its appeal.

Leaving Mill Creek Lodge, situated in an absolutely beautiful location, I traveled to Purgatory, a short distance south. The place was a beehive of activity with heavy equipment digging power and water lines and moving dirt, while a multitude of building trades scampered about working on the day lodge. I wandered around looking for Ray Duncan and came across my old friend Jim Akin. He mentioned that Homer Hartley, Swede Alexander, Shorty Porter and some others that had worked at Colorado Trails were working at Purgatory. I came across Swede and Homer and we chatted briefly. It sure was good to see them. Eventually I saw Ray Duncan who after greeting me, showed me around and told me what his plans were with respect to the building program which included the day lodge and another building he referred to as the maintenance shop. That was it! They were putting in a Riblet double chair lift and he said the towers for the lift were in place but the cable had to be strung and the chairs installed. He also showed me where he planned to build a T-Bar lift on a small slope close to the lodge.

I reckon the whole meeting didn't last an hour, but I told him I was interested in taking the job. It was obvious he needed someone to coordinate all the loose ends and bring it together in time to open by early December. I can't say for certain, but I think he offered me a salary of $75 a week. Now, that may not seem like a lot of money to you, but from where I stood at the time, $75 a week was about $75 better than what I was earning just then. I took the job.

One afternoon some weeks later, I got a message that Duncan wanted to see me at his Durango office in the West Building. The next morning I went waltzing up to the fourth floor (actually, I used the elevator) and Ray invited me in and told me to have a seat. He asked his secretary, Mrs. Joella Dunigan, to bring me a cup of coffee, which she did. After some preliminary chit-chat about how the construction was going, Duncan got down to business. He asked if I would like to manage the food and beverage operations at the day lodge. I wanted to know what that entailed and he said, "Hell, I don't know. Whatever you need to do to provide meals and run the bar. You've been doing that sort of thing at your dude ranch, haven't you?" I nodded my head. "I don't see how it would be all that different from what you must be doing at your ranch. You *can* do that can't you?"

"Well yes. I can handle it, but what kind of food are you talking about, just lunches, short order stuff?"

"No. I've got something a little more elaborate in mind. I've ordered some very nice furniture, square and round tables, captain's chairs with leather backs and seats, real nice stuff. Trader Jack up in Denver is building it special for me. I think we should serve breakfast and lunch sort of cafeteria style like they do at Aspen and Vail and then do a high end kind of dinner with, you know, white table clothes, candles, good looking waitresses, nice wine, all that sort of shit. In other words, more like the kind of thing you'd find at a nice restaurant at Vail Village."

"Really!" I didn't have a clue what he meant by "like they do at Aspen and Vail," or even what a "ski village restaurant" was. Had I known anything at all about ski areas, I would have probably asked some serious questions about what would be prudent and practical for a little start up ski area, north of nowhere. But as with dude ranching when we first started, I didn't know shit from apple butter about ski areas and what they do and how they do it so if he was looking for intelligent advice from me, he sure came knocking on the wrong door. Those thoughts passed through my mind but all I said was, "Really. So you want to serve three meals a day? Seven days a week?"

Duncan tilted his chair forward and earnestly said, "That's right. Now what I want to know is, can you do it and will you do it for ninety bucks a week?"

Without hesitation I shot right back, "I can do it!" then borrowing from George Horton added, "No problem. Will I do it depends on how much freedom you'll give me to do the job the way I feel it needs to be done and with the staff I'll need." Then I quickly added, "Of course, all within the boundaries of your food service policies. As for the last part, will I do it for ninety a week?" I paused and looked him straight in the eye and said, "No. I need at least a hundred."

I think I caught a glimmer of a smile on Ray's face as I'm sure he was thinking, *I can't believe I'm getting off this cheap*, but what he said was, "You won't take less?'

"I think a hundred is damn reasonable. I'll be working seven days a week for gosh sake. I'll be lucky if I get any time off all winter."

Duncan leaned his chair back and smiled. "Ninety a week and you'll be in charge all the way."

"Afraid not." This was a poker hand and I wasn't going to let him bluff me.

"Okay. You got it." We both understood that Ray Duncan got a real bargain but I needed the work and I guess he knew it. "I'll have Joella set up an office for you and you can start hiring people, work up menus, order what you need and all that kind of thing."

I had some questions. "The space allocated for the kitchen isn't very large. My kitchen at the ranch is three times the size and I didn't see a walk-in cooler or freezer in the plans. What about kitchen equipment? Do I order that?"

Ray stood up indicating the meeting had come to an end. "You won't need to worry about that. I've had a kitchen planning company figure out what we need and all the equipment has been ordered." Duncan reached across his desk and extended a hand. "Well, thanks for coming in and welcome to Purgatory. We're going to be the best damn little ski area around and I'm counting on you to help us. By the way, what do you think of this slogan? *Purgatory, a hell of a place to ski.*"

I told him I liked it, then we shook hands and I left. My head was spinning. I thought, what the hell do I know about running a restaurant? Marye took care of all the food service at the ranch. About the only thing I had to do with food was to eat it then say to her, "That was good," or "Let's not have that again." But, Marye was gone and I figured I would be able to hire people who knew what to do. Besides, everything I learned running the food service at Purgatory would help me do a better job the following summer when neither Marye nor any of my partners would be present.

Keeping an eye on construction, while getting my office organized in the West Building, kept me plenty busy. Regardless, I still had to get ready for the fast approaching hunting season that would begin the third Saturday of October.

CHAPTER THIRTY NINE

It was my trigger finger.

In early October of '64, I went down to Gardenswartz Sporting Goods in Durango and bought some better camp equipment, including an old Marlin .32 caliber lever action rifle that was like the 30-30 I acquired in '61. I purchased a much warmer sleeping bag, two used pack saddles with canvas panniers, some lash ropes, and other items all on credit.

Taking a chance, I raised the fee to $150 for a six day hunt. Despite the higher fee, we booked six hunters. A week before the hunters arrived, we packed all the equipment and supplies to our base camp in the San Juan National Forest on Shearer Creek some five miles north of the ranch. It was a great spot. We built a pole corral to hold the "night horse," made a nice rock-lined fire pit, pulled up some logs around it for seating and placed the tents on flat grassy ground nearby.

Our six hunters came with enough artillery to hold off Geronimo and the Apaches. It was ridiculous! We took the men to the rifle range so they could sight in their guns (adjust their scopes or iron sights). Afterward, they went up to their cabins to clean up for dinner while Hilton and I went down to the corrals to feed the horses. I climbed up into the old International where the hay was stored and threw the flakes of hay out to Hilton who spread it around the corral. Some of the horses began running through the piles of hay making a mess, so Hilt put Johnson halters on the worst offenders and tied them to fence posts while they ate.

I jumped off the hay truck smack dab onto a round rock that gave my ankle a hell of a twist. I was sitting on the ground rubbing my ankle and cursing the bad luck when I heard a scream. I hobbled around the truck and looked over at Hilt who was jumping up and down and shaking his left hand.

"What's the matter?" I yelled over the top of his screaming.

"It's my finger," he cried. It's cut plumb off!"

I hobbled over to him and sure enough, the first finger on his left hand had been severed just above the second knuckle. He was dancing around in pain so I grabbed his arm and with my bandana, made a tight wrap around his hand. "Where is it?" I asked.

"What?"

"The finger," I shouted. "Where is it? What did you do with it?"

"I don't know. Must still be in the glove."

"Well, where's the fucking glove? I don't see it."

Holding his left hand with his right and grimacing with pain, Hilt sobbed, "Must be over in them weeds yonder. I reckon I just flung the glove off. I gotta git ta a doctor pronto. Can ya git yer machine and take me ta town?"

I searched in the weeds, which actually were stinging nettles, but could not find the glove. Hilt asked me what the heck was I doing and I told him that if I had the rest of his finger, I could pack it in ice and maybe the doctor would be able to sew it back on. Hilton was getting "shocky," his face became pale and he was beginning to wobble around, so I gave up the search, led him out of the corral, put him in the car and off we went to Mercy Hospital. On the way to town, Hilton, who prided himself on being a crack shot especially, with a revolver, looked at his injured hand and muttered something.

"It'll be okay," I told him. "They'll fix you up."

Shaking his head, on the brink of tears, he turned to me and in a whisper said, "It was my trigger finger."

While at the hospital, I asked a doctor to have a look at my ankle, which had become so painful I could hardly walk on it. He told me that he didn't think it was fractured, probably just a bad sprain. He wrapped the ankle with an Ace Bandage, gave me some pain pills and told me that I should keep off of it for a few days. Right! Hunting season was to start in a day and we had six hunters to pack up to camp. Great! We had a man missing his trigger finger and a one-legged guide and no way to get hold of George who had taken time off from his job and was up at the base camp getting things ready.

On the way home from the hospital I asked Hilton, "What the hell happened back there? I didn't see no knife. How in the hell could you loose a finger just like that?" I snapped my fingers.

He gave me a blow by blow accounting and here's the long and short of it: When he saw the horses running around, kicking at each other and messing up the piles of hay he had laid out, he got irritated and haltered and tied the three worst offenders. Everything was fine until he began to remove the halter from an old mare named Kate. The Johnson halters were made from rope that looked like old-fashioned clothesline. Knowledgeable horsemen know that you always untie the rope before removing a halter. Hilton must have had a memory lapse or something because without untying the lead, Hilton just slipped the first finger of his left hand under the halter behind the horse's ear. As he pulled the halter over her ear, Kate pulled back hard, the rope halter bit into his gloved hand and it was adios trigger finger.

The thing that pissed me off, and I told him so, was the fact that he knew that Kate was a mare that hated to be tied. She frequently pulled back with such force that the tie rope would break.

Looking down at his professionally bandaged hand, Hilton shook his head up and down. Not only did he loose his favorite finger, now "The Brain" was giving him hell for being stupid. "I know, I know. I shoulda knowd better. Well, I'm payin' fer it now, that's for dang sure."

Then I felt bad about chewing on him. So I offered him a tailor made and said, "Well, it's done and I reckon that's one mistake you won't make again. It's okay. Don't you worry none. I ain't gonna let ya go." Hilt looked at me and smiled, so I knew it was all right.

Did he get workers compensation for the loss of his finger while on the job? Are you kidding! The man was a cowboy! I don't think he ever heard the term, "Workers Comp" and even if he had, he had too much pride to ask for it. Furthermore, I'm sure we didn't have it.

Next morning I saw Hilton, a shovel in his right hand, walking up the trail to the dump that was located near our west fence line. I ran out and intercepted him. "Where ya headin'?"

"Up ta the dump. Found the dern glove with my finger still in it. It was a ways back in them nettles." He pulled the gauntlet glove from inside his jumper then took a folded white cloth from his pocket. Unrolling the material, he showed me the missing finger, then carefully wrapped it again.

"So, whatcha gonna do with that shovel?" I asked.

"Well sir, if ya must know, I'm fixin' ta bury my finger and say a prayer over it. That's what I'm fixin' ta do." I guess I must have given him a weird look or something because he went on, "Ya know, I'm a Catholic and I sure do believe in the life hereafter and when I git there, I want ta have all my parts where theys supposed ta be. Ya savvy?"

"Well, sure you do. I understand and I reckon that's a fine idea, so I'll just leave you to it. This is something you need to do by yourself." With that, I turned and walked away.

Later on, when I felt he would be okay with it, I asked Hilton about burying that finger. He told me that he believed that if he gave his finger a proper burial in the Catholic tradition or his version of it, that when he died and went to Heaven, his trigger finger would be back and he could shoot again like he always had. But, if he hadn't done the burial ceremony, then he wouldn't have the missing finger for all of Eternity and that was a prospect he just couldn't deal with. It sure made sense to me.

The next morning after a huge breakfast, and those guys could eat, the hunters drove to the corrals. Behind their car was a medium size trailer in which they had all the stuff they wanted packed up to camp including a bazillion rounds of ammunition. Not only would the ammo take up a lot a space in a pannier, it was very heavy.

"Do you really think you're gonna need all of this ammo?" I asked them. "I'm taking the seven rounds in my 30-30 and a few more in my pocket." Pointing to their suitcases of ammunition, I continued, "If any of you boys need that much ammunition to kill a half dozen animals, then I think we better spend some more time at the rifle range. Tell ya what. Each of you can bring one box of 25 rounds in your saddlebags. How's that?" The hunters became contrite!

They had cots, they had a table with folding legs, really! They had more damn stuff they wanted packed into camp than you can imagine, including several canvas zipper bags in which were bottles of whiskey. I reminded them about our drinking rule: No drinking until everyone was back in camp. I told them I wasn't about to have some liquored-up hunter kill somebody. I got no argument from them, however we did pack some of the booze, although not anywhere near all of it.

I also told them that we could only take the essential items. They started bitching and moaning but I just kept on sorting out what I would pack. Then it started to rain and within seconds we were smack dab in the middle of a regular "frog choker."

We quickly gathered the pile of stuff we had selected and put it under a shed roof. Then we led each packhorse under the roof and packed him right there. It was a mess. Pouring down rain, a bunch of grouchy hunters, Hilton with a hand all bandaged up and me hobbling around like a ruptured duck. The hunters wanted to get their hands into the packing and lashing of the panniers, which made matters even worse. Then a good thing happened. The rain stopped as suddenly as it had started, the sun popped out and all seemed right with the world. We had lined out each of the hunters with a horse and saddle so we didn't have to go through that exercise. Eventually the packhorses were strung out, the hunters were in the saddle and we headed up the trail.

About fifteen minutes out and while still on the ranch, we crossed Shearer Creek and continued on the west side past the big rock slide where we gathered much of the stone we used while building the lodge. We came across a large boulder that had slid down the hill and landed in the middle of the trail. There was enough space to the left of the rock to get through and I cautioned the hunters to just ease their horses between the rock and the hillside. I also said, "Make sure you rein left now before you get to the rock otherwise your pony just might head into the bushes and you don't want to go there." The sight of a big boulder in the middle of the trail was traumatic for the horses. It wasn't the boulder that bothered them, they had seen a million of them. The problem was the *location*. That was new and scary.

My horse danced around a lot but eventually went where I wanted him to go and once past the boulder, he settled right down. The packhorse I was leading followed right along. Hilton and his two packhorses had no problem. The next horse danced a little but came on through okay. The rest of the horses, except the last horse, having seen their mates go past the rock unscathed, went by without a blink. The last horse started to go to the right toward the chokecherry bushes that grew along the creek bank. I yelled to the rider, "Stop and turn around and try again. Rein him to the left and use your right leg." The hunter turned the horse around, reined hard to the left and was kicking like a mule but, just about the time they got up to the rock, the horse panicked and bolted into the bushes, damn near loosing the rider. In a matter of seconds, the horse came busting out of the brush and galloped up to the other horses. It was pitiful! The rider lost his glasses, his face and hands were all scratched and cut and parts of his jacket hung in shreds. The guys laughed their heads off, but I wasn't the least bit amused. The horse was all scratched up, the canvas saddlebags, which were ours, were ripped and the contents scattered in the brush. Hilton and I dismounted, tied our saddle horses and the pack string to some tree branches and went into the brush to retrieve what we could, including the eyeglasses that Hilton found by stepping on them. One lens was totally gone and the other had a crack in it. I handed the glasses to the hunter and asked if he brought along a spare. He said he didn't bring another pair and how was he going to shoot anything when he couldn't see. I told him I sure was sorry but he hadn't controlled his horse and sometimes shit like that happens. He was pissed off of course and embarrassed as well, so I left it at that, mounted up, gathered the pack string and headed north.

George must have wondered what happened to us because about the time we got to the forest service gate at the north end of the ranch, I saw George crossing the creek. He yelled, "Where the heck ya been? I thought you would be in camp by now."

"It's a long story Hap, but let me tell ya, what with one thing and another, it hasn't been a real pleasant morning."

"I probably should a come on down and give ya a hand. Hey Hilt, I'll take one of them pack horses. Say, what the hell happened to your hand?"

Hilt just shook his head while I answered, "That's another long story but it'll keep 'till we get up ta camp."

George, AKA Hap Horton, and I stepped off our horses and went around checking cinches then remounted and headed up U. S. Forest Service Trail number 1557. At the time the trail hadn't been touched by any maintenance crew and was one rough son of a gun. It was rocky, often very steep, maybe only sixteen inches wide where it just kind of hung on the hillside and there were large deep muddy places at most of the creek crossings. In other words, Trail 1557 was not exactly what your average backyard amateur rider would be comfortable with. However, we made it up to camp without further incident about the time the sun began to set.

Once in camp, while pulling the saddle off my horse, I overheard one of the hunters say to the guy next to him, "I hope they give us something to eat pretty soon. I'm so hungry I could eat a horse."

Said his companion, "Do me a favor will ya. Eat *mine!*"

CHAPTER FORTY

The fairy tale hunt

You would think that a deer and elk hunt in the pristine San Juan Forest would be a dream come true for any red-blooded American man. Maybe so, but for me it was just plain hard work. It got very cold at night and my fancy new sleeping bag failed to keep me warm. Getting up hours before sunrise to gather the horses that had been turned loose to graze overnight was no fun either. Once back in camp, they had to be groomed and saddled before the hunters had breakfast. We made a huge breakfast for the men consisting of eggs, bacon or sausage plus a steak, pork chops or a thick slice of ham. Side dishes included potatoes or grits and biscuits with sausage gravy. Some mornings I prepared buttermilk pancakes, the kind I made for our summer guests. Breakfast for a hungry hunter, who had never heard of the word cholesterol, had more calories and fat than you would consume in a week . . . better make that, in two weeks.

While breakfast was being prepared, the horses were fed grain in morales (nose bags). Hilton stayed in camp to clean things up and gather wood. You can never have too much wood especially with a bunch of city guys who use a chord of wood every night stoking a huge campfire. I swear, some nights I thought they would burn down the forest. Tony Burch, a Southern Ute Indian working with us, evoked an ancient maxim: "White man build big fire, stand far away, use much wood. Indian make small fire, stand close, use little wood." When it came to burning wood, our hunters had neither heard of that insightful Native American saying nor was the word *conservation* in their lexicon.

In addition to guiding hunters, Tony had the job of "gutting" and hanging any game that was brought to camp, although, in theory, the hunter should gut his own animal right after the kill. The idea is to get the meat cooled down quickly by removing the hide as soon as possible, the way it's done in a packinghouse. I'm sure you have heard the term "gamy," referring to that certain taste that venison frequently has. Much of the meat is handled so poorly by hunters that it is actually spoiled, hence the "gamy" taste. During hunting season we would shake our heads in disbelief as we witnessed hunters heading out of town with a deer or elk, hide on, lashed across the hood or laying in a trailer going all the way to Texas or some place. There can be no doubt that meat was "gamy" by the time it got to the table.

Having discussed in advance the general area where we would place each man, George, Tony and I each guided two hunters to a stand where game might be traveling. We also wanted to make sure that they were not in anyone's line of fire.

Game trails to the creek were well defined and Tony had been observing which ones the deer and elk used.

We placed each man at his stand, exchanged the bridle for a leather halter, then tied the horse to a tree with a stout tie rope and loosened the cinch. After making sure each hunter knew exactly where *not* to shoot, we left them. Our job was to circle well around and at first light, push game in their direction.

The first day our hunters bagged three deer. After bringing his deer into camp, one of the men rode out again and just at dusk, shot a nice bull elk. Throughout the next five days, all but one of the hunters had bagged a deer plus we had two elk hanging in camp. Late in the afternoon on the last day of their hunt, all but two of the hunters were in camp when we heard two quick shots echo off the rock walls above Shearer Creek. George quickly threw a saddle on his horse and rode up the canyon. About an hour latter, George walked into camp leading his horse with a deer lashed across the saddle. The two hunters were directly behind him wearing broad smiles and jabbering like a couple of magpies. One of the hunters was the guy with the busted glasses, the sixth one to bag a deer making our success rate for deer one hundred percent and for elk, thirty three percent. The average that year in our area was something like seventy percent for deer and twenty-five percent for elk.

George had gutted the deer before bringing it into camp and now we helped him get it off the horse. Wedging a stick in the cavity to hold it open, we poured cold creek water on the carcass so it would cool more quickly. As we were hanging the carcass from a tree limb, George said in a whisper, "I heard two shots, didn't you?"

"Yeah. There were two shots, sure. What about it?"

George moved close to me and whispered again, "I don't see but one bullet hole in this ole boy. I think

Walter [the eyeglass guy] missed his shot and Pete went ahead and killed the deer for him. Don't think that's legal but let's not say anything 'bout it, okay?" We didn't! So much for the "Rules."

There were toasts all around and everyone was feeling fine. George and I were pleased even though it had been a lot of work and the hunters had been a royal pain in the ass the first few days, but now we were all buddies. It had been, as the hunters told us, "A great hunt. It couldn't have been better." One of them claimed it was like a "fairy tale hunt." For the avid hunter, this hunt was the stuff of dreams.

Riding back to the ranch the next morning and approaching the place where the boulder had rolled on to the trail, I turned in my saddle and yelled back, "Here's that rock where Walter lost his glasses. Tell him to watch it this time." George heard me yell out the warning. Walter was riding directly in front of him, so George cautioned Walter to make sure his horse didn't run through the brush again. Most of the horses paid no attention to the rock and walked right past it. The horse in front of Walter shied a bit but the rider got him lined out. Walter was about five feet from the rock when, without warning, his horse jumped to the left and shot right into the brush. It was unbelievable! Walter came trotting out minus his hat, all scratched and torn up again. This time he was laughing and so was I.

We charged each hunter $150 for the week. A dozen years later, I was charging that much a *day*! Six hunters gave us a total of $900. What with the cost of food, (and those boys sure could eat) and the cost of the equipment, rent for the horses, wages and so on, we only *lost* a couple thousand dollars. The truth is, we would have been better off had we not hunted.

I told Jim Dodson about our hunt and how all the work had actually netted a loss. He simply repeated a phrase he frequently used: "Seems like we just can't win for loosin'. Well, look at it this way. We was in a hole t's-tart with and now it's got just a little deeper, that's all." I was reminded of a Will Rogers line: "If you find yourself in a hole, the first thing to do is stop digging."

George didn't say, "No problem" this time. He was well aware of the situation we were in and was plenty worried about it. I too, was fretting about what might happen to us although I didn't articulate it. It sure looked like we were not only in a deep hole, but the bottom was pure quick sand. It was going to be mighty hard to climb out when we were getting sucked in deeper each day. Maybe, I thought, we should *stop digging.*

The only bright spot on a very dark economic horizon was my impending job at Purgatory. It was exciting to think that I would finally be making almost as much money as I did when I first went to work for my dad in 1950.

CHAPTER FORTY ONE

Living and loving in Purgatory

I had booked hunters just for the first week of the season and as soon as they left, we got the ranch buttoned up for the winter, George went back to Ohio, and I enthusiastically plunged into my new ski area job.

I began by writing menus and lists for the liquors, beers, wines and other things I needed for the bar. At least I knew something about that! When I had figured out conceptually what needed to be done and how to do it, I conferred with Ray Duncan who approved my plan. The only suggestion he offered was to have plenty of Cutty Sark Scotch whiskey on hand. He was adamant that our dinner service be quite elegant, "Just like the better clubs at Vail," which incidentally, is where he owned a condo. To make certain I knew what he meant by "just like," he sent me to Vail and Aspen along with the area manager, Chet Anderson.

Chet had been with the Forest Service and had studied snow conditions in the Purgatory Creek area north of Durango for many years. He determined that the mountain, the snowfall and other winter conditions were perfect for a ski area location and somehow managed to convince Ray Duncan and his brothers Walter and Vince, to build it. Chet laid out the runs on the mountain and provided most of the expertise for the skiing side of the project. Ray

Duncan became the active CEO and Chet was picked as Purgatory's general manager. During our trip to Vail and Aspen, I learned that he was a well educated, many faceted individual, a great guy and one hell of a skier.

At both Vail and Aspen, I talked to day lodge and restaurant managers. We ate dinner at some very good places and I tried to learn as much as possible about how things were done. For example, I observed how day lodges arranged their food on the cafeteria line, how they handled the money, how they priced their products and so on. One of the perks (that word wasn't around then) that came with the trip was a chance, actually a need, to ski to restaurants and day lodge locations on the mountain above the base areas. By the time we returned to Durango, I had some definite ideas about how I was going to manage the food and bar service at Purgatory.

Determined to do a first-class job, I furthered my education by frequently picking the brain of my buddy, restaurant owner Pat Howley about all aspects of food service and how to efficiently run a restaurant and, more particularly, how to manage a commercial kitchen. I consulted with bartenders and bar owners and anyone else who I thought could assist me. When it came time to hire a crew, I selected a good one. Don Ross was attending Fort Lewis College and working part time as a bartender at the Diamond Belle Saloon. Don agreed to work for me on weekends and holidays. I hired Ming Wong as my chef. He was the son of Whey Sam Wong who had owned the Mandarin Restaurant in Durango. Ming had been working as a cook for Woody Wong (no relation to Whey Sam) at the Western Steak House. Ming had the ability to whip up just about anything I put on the menu. I hired Maxine Thompson, a country lady, to bake pies at her home and bring them up to the lodge. (We didn't have a bake oven.) Maxine also worked as a cook. For the cashier, I hired Bobbi Courtney from our ranch staff and several other girls from CTR to staff the serving line.

I employed two cocktail waitresses for the lounge adjacent to the bar room on the third floor and had Tyrolian-like costumes made for them with puffy sleeved white blouses and bright red short pants with suspenders. Angie Candalaria had worked with me at the Full House, the other was Ming Wong's sister, Nancy Wong. Ming was as ugly as a cedar post but Nancy, a little thing who could not have weighed more than ninety pounds, was absolutely gorgeous. I never did figure that one out. I hired students from Fort Lewis College to fill jobs as line servers, bus boys and grill cooks. The kitchen was tiny and it took a lot of planning and coordinating to accomplish a practical method of getting out the required volume of food.

Chet Anderson and I shared an office on the first floor of the lodge. Chet's management style was much different than mine. He was very loose and seemed to pay little attention to detail while I was the kind of manager that attempted to know what was going on everywhere all of the time. I was able to avoid most problems because I identified them early and took corrective measures before they became big problems. That was my style at Colorado Trails Ranch and that was exactly the way I managed the lodge at Purgatory.

Opening day at Purgatory was sort of a semi-controlled mayhem. The restaurant and bar were ready for the onslaught of curious locals but they were still putting the ski rental shop together and there was a lot more work to finish elsewhere.

Regardless of the obvious shortcomings, the grand opening was a huge event. Ray Duncan had invited Governor John Love and his wife to attend the gala festivities and when they arrived, much to the surprise of everyone, the ceremony began with the governor's wife "christening" the Riblet chair lift with a bottle of champagne. Her words as I recall them were, "I hereby christen thee chair lift number one." The chairs were put in motion and the first official run with skiers ascended the mountain.

Afterwards, I served lunch with wine, delectable desserts, the whole nine yards . . . and it was good! The Governor loved Maxine's homemade pecan pie so much that I gave him a whole pie before he left, and every time he came down to ski thereafter, I always placed a whole pecan pie before him. On his fourth visit he told me, "You know, I really appreciate the pecan pies but I would love to try a slice of the lemon or cherry some time."

Ray was pleased with how well things went in the lodge and he commented favorably on the quality of the food. A couple weeks later, we both were in the men's room just down the hall from my office. We were standing next to each other washing our hands, when Ray turned to me and said, "You've been doing a great job. I'm impressed." I thanked him and was about to leave when he added, "Wait a minute, I have something for you." With that, he handed me a small box containing a Cross pen and pencil set, in gold, no less. I thanked him again. "And by the way, I'm raising your salary to $125 a week."

A by-product of that winter at Purgatory was a relationship that developed between Bobbi Courtney and me. Bobbi was a twenty-one year old from Palmetto, Florida when I hired her to work at the ranch. Her manner of speaking and the timbre of her voice sounded something like a cross between southern and hillbilly.

I had hired Bobbi to be our children's counselor and she proved to be a dandy. She was a good rider, was great with the kids, had an affable personality and she sure wasn't afraid of work. She was about 5'5", very trim, always wore jeans, boots, a loose fitting shirt and a cowboy hat. She kept her long black hair tied up in back and she never bothered with make up. Bobbi was a nice looking girl, but I would not have called her any kind of a beauty. She had the right attitude and that is what I liked most about her. She was there to do a job and she did it without fuss or fanfare. I like those attributes in an employee. I took no more or less interest in Bobbi during the previous summer than I did with any other member of our staff.

After our guest season was over, Bobbi stayed on to assist with the hunters and to work with me at Purgatory. It was during this time that Bill Steward, a local guy who had dated one of our staff girls during the summer, arrived to pick Bobbi up for a date. I was in the lodge kitchen when Bill came in and Bobbi was upstairs in her room getting ready. Bill and I were talking when Bobbi walked into the kitchen. I guess my mouth must have dropped open because Bobbi asked me if something was wrong. Actually, everything was right! Bobbi was beautiful! She was wearing a good looking dress that showed off her lovely figure and her slim legs. I couldn't believe it. What a metamorphosis! I began seeing Bobbi in a whole new light. One evening Bobbi and I were alone sitting in the dining room staring into the fire when suddenly I kissed her. She returned that kiss and we were off and running. Sex (intercourse) however, did not happen then or for a long time thereafter. Bobbi was a proper girl with high morals and definite ideas about what was appropriate behavior. I respected that and never pushed her. When the ski area opened, she lived in an apartment with another girl while I lived in a room at the Alpine North Motel. We never lived together nor did we ever consider it!

We didn't have much time for ourselves. We started work by seven and didn't leave until ten or eleven at night. It's hard to come up with enough energy for anything after working that many hours. The attraction was both mutual and certainly much more than sexual. Everyone at the ski area was aware that we were *an item*, including Ray Duncan who invited us to his home for dinner, prepared by his lovely wife, Joan.

After the Christmas and New Years holidays, we stopped offering evening meals because there was insufficient interest. Don Ross, his girlfriend, Elaine (Bobbi's room-mate), Bobbi and I would frequently go out together after work. In spite of the fact that I was thirty-eight and Bobbi was twenty-one, it didn't seem to present a problem for us, although I'm sure some folks thought it a little weird. It seemed that the relationship might be ready to step up a notch or two and I'm sure it would have except for one thing: Mary Ann Davis! The thought of her kept gnawing away at the back of my mind and occasionally I tele-phoned but she immediately hung up. I was continually trying to think of a way to convince her to see me again. I persuaded myself that I absolutely had to find out if I was dealing with nothing more than just another romantic fantasy.

Bobbi was aware of my abstract relationship with Mary Ann, which in fact, was no relationship at all. In early spring, I hit upon a plan. Bobbi said I was crazy and should give it up and I was tempted to do so, but in the end, I decided to make one last effort to see Mary Ann.

The scheme I had in mind required an intermediary and an accomplice. I knew precisely who to call. I picked up the telephone one evening and dialed the number.

CHAPTER FORTY TWO

All day, all night, Mary Ann

I was nervous as I dialed the Phoenix number. "June, it's Dick Elder, how ya doin'?" I asked if Dick could pick up an extension so the three of us could talk. Dick came on and we chatted briefly. "Listen, I have a big favor to ask of you. Don't feel like you gotta say yes because if you'd rather not do this thing for me, it's okay."

Dick Bridges answered, "Sure. Fire away. We're glad to help the ranch any way we can." June agreed.

"No, this isn't about the ranch, this is about me and a certain lady who lives in Phoenix." Then I told them the story and added, "Here's where you two come in. The problem is that Mary Ann refuses to answer my calls. As soon as she hears my voice, she hangs up, so I can't tell her that I'm divorced now and want to see her again. What I'd like you to do, June, if you're willing, is call and tell her I'm free now and want very badly to see her. Now, I know she'll want to turn me down, but you could say that you and Dick will pick her up and the four of us will go to dinner. After dinner, we'll come back to your house so that she and I can chat but you folks will be there in the house so she has nothing to worry about. After a half hour or sooner, if she wants, Dick will take her home. I think the main thing is to assure her that she'll not be left alone with me from start to finish." I took a deep breath. "So, what do you say? There was a long period of silence. I suppose both of them were waiting for the other to speak so I interjected, "You can talk it over and I'll call back tomorrow evening. How would that be?"

June answered, "Maybe that would be better."

Dick said, "Oh hell June, we can try to help the poor guy out. Can't you see he's in love?"

June answered, "Sure. Okay. She may not want to talk to me either but sure, I guess I can give it a try."

We worked out the details if Mary Ann agreed and then I told them, "If you can pull this off, you've got a free vacation next summer."

Together they said, "No, no, you don't need to do that." Dick added, "We're happy to help if we can. We'll call you."

MY DIVORCE FROM MARYE HAD GONE SMOOTHLY, AS COLORADO had recently passed the "Dissolution of Marriage" law. This law established criteria that if both parties agreed to the terms of a Separation Agreement, then normal divorce proceedings could be waived and the marriage dissolved. Larry McDaniel represented both of us, as Marye and the children were living with her parents in California. There was no haggling and no hassle. Marye got her share of CTR stock and notes plus child support from me. Seventeen years of a rocky marriage ended . . . a marriage that, as I have stated all along, never should have taken place.

After the Christmas holidays, I set up my ranch office at the Alpine North Motel in an alcove adjacent to my bedroom. The space was about the size of a small walk-in closet. I put my old Royal typewriter on a little table with boxes of brochures, stationery and other office items stacked below. After leaving the ski area, Bobbi and I would dine at the Western Steak House. Sometimes, we would live it up a little and eat at the more prestigious Sweeny's Grubstake or the Assay Office. After dinner, I took Bobbi to her apartment, and then went to the post office and got the mail out of box 848. Back at my motel, I would answer inquiries, job applications and other correspondence. I rarely made it to bed before one in the morning. This routine continued throughout the winter and early spring. I did not take a day off from the time the ski area opened in early December, until closing day, Easter Sunday.

The lodge food and bar operation was the only department that showed a profit for The Durango Ski Corporation. Ray Duncan was very happy with what I had accomplished and invited me to run the lodge the following winter. I agreed. It was a lot of work, the hours were ruthless, but unlike the ranch, I was at least able to make some money.

I received a call from Dick Bridges. He advised that Mary Ann had agreed to see me under the stringent conditions June had defined. However, there was no way that I could get away from Purgatory until the ski season ended. As quickly as possible thereafter, I traveled to Phoenix for that much sought after and long anticipated encounter. Bobbi was intensely upset with me and rightly so, but I told her that perhaps nothing would come of my meeting with Mary Ann. Besides, I argued, we both needed to put the Mary Ann thing to rest one way or the other. Then, for a capper to the argument, I said something that made her furious: I told her she needed to find someone closer to her age.

The meeting took place on the appointed evening. Dick Bridges picked her up, returned for June and me and we went to a restaurant for dinner. It had been more than a year since Mary Ann threw me out of her home. I sat in the front seat with Dick and Mary Ann chatted amiably in back with June. We said only a few words in the car, but during dinner we began a somewhat tentative, if not strained dialog that became more relaxed over time. Back at the house Mary Ann and I sat in opposing chairs and talked for the proscribed half hour. Just before Dick took her home, she agreed that we could go out on a date by ourselves. If she had been seeing other men in the interim, she didn't mention it, and I didn't ask, nor did she question me on that subject.

While in the Phoenix area, I made follow up calls on travel agents, airlines and the recreation council (IRC). I had been staying in touch with these sources throughout the winter. In the evenings, Mary Ann and I went out or she cooked a meal at her place with Gene and Sally, her two children joining us. The kids and I got along fine and the magic that she and I experienced before quickly returned and began to blossom. I was invited to the Gaglioni home in Mesa for another Sunday dinner and it went well.

Driving back through town after that meal, a '63 Ford Thunderbird on a dealer's lot caught my eye. It was in perfect condition, had low mileage and the price, as I recall, was $1,800. (The car probably sold new for $2,500). The next morning, I called my friends at the First National Bank, arranged for a loan and bought the car. Since going to work for Purgatory, my credit status had greatly improved.

Driving home in the T-bird, I was one happy son-of-a-gun having finally revived my relationship with Mary Ann. I was whizzing down the nearly deserted highway on the Navajo Reservation at over one hundred miles an hour (that big V-8 hardly working) and making up a song as I went along. I recall one of the verses:

I've got a Thunderbird and I've got a Mary Ann,
And I've got a star in the sky.
If you had a Thunderbird and you had a Mary Ann,
You'd be as happy as I.

Now, I thought, all I had to do to make the picture perfect was get that damn ranch on its feet and marry Mary Ann! The Mary Ann part turned out to be a lot easier to accomplish than the ranch part.

After our guest season of 1964, we were $28,000 in the hole, but we did manage to make our mortgage payment to Camp Silver Spruce. Our 1965 season brought in gross income of $28,500, which resulted in a loss of $3,721. Cash on hand was only $283 and the SBA loan went unpaid. We were deeper in debt than before. The balance sheet listed earned surplus as *minus $35,231*.

I wrote a letter of desperation to the stockholders in which I all but begged for help. Are these not the words of a desperate man?

The very bad weather in late June and early July last year hurt us. We received numerous cancellations after Colorado was declared a disaster area and we lost quite a few guests who were unwilling to sit out the rain and left after only a few days.

Since SBA has turned down our request for deferment of the principal payment this year and since we will not have enough cash left over to make the payment, please give consideration to the possibility of making an additional investment however small, so that we can meet our obligation to SBA and stop foreclosure. If you can see your way clear to investing some more, I can assure you that this investment will bring you a handsome gain later. Please keep in mind that with your support now we will see the day when we will be able to sell this place for $300,000 or more. If you are looking for a good growth stock, with security, this is it! Help this ranch now and help yourself. Borrowing additional money to build is out of the question. The only way we are going to get those extra rooms we need is if those of you who can afford it will invest a little more by no later than April. [1966]

I think you will agree that those statements constitute begging and at that point, I sure wasn't above doing it.

Apparently my partners had given up on the deal and were ready to write the whole thing off because no money arrived. The only response was a letter from George Horton dated July 1, 1966. Here is part of what he wrote:

You said in your letter that you want to sell for a profit but I for one feel like at this time that if we could break even we would do well. You may be able to hold off for six months, but in case it isn't sold by then it would of course go up for Sheriff's Sale, and we'd be lucky to clear the SBA loan and the first mortgage. As you know, in a case of a Sheriff's Sale, this is all they are interested in. Well, all I can say Dick is, let's hope we make out selling it, and if any other thing comes up pertaining to this, please let Mel, Jim or I know. See you and Good Luck. Regards, George."

I'm sure the three of them had talked it over, decided that there was no future in it and the best they could hope for was a sale where they would get their money back. But I wasn't ready to go down that road, not yet.

Using some money I had saved from my Purgatory job, I pushed on and went about the annual task of hiring staff and getting the place ready for guests. I was on my own this time with no wife, no partners, just me. That's not altogether true; I did have help and lots of it from Bobbi, Bob Bellmaine, Shorty, Cecil and Faye Mars, a few members of our '65 staff and a bunch of new college kids. One new staff person was an eighteen-year old from Redlands, California, named Jeanne Fullerton. Jeanne worked the previous summer for Bob Jacobson, the owner of Wilderness Trails Ranch and it was he who had recommended her. She took a job as a combination waitress/housekeeper at $60 a month plus room and board. The reason I mention her is that Jeanne is *still* working for Colorado Trails Ranch as I write this in the year 2002. That, you must agree, is pretty amazing!

I flew down to Phoenix several times that spring to spend weekends with Mary Ann who I was now calling Dolly. It was in May during one of those visits that we decided to marry and we set a July 1 date.

Meanwhile at the ranch, we all worked very hard to get everything ready for a mid-June opening. I am unable to accurately relate all of the pertinent details of that summer, except for financial information, so I'll just have to wing it.

One event that is etched in my memory was my wedding day and the rehearsal the day before. Dolly was dressed very nicely, as always, when we walked into the chapel, but I was in my usual garb of boots, jeans, cowboy shirt and hat. After we rehearsed the ceremony to the minister's satisfaction and were about to leave, he took me aside and asked if I had a white shirt, tie and regular pants, not blue jeans, that I could wear for the ceremony. I laughed and told him not to worry that I would be presentable. I had one suit left over from my prosperous days in Ohio that I had not worn since 1959. I wore the suit with a white shirt and tie and even bought a pair of regular shoes. When I took my place before the minister, he wasn't convinced that I was the same guy he had seen the day before.

It was a somewhat perfunctory ceremony, although not unpleasant and certainly, Dolly and I were all smiles as we exited into a sweltering 115 degree July afternoon. Dolly's relatives and friends attended but I don't recall inviting anyone except my best man, Don Stickle, the DJ from KDGO. We had an enjoyable reception with champagne and food then spent our wedding night at the Mountain Shadows Resort in Scottsdale. The next day we drove her Chevy to Durango. Since we were in operation by the time Dolly joined the ranch, she had to learn what it was all about without much help from me as I was busy eighteen hours a day. She took over the office, got it well organized and running like an eight-day clock in no time. The downside of it was that we were newlyweds living in the middle bedroom of the lodge. The other three rooms housed our young staff girls, including Dolly's daughter, Sally. At times it was comical, especially when all of us needed to use the only bathroom or when Dolly would knock on the wall and say, "Okay girls. That's enough talk for tonight. Go to sleep now." Then the girls would take turns answering, "Good night Dolly. Good night Dick." Of course, we had to reply to each of the ten girls in turn. Is this not the stuff of a television sitcom? It sure seemed like it to us and to our guests who thought it quite amusing.

I had no doubt whatsoever that we had all the ingredients for eventual success with just one exception . . . money! The SBA was getting nervous and sent a couple men down to have a talk with me. While there, the men listed all of our assets, right down to the carpet sweepers, pots and pans, everything. That made me extremely nervous. I was smelling foreclosure.

CHAPTER FORTY THREE

*The Indian Snow Dance
isn't an exact science, or is it?*

I didn't book any hunters, as I wanted to get a head start on my ski area job. Although I had not talked to Ray Duncan, I was certain that my job as Lodge Manager was secure. Additionally, I wanted to be able to spend some quality time with my new bride.

When I met with Duncan at his office in the West Building, I planned to make the first order of business a discussion of my salary requirements. I intended to ask for $250 a week and let him beat me down to $200, but after a minute of small talk, he launched into a subject that at first had me very worried. The conversation went something like this:

Ray: "I've been giving this food and beverage thing a lot of thought and I'm pretty sure that I don't want you to manage the lodge this year."

Me, aghast: "Huh?"

Ray: "No, I have a better idea that will be good for the both of us."

Me: Mouth open and speechless.

Ray: "Here's what I'm proposing and listen to the whole deal before you say anything, okay?"

Me: Speechless, but I nod.

Ray: "Instead of managing the lodge I want you to

lease, that's right, lease the restaurant and bar from Durango Ski Corp. You understand what I'm saying? Everything that happens in the lodge will be like your own business. You pay your employees, you buy the food, you will be responsible for all of your costs and you pay Durango Ski Corp. fifteen percent of your gross sales as rent for the building and equipment. How's that sound?"

Me: "Sounds a hell of a lot better then what I thought you were going to tell me."

Ray: Leaning back in his chair and laughing, "Did you think I was going to fire you?"

Me: "It did cross my mind for a minute there. Sounds pretty good, but who pays for the restaurant and liquor licenses, insurance, electricity, equipment, building repairs, all those things?"

Ray: "We'll pay for all of that just like before. You just pay your direct costs and your workers comp insurance. How's that?"

I started to say that his deal sounded all right but changed my mind and said, "Basically, it sounds great but you know there's not a hell of a lot of profit in the food part, at least not at the prices we're able to charge. How about this? I pay you ten percent of the restaurant gross and fifteen percent of the bar gross. Those percentages will make it possible for me to show a reasonable profit. If I can't average a couple hundred dollars a week, your deal won't make any sense."

Ray: Without hesitating: "Okay. Ten and fifteen." He stood up, reached across the desk and we shook hands. "I'll get the contract drawn up and call when it's ready for you to look over."

Me: "Just a couple of other things Ray, if you don't mind." Ray sat back down. "I want to enclose that little porch off of the kitchen back door and install a convection oven so we can do our own baking and roasting on site." I was going to stop there but I figured, what the hell, the most he can do is turn me down. "And I need a lot more refrigeration space. What we need is a walk-in cooler. We could install it in the storeroom."

Ray: "What storeroom?"

Me: "Well, I heard you were going to build another building to house the ski rental shop, which I think is a damn good idea. I want you to give me the space the rental shop had in the lodge for storage and for the walk-in cooler."

Ray: Giving me a long hard look: "Who pays for all this?"

Me, smiling: "Why, Durango Ski Corp, of course."

Ray laughed loudly: "You're something Elder, ya know that? Okay, let me think about it." He stood up, looked at me intently and said, "You really need those things?" I nodded. "Aw, the hell with it. Go ahead, but let me know what all this shit is going to cost before you buy it."

The best thing about working for Ray Duncan was we understood each other and that made the relationship, at least from my perspective, a good one.

The Purgatory lease deal was a good break and I was confident that I would be able to make some serious money that I could use to aid Colorado Trails. Dolly was delighted with the arrangement and our expectation was that we would do well.

I hired a good staff that included a number of key people who had worked for me before. However, Bobbi, having returned to Florida in September, was not one of them. I proceeded to have a small room built adjacent to the kitchen to house a Blodgett convection oven. The ski rental shop did move into the new building and I was given the space for a large walk-in cooler and for food storage. By Thanksgiving, the entire ski area was ready to go except for one thing . . . SNOW! Snow is something you simply must have if you want to ski and Purgatory had no snow and no snow making capability.

December rolled around and the forecasters were predicting nothing but clear skies. On December fifth I got a call from Ray Duncan telling me to come over to his office pronto. (He didn't say ASAP, because that term hadn't been born yet.) It didn't take me long to get down to the West Building and run up to the fourth floor.

The conversation we had that morning was both bizarre and comical, but Duncan was serious as a heart attack. He told me that we needed to do something about the snow situation right away because Christmas vacation time was coming up and he exclaimed, "If we don't get enough snow to open, we'll be screwed."

I just sat there for several moments in disbelief. "What the hell am I supposed to do about it? I'm the Lodge manager." He told me what he wanted me to do. Are you ready to hear this?

Ray leaned forward and in a somber tone said, "I want you to get a hold of that Ute medicine man you know and have him come up to the ski area and do a snow dance."

I started to laugh, but immediately stifled it as I could tell that Ray was not trying to be funny. He jumped up and said, "Hey, I'm dead serious about this. We've got to have some snow and I'm willing to try anything to get it. I heard this guy went some place that needed rain real bad and he did a rain dance and by Christ, they got more damn rain then they knew what to do with. So get this guy, pay him whatever he wants, but get him the hell up to the area."

I had my marching orders and they could not have been more explicit. I drove to Ignacio hoping to find the Southern Ute Tribe's Medicine Man, Eddie Box. The tribe's administration facilities are in Ignacio, a little town some twenty-five miles from Durango, on the Ute reservation. I knew Eddie Box through Tony Burch and had him and some of his tribal dancers at Colorado Trails during the summer to dance for our guests.

It took a while, but eventually I located Eddie and told him what we would like him to do. He said he would dance for snow but he couldn't do it right away, although he promised that he would let me know when the dancers would come up to Purgatory. I begged him not to wait too long because so many jobs were dependant on the ski area. He reiterated that he would be there as soon as he could. I offered as payment for his services, a full course steak dinner for everyone he brought with him. He told me that that would be payment enough.

I reported to Ray that the Indian dancers would come up to the area and perform the snow dance. He was pleased, but when a week passed without a call from Eddie Box, Ray got crazy and told me to do something. The problem was, I couldn't find Eddie and no one at tribal headquarters in Ignacio seemed to know his whereabouts. December 17 rolled around and I still had not heard from the Medicine Man. By this time, the whole town of Durango was getting the jitters. The sky was crystal blue, we hadn't seen a cloud in weeks and the forecast called for "continued clear and dry with no moisture in the foreseeable future."

Before sun up on Thursday, Eddie called to tell me that the dancers would be at Purgatory about eleven o'clock on Saturday. I was tickled pink (as we used to say) and called Ray. He was tickled more pink than I. At the end of our conversation, I added, "I hate to mention this Ray, but you know, it is possible that Eddie and his guys can dance their brains out and we still might not get any snow." No response from Ray, so I continued, "You have to understand that this snow dance thing is not an exact science." Still nothing but silence, so I plunged ahead. "Did you hear the forecast on the radio this morning? It was for continued clear and dry. Anyway, I just thought I'd mention it." I don't think that was something Ray wanted to hear.

I placed ads in the Friday edition of the Durango Herald advising that the Southern Ute Indian Dancers would be on the sun deck of the lodge at Purgatory on Saturday at noon and all were invited to watch the ceremony and incidentally, enjoy lunch while they were there.

A very large crowd assembled to watch the Ute Dancers perform the sacred "Dance for Snow" on the sun deck. Dolly and I stood on the third floor balcony and watched the activity below. I looked up at the clear blue ski above the run called *Pandemonium* and remarked, "No way in hell are we gonna get any snow today." Dolly agreed.

The dancers below were well into the ritual as Eddie chanted the words his ancestors had sung. The relentless sounds of beating drums echoed from the surrounding mountains. Then suddenly, to my amazement, clouds began to roll over the mountaintops from the west. The drummers beat a faster tempo, the dance became a flurry of energy as snow flakes, the size of silver dollars, came floating down. The drums became silent, the dancers were still, the spectators stood motionless. That great crowd of people quietly staring, unbelieving, into the snow filled sky. It was like a freeze frame in a movie. Then, just as suddenly, all hell broke loose. People were yelling and jumping up and down and laughing and hugging and generally going mad. I ran down the stairs to the dining room, Ray was just coming in from the sun deck. "This is unbelievable," he shouted. "Look at that, will you. It's snowing!"

Eddie and the dancers got a full course T-bone steak dinner, I got a lodge full of people and a jammed bar and lounge. The ski area got what it wanted too. Snow! It snowed for two days. Our one snow packing machine couldn't begin to keep up with it. The ski season at Purgatory was off and running. Now we heard the joyful sounds of cash registers ringing, of skiers laughing, of ski boots resounding on wood floors and Swiss yodeling blaring from loud speakers. The awesome morning runs on the uncut powder skiing with Chet, the ski school instructors and ski patrol, all of it was perfect.

Life was good until January 12, 1967. Chet and I were shooting the breeze in the office we shared when someone knocked. Chet unwound his long frame and opened the door. A middle-aged man wearing a suit and holding a brief case stood in the doorway. He looked around and inquired, "Mr. Elder?" Chet nodded in my direction.

The man glanced at Chet, then turning to me said, "Mr. Elder is there some place where we can talk?"

Chet jumped up. "It's okay. You guys stay here. I gotta go anyway."

"What can I do for you," I inquired.

The man reached in his pocket and handing me his card said, "I'm Joseph Madera with the SBA. Mr. Elder, I'm afraid I have some bad news for you."

I glanced at his card and immediately felt my gut contract. What the hell did the Small Business Administration want now? I spoke, "What bad news?"

Madera opened his briefcase, pulled out some papers and laid them in front of me. "I'm very sorry sir, but I'm afraid the agency has no other options. We forgave last year's payment and now your mortgage payment is four months overdue. Frankly, we don't think your dude ranch business is going to survive. You actually lost more money this year than you did last year. That isn't too encouraging now, is it?"

While he was talking, I scanned the documents, then looking at my visitor, who was obviously uncomfortable, declared, "You're foreclosing? Is that what this is about, foreclosure?"

"Yes sir, I'm afraid so. We are sorry, honestly, but we have an obligation to the taxpayers to keep our losses to a minimum."

"No, I sure as hell don't understand. I'm a taxpayer. Don't you have an obligation to me? I told Mr. Jaramillo we would need a couple more years to get the thing rolling. I told him I had this job at the ski area and that I'd personally make good on the mortgage payments after the ski season was over. He told me he would lower our payments to $6,000 for the next few years. Now, you're telling me that he's not going to do that and you're shutting us down just like that?" I was getting hot, my voice and temper rising. "Jaramillo was feeding me a line of crap, is that it? Why didn't he just come right out and tell me he was going to foreclose." I tried to control it, but back in the sixties I had a problem keeping my temper in check.

The man stood up and closed his briefcase. "There is no point in getting upset with me Mr. Elder. I'm only carrying out my instructions. Good day sir." With that, he walked out of the office, closing the door quietly behind him.

I was in shock! I never thought it would come to this. Seven years of work, beating myself up, going through all the crap and now this? If those bastards at SBA would have just given us another year or two . . . I killed the thought. They're foreclosing and that's that. I was getting a headache.

I left the office and slowly climbed the stairs to the third floor. It was early, the bar was deserted. I picked up a bottle of Ancient Age, sat on a stool, elbows on the bar, head in my hands. Looking up, I saw my reflection in the back bar mirror and muttered, "Damn those horses."

How, I mused, had I let myself get into this mess. There sure hadn't been any shortage of advice. Good advice! Don't do it they said. Did I listen? Hell no! I thought I knew what I was doing. I must have been crazy to think I could actually pull it off. My dad was right after all. He said I was nuts for not having the financing figured out before we started. I finished off the bourbon and poured another. If I hadn't let myself get so wrapped up with the damn horses, I'd still be living a normal life back in Chesterland, Ohio. Damn those horses!

Searching my reflected image intently, I wondered, who is that guy? Oh, I remember . . . he's the hotshot horseman who wanted to be a Colorado cowboy. He's the idiot who claimed he was going to build the best damn dude ranch in Colorado.

"Well, smart-ass," I said aloud, "go home and explain all this to your wife."

CHAPTER FORTY FOUR

Two Angels pluck me from Hell

D olly and I reviewed the SBA foreclosure documents and after the initial shock subsided, we discussed our options. We concluded that we had only two: make the overdue payments, or convince SBA to lower our payments to a number we could realistically afford. Since there was no immediate way we could accomplish the first, we were left with no choice but to go up to Denver and, as Dolly put it, "Explain everything and then throw ourselves on their mercy." The SBA, as I had come to know it, was not the sort of entity that routinely practiced financial decisions based solely on 'mercy.' Regardless, I called our loan officer, made an appointment for a meeting and a week later, drove to the Small Business Administration offices in Denver.

Dolly and I sat in the little office of Mr. Charles Jaramillo, the man responsible for managing our loan, discussing our plight, assuring him that in a matter of a year or two, Colorado Trails would be operating in the black and making mortgage payments on time. I reminded him that he had promised to get our annual payments lowered, but he claimed that the loan committee wouldn't go for it. Though he was sympathetic to our pleadings he refused to stay our execution. Disheartened, we were about to leave when the telephone rang. He picked it up,

"They're in my office now. No, I didn't see any way to. Very well, I'll bring them right up." Laying the receiver down, Jaramillo turned to us and said, "Mr. Wilkerson has asked me to bring you folks up to his office."

Lacy Wilkerson was a retired bank president who now held the top SBA position for the four or five western states region. A very tall, distinguished looking man with white hair, I judged him to be in his mid-sixties although he may have been older. He excused Mr. Jaramillo and invited Dolly and me to take seats in his spacious and well-appointed office. I made a mental note that I could have built and furnished three cabins for what the government had paid for Mr. Wilkerson's office décor.

"I'm Lacy Wilkerson and I'm very pleased to meet you," he said as he shook hands with each of us. "May I get you something, ah, some refreshments, coffee?" We thanked him but declined. Wilkerson sat at his large desk, pushed his chair back, crossed his legs and in a fatherly tone began, "I happened to hear about your case during a meeting last week. They told me that you were planning on coming up here. Frankly, I was somewhat intrigued with your notion to build a dude ranch. That sounds like a romantic sort of thing and I should think, a most interesting line of work." He had our file on his desk and paused momentarily to flip through the pages. "Personally, I would rather not take you through the foreclosure process at this time and I'll tell you why. Although some individuals in this agency might disagree, I think our overriding purpose here is to help business people such as you get through the rigors of starting a business. I do not think that we should become overly zealous in our quest to protect the government's position and end the start-up process before a sufficient period of time has passed to allow you to demonstrate your capabilities. So please tell me why you think your company will prosper and what you think we at SBA should do to help you."

I looked at Dolly. I'm sure she was thinking the same thing I was: *What is going on here? He's not talking at all like a government bureaucrat. He actually sounds like a caring human being.* Between the two of us, we spent the best part of an hour telling Lacy Wilkerson about how we hoped to implement our business plan. I particularly emphasized some points that caught his attention. I asked, "What is the harm in giving us a few more years to get on our feet, particularly since we only owe $50,000 and the present value of the land and buildings is at least twice that much. If we had lower annual payments and if SBA would give us a few more years to grow, we would be in good shape."

"If we don't make it," I continued, "SBA still has the option to foreclose with the assurance that the property would sell for considerably more than the outstanding debt." I wound up my pitch with, "It all boils down to these two basic elements: One, we have more than enough equity to cover our loan in case of default, so you have virtually no real risk. Two, if we do thrive as a profitable new business, then you folks will have accomplished your agency's mission, which I understand is to help small businesses get started and become profitable."

Wilkerson listened intently, occasionally nodding his head in agreement with something I had said, but remained silent. When we had concluded, he thanked us for, as he put it, "Enlightening me." He said he was glad that we had come to Denver to give him a more comprehensive view than that which he received from his staff. After scanning our file again, he picked up the phone and dialed. "Listen Charles, I have had a very illuminating and productive discussion with the Elders and I am sending them back down to you. I want you to organize their repayment schedule along these lines. I should think annual payments of $6,000 should work well for them for say, the next three years with incremental increases thereafter. Doesn't that seem like a more appropriate way of handling this case? Good. I'll just send them back down to you. Oh, and Charles, best get cracking on canceling that foreclosure order, eh? Fine."

Wilkerson swiveled his chair in our direction and smiled. "I'm sure you are going to be just fine. Be careful, stick with your principals and your plan." He showed us to the door. I thought Dolly was going to kiss him. I darn near wanted to kiss him myself. Holding the door open he said, "Good bye and good luck. Write to me in a year's time and let me know how you are getting on."

Lacy Wilkerson, as they say now, saved my ass. He was the first of two angels who significantly assisted me as I fought to keep Colorado Trails Ranch alive.

We had a wonderful run at Purgatory and made a significant amount of money. Six- thousand dollars went to the SBA and a good portion of the remainder was deposited in the Colorado Trails bank account. When the ski season ended, we busied ourselves with the annual routine of hiring staff and getting the ranch ready for guests. We purchased the home we were renting from David Bechtel, the same minister startled by Bradley's inappropriate vocabulary. It was a rather large house if you counted the full basement. We paid $25,000 for the three-year old home and I sold it for $70,000 in 1977. It last sold a few years ago for more than $250,000. You got to love it!

The annual meeting of the stockholders, held on April 1, was adjourned as no one showed up. Apparently, none of them wanted to incur the expense of traveling to Durango. Since there were so many issues that needed to be addressed, Dolly and I felt that we should hold the meeting in Ohio. We had a great time crossing the country in the Thunderbird, following the route of the International truck across the plains of Colorado and

Kansas. Dolly enjoyed hearing the stories of our original trip in the old binder back in 1960. I told her about Leonard and Wolf Creek and all the rest of the now-fabled history.

My parent's anniversary was on May 5 and they and my brothers had their first introduction to Dolly at that time. It went well although they loved Marye and were not yet reconciled to my divorce, the first in the history of the Elder family. Anyway, Dolly captured them as she did most everyone she met. My brother Bob gave us his five shares of Colorado Trails stock as a wedding present. In truth, the shares were almost worthless, but over time, it turned out to be one hell of a gift. The next day, we held a meeting at Mel's Ridge Top Farm in Willoughby. Attending were the Shaefers, Hortons, Dodsons, Dolly and me. There was an unmistakable chill in the air as I introduced my new wife. Twila and Donna did not much cotton to this intruder, as Marye was their good friend. Many months later Twila told me that when Donnie learned my wife's name she snorted, "I'll just bet she's a *Dolly*."

To relate the significant issues of that meeting, I'll quote directly from the minutes:

The President gave his annual report to the stockholders, in which he advised that reservations for the 1967 summer season were running well ahead of the previous year and that he anticipated a good season. He also advised that he had completed arrangements with the Small Business Administration in which he had renegotiated the payment schedule and that payments for the foreseeable future would amount to only $6,000 a year including principal and interest. [Previously, about $15,000.] He distributed copies of a letter dated April 14, 1967 from Mr. Charles Jaramillo which explained in detail the conditions and modifications of the new schedule.

The following is something you may find hard to understand:

The President advised the stockholders that he had listed the ranch for sale with various reputable real estate firms, but as yet had received no offers. He suggested that ads placed in trade journals and other media might be a method of securing prospects, however, he advised that there were no funds available for the placement of such ads. He asked the stockholders if any of them would care to contribute to a special fund for the sole purpose of advertising the ranch for sale. None of the stockholders indicated a willingness to contribute.

Not one stockholder offered any opposition to selling the ranch and yet none were willing to contribute money to facilitate a sale. After all these years, I can't say for sure what my feelings were in this regard, but I think I had come to the point where I just didn't want to continue the fight all by myself. It was obvious that my partners had given up on me and on Colorado Trails and were willing to sit by and let it go. Perhaps they were hoping that if the ranch sold, they might recapture some, if not all, of their investment. Certainly, that letter from George suggested it. My position must have been ambivalent. I had a new wife, a good job with a bright future and I undoubtedly determined that it would be in my best interest to pursue the easier and more secure course. Or, it could be that I had just reached the point where I thought that if the others were not interested in the ranch, why the hell should I knock myself out?

Regardless, I was reelected as President, Mel Schaefer, Vice president and Mary Ann Elder became our new Secretary/Treasurer. My annual salary of $4,800 was renewed. I had not received any money during the previous year but I agreed that I "*would defer demand for payment until some future time when the company's financial position would warrant the disbursement of funds to make up the deficit."* I don't believe that anyone at that meeting actually thought such a time would ever arrive.

We opened the ranch around the middle of June, 1967 with a light-hearted optimism fueled by the twin possibilities that my Purgatory lease for the coming winter would be renewed and the likelihood that we might sell the ranch and recoup our investment. It was a good summer and there was little doubt that we were getting more adept at managing the outfit and organizing and implementing better than average vacation programs. Any job becomes easier and performance improves when you know what you are doing and more importantly, *why* you are doing it. We stuck to our goal of making sure that every guest had the best vacation we could possibly provide. All other considerations were secondary. We were getting a good percentage of repeat guests and a large percentage of our census was the result of word of mouth recommendations from former guests. A new brochure that year with many more pictures, some in color, helped our advertising effort as well.

Admittedly, our facilities remained as before. The lack of cash precluded our making improvements or adding amenities, but we had an energetic and attractive staff who literally knocked themselves out day after day. The guests recognized and appreciated the huge contributions by the staff and weekly tips frequently exceeded weekly salaries. We worked hard to live up to our mottos, *Colorado's friendliest* and *More than just a great vacation* with a program that was ambitious and entertaining. The proof that our guests were more than satisfied with the quality of their vacations was reflected in the number who reserved for the following summer.

The second angel arrived in July, not on gossamer wings, but in a yellow Lincoln. This angel was from Richmond, Kentucky and his name was George William

Begley. His wife Geneva, sons George Richard and Bruce
Bernard and secretary, Mary, accompanied him. They
had called the week before from Eaton's Ranch where,
they claimed, they felt like outsiders and thus were not
having a very good time and wanted to make a change.
Fortunately, we had a cabin available for them.

I thought George was quite a bit older than me, he certainly looked it and he seemed to have trouble getting
around in the high altitude. Actually, he was my senior
by only a year. He drove his car everywhere. When he got
out of the car, he left the door open. I was teaching
archery one afternoon and George arrived in the Lincoln
with the secretary, Mary. When it was his turn, he shot
his six arrows and when everyone was instructed to
move up to the target and retrieve their arrows George
said, "Mary, go fetch my arrows," which she did. Mary
was George's gofer in every event that required some
walking. The guests were amused, as was I.

On Wednesday evening, I found myself sitting next to
George on the lodge porch. He told me how much his
family was enjoying their vacation then he said in his
slow, southern, almost hillbilly dialect, "Son, I can see
that you need some things. They tell me that y'all do
your dirty dishes by hand in a sink." I told him that was
correct. "And, do you and your missus live up there with
all those young girls that work here?" I nodded. "Lord
have mercy," he exclaimed. "Well sir, that's just not
right. Y'all need some privacy and I don't reckon y'all get
any up there right in the middle of that passel of girls."

"No," I replied, "there's not much privacy, that's true."

Then he asked me how we were organized and I told
him we were a corporation. He wondered if we had any
stock for sale and would we be interested in selling some.
I told him yes, we would be delighted to sell him some.
Then he said, "When I said that I could tell that y'all
needed some things, I didn't mean to be disrespectful in
any way, I was just making an observation."

I laughed. "Well, you're right that we need some things. Hell, we need a ton of things but . . ."

George interrupted, "I understand and I think y'all are doing a fine job with what y'all have. I also think there's the potential to do a lot more if you had just a little help." He stubbed out his cigarette and immediately lit another. Looking at me, he said in a hushed voice, "I came out here for this vacation but also to buy me some pure bred Semental cattle that are being raised by a fella named James somewhere north of Durango. I brought along $25,000 for that purpose. What I'm thinking is, maybe I'd be better off investing that money with y'all because I think that with a little help, this place could turn into a first class resort. I know a little bit about making money and this place *will* make money. In just these few days, I can see that you have what it takes. Before we leave, I'd like for you and me to get together and work out something, that is, if you're interested."

Begley had only been on the ranch for a couple of days, I barely knew him and he sure didn't know me, yet on Friday at the office in Coney Cove he purchased forty shares of Colorado Trails Ranch, Inc. stock at $100 a share. He also agreed to accept a promissory note with a face value of $20,000 with interest at 6%, as did all other stockholders. George said that the first thing he wanted me to do with part of the $24,000 was, "Build ya a place for you and your missus."

Those two events, triggered by Lacy Wilkerson and George Begley, proved to be the most significant in our history. Had Lacy Wilkerson allowed the foreclosure to proceed, Colorado Trails Ranch would have expired then and there. Had George Begley not shown his faith in me and in the future potential of the ranch, chances are I would have sold it. Now, however, all thoughts of selling the ranch evaporated. We were financially able to get in gear and move ahead. The Colorado Trails dream was reborn and as they say now, I was "pumped."

CHAPTER FORTY FIVE

"Get out of there, you damn hussy!"

I wrote a long letter to the stockholders on August 10, 1967 to, "advise how things are going." Here's some of that letter:

It looks like we'll record the largest gross in our history this year. Because we are booked solid, we've been renting some cabins across the road and putting our overflow there. If we book just two more families, we will hit our goal of $35,000, the magic number I've been looking for all of these years!

So far as the sale of the ranch is concerned, we have had no action at all from the various realtors with whom we are listed and I cannot justify taking money from our working capital for the purpose of advertising [the sale of the ranch]. As long as things are going alright and we're able to keep current on our bills and pay our mortgage, I'm satisfied to let it go at that until the right party happens along. If nothing more, we are getting the place paid off and certainly our equity is appreciating yearly.

I included with that letter a copy of a long and highly complementary newspaper article about us.

In September I wrote a short letter to my brother Bob which dealt with his wedding present of his five shares of stock. I closed with this paragraph:

Once again, you are under no obligation to transfer this stock and we hereby release you from all previous commitments, particularly in view of our rather good year this year, our $24,000 windfall from Begley and our new arrangements with the SBA.

True to his character, Bob signed over his stock as promised and, as I mentioned earlier, that turned out to be one hell of a gift.

When the last guests departed in September, we immediately began spending some of Begley's invested money. Dolly and I agreed that we would be pragmatic and postpone building our personal cabin and use the money for much needed improvements, the first being a commercial dishwashing machine. The second project was a 12 x 20 foot addition to the lodge to be built with the help of my old friend, Homer Hartley. The addition would become a laundromat with three coin operated washers and dryers. Interestingly, a laundromat was the most frequently guest-requested amenity while the dishwashing machine was the number one staff request. Another popular guest entreaty was for carpeting the bare wood cabin floors. One of my former radio customers, Durango Furniture Mart, gave us a good price for enough wool carpeting to carpet all of the cabins.

Another project we tackled that fall was replacing our 1800's style cesspools with septic tanks and leach fields, the modern and proper way of handling raw sewage in a rural setting. I hated spending our precious capital on it, but a dramatic event convinced me that I had no choice but to do something about our archaic sewage system.

One afternoon during the summer, I saw a little girl running up the cabin road yelling, "There's a horse in the water, there's a horse in the water!"

I quickly ran over to her and asked, "Where's the horse?"

"In front of our cabin," she breathlessly replied.

I had no idea what she was talking about, but she insisted that I come with her at once. Together we ran down to *Valley View* and when we rounded the corner of the cabin, I immediately knew what she was talking about. There *was* a horse in the water. Brownie, a large bay mare, had obviously been grazing on the lush grass that always flourishes around septic systems and when she stepped onto the wood planks that covered the cesspool, boom! The wood gave way and Brownie fell in. The mare was standing belly deep in sewage water, mindlessly grazing on the thick grass that rimmed the edge of the hole. "See," said the little girl with obvious satisfaction, "I told you."

Much to my dismay, a crowd of guests gathered around eager to see what was going on. The worst thing was having the guests see how primitive and unsanitary our sewage system was. Shorty Mars arrived with a stout halter and some ropes and the first thing he did was have a good laugh. "I'll be dogged. This sure is one for the books. Well, let's see what we kin do about it." With that, he kneeled at the edge of the foul-smelling pit and put a leather halter on the mare then snapped on two stout leads. Handing me one of the lead ropes he said, "Let's see if we can get her to jump out of there. Ready? Pull!" We pulled but she didn't budge. She seemed to be quite happy right where she was. We got another rope behind her but that didn't work either. By now, just about every guest was watching this spectacle and we were being bombarded with suggestions of how to handle the operation. An unfruitful half hour had elapsed when the exasperated wrangler concluded that he had spent enough time fooling around and asked the crowd to move away. He then whacked off a long stout branch from a nearby spruce tree and whickered out a whip. Telling me to take hold of the lead rope and pull, he got behind the horse and whipped her rigorously on her backside while yelling, "Get on out of there you damn hussy." Brownie was no dummy. She set back on her haunches and made a giant leap plumb out of that hole. The crowd cheered and clapped and Brownie gave a big shake, spraying the celebrants with foul smelling sewage, sending them dashing for cover or more likely, to their showers. That, my friend, is why I decided to spend a large portion of Begley's money on septic tanks and leach fields. I'm sure that had the guests known from whence came those foul odors detected near their cabins, they would have listed improving the sewer system as number one on their list of requested upgrades.

All of my children spent the summer at Colorado Trails and it was great having them with us. They accepted Dolly as a friend and got along wonderfully with her. Nancy was a good worker and a big help, except at times she tended to lead some of the staff girls astray. Most of these misadventures were harmless enough but keeping the lid on the comings and goings of a bunch of young men and woman was an ongoing problem, so much so that it inspired high minded speeches from me at the beginning of every season along with weekly reminders. I made sure that our young staff was keenly aware of the temptations to which they would be exposed and certainly, I knew all about that. I cautioned them to maintain high moral standards throughout the summer. Don't fall in love, I warned the girls. Have a good time, enjoy making new friends but DON'T FALL IN LOVE! That admonition, no matter how frequently repeated, never resulted in the desired outcome. The phrase *fooling around* was not part of the popular compendium of 'cool' expressions back then, but I'll use it now. There was an abundance of fooling around, I just didn't know about most of it. Once in a while Jeanne Fullerton or some other staff confidant would tell me about staff misdeeds, then I would launch into a righteous sermon but with little long-lasting consequence. My marriage to Mary Ann,

AKA Dolly, launched a totally pure phase in my life. I was the quintessential husband. Like a person who has just quit smoking, found Jesus, or become a vegetarian, I decreed that all those working in my domain should likewise be as pure and upright. It was a crock of you know what, but I pursued it with the passion of an evangelist!

Staff members were not permitted to go out with guests and were ordered, yes, *ordered*, to "never, ever, do anything with guests outside the scope of your job, no matter how innocent." I instituted a stern schedule of fines for misconduct and enforced them. Can you imagine that happening now? If the foregoing gives the impression that I was a cruel taskmaster who delighted in browbeating employees, please be assured that was not the case. I enjoyed my relationships with the staff and got along with them very well. However, we had rules and back then, rules were not something to be ignored.

THESE ARE THE FINANCIAL STATISTICS FOR 1967: TOTAL Income, $38,764, surpassing my stated goal of $35,000. Net Operating Profit, $3,840. Net Loss, after depreciation, $1,141. Notes Payable to SBA (they had paid off Camp Silver Spruce in order to hold a first mortgage), $44,616. Cash on hand, $8,429. At least we didn't end the year in worse shape then when we started.

I didn't book hunters that fall, instead I worked with Homer on the Laundromat addition and with Jerry Luther, a first class back hoe operator skilled at installing septic systems. My lease contract with Purgatory had been renewed with the same terms as before, and much of the task of hiring staff had been completed, so we thought we would take a little break. Dolly and I had been invited to visit the Hafer family, guests who lived in Chicago, and we thought that the drive would be a nice break before the ski season began. We contacted other guests along our route and without exception, every one we called insisted that we stay with them. That trip was great fun and staying with many wonderful people along the way made it even better. Our guests introduced us to their friends who later vacationed with us.

Many more skiers enjoyed the slopes at Purgatory during the winter of 67/68 than during the previous two years. We were serving lunch to over 2,000 people a day on weekends and more every day during the Christmas holidays. It was wild! The dining room, sun decks, third floor lounge, bar and even the picnic tables around the base area were packed with hungry and thirsty skiers. I had two bartenders and they were fast. Even so, I had to get behind the bar after the lifts shut down and help out. It was great for Dolly and me. We worked our butts off seven days a week, but we sure made some money, actually more than our gross income at Colorado Trails.

Winter turned to spring, and after Purgatory closed, we began getting the ranch ready for another summer. I had put together a new and much improved brochure, and partly because of it and the continued success of the word of mouth advertising, inquiries were running well ahead of the previous year. We put our crew of college kids to work painting bathrooms, polishing up the cabins and cleaning up our entrance area. We built a pole structure with two wagon wheels at our entrance, set up a new sign, spruced up our archery, riflery and trap ranges, bought some new equipment, hacked out some more riding trails, fixed fences and more. I thought we did a hell of a lot of work and improved the ranch significantly. Realistically, it wasn't all that much, but the returning guests definitely took notice.

I was surprised when Mel Schaefer called to advise that George and Donna Horton had offered to sell him their entire CTR equity. I was caught off guard by this news and dismayed that George and Donnie wanted out just as things were looking up. Mel asked if I wanted my preemptive share. I said I just couldn't buy any of Horton's stock but that he should feel free to do so. I don't think he told me the price and I didn't ask, although I assumed that he would pay at least what the Hortons had invested. I was tempted to call George and Donnie and try to persuade them not to sell. I wanted to tell them that I was positive that their equity would be worth considerably more within a few years. Appearances were important to them and they probably would have been embarrassed to tell me that they needed the money, so I did nothing.

Mel bought the stock and thus ended the participation of two of my original partners. It had all begun over bowls of steel cut oatmeal in the Hortons home ten years before, and now the H-E-A-D Ranch partners and best friends had unraveled.

The day that Mel called to tell me that he had completed his deal with the Hortons is a time I recall to the last detail. I saddled a horse and rode up Texas Creek Road to the trail that led to the top of Eagle Ridge, the same ride that George and I had made nine years before.

Reaching the top, I stepped off my horse, sat down on a rock, and thought about what we had been through together. Those long days of hard work, the laughter, the tears, the frustration and now the disappointment they must be feeling. It had been every bit as much their dream as it had been mine and now it was over for them.

I rode back down the hill, the same hill on which we had gathered stone for the lodge building. My horse stepped on a large flat rock and skidded on her tail, the way Hap Horton's pregnant mare had years before. A deep feeling of sadness suddenly swept over me and my eyes filled with tears, for I realized that I had lost something that I would never have again.

CHAPTER FORTY SIX

Wildflowers would be fine

During the summer of 1968, we unquestionably hit a home run with the bases loaded. Suddenly, somehow, it just all came together and George Begley was the catalyst.

Who was George Begley? He invested $24,000 in 1967, but our limited conversations had not revealed much of his true nature. Why he did what he did remained something of a mystery to me. When I told Mel Schaefer about Begley's investment, he was as perplexed as I and wondered what Begley's motivation was.

The Begley family, along with George's secretary and her son, returned to the ranch for a two-week stay. During that time, George and I had many long talks in which I gained some insight into the character of the man. I concluded that George Begley was the most decent, honorable, charitable and unpretentious man I had ever met. Were I to select an example that best personified the term *Real Christian*, George Begley would be it.

Not withstanding his impeccable character, I do not believe that George was a particularly happy man. He did not carry himself assertively, quite the opposite. He was perhaps 5'9" tall, somewhat overweight but not obese. Commenting on his protruding belly, he told me that he "hadn't seen his privates in years." He was someone who, for whatever reason, didn't make, or perhaps wasn't allowed to make, many personal choices. He appeared to be a prisoner confined by the self-imposed rituals of his daily routine. His wife purchased all of his clothes and selected what he would wear each day.

George worked in the drug store business started by his pharmacist father and his uncle whom he referred to as *Big Bob*. After George's father died, his uncle became the head of the company and George became what we would now call the chief financial officer. The company prospered and their chain of drug stores became a dominant player in the market. Six days a week, George went to work, did his job and did it well. Additionally, he managed his several farms staffed with share croppers, his hundred plus cattle, which he called *mortgage lifters*, and a sizeable tobacco crop, a fair portion of which he and his wife smoked. George was a busy guy, too busy to get out much and see what was going on in the world. He talked slow, he moved slowly, but he obviously accomplished a lot. It has been suggested that George may have envied me in some peculiar way for my determination to succeed, but more importantly for my lifestyle which he characterized as *being free*. Given his highly regimented life, I reckon that by comparison, I appeared to be a free spirit, doing what I loved and living in what he considered a spatial paradise.

One afternoon I asked George if he would like to take a drive with me to pick up some groceries at City Market, a modest size supermarket. I pushed the cart and selected items while George, wide eyed, walked beside me uttering phrases like, "Lord have mercy," or "Dear Jesus." At the checkout counter George said, "I had no idea." I asked him what he was talking about. "I had no idea," he replied, "that there was all these things a person could buy—hundreds and hundreds—Lord have mercy!" George W. Begley knew his way around a balance sheet and a statement of profit and loss, but he had never been in a modern supermarket.

The summer was something like a little snowball rolling down a hill, increasing in both momentum and size. Begley started the ball rolling and got me energized. I renewed my efforts to sell stock to those guests who I thought could afford it, who I liked and who elicited immediate interest when I brought up the subject. Primarily, I had to *like* a person before inviting them into our "family of owners." That home run was just the beginning of an all out win.

While vacationing with us, two widow ladies from Texas, a commercial pilot from California, a doctor from Oklahoma, a businessman from Illinois, another family from Oklahoma and two ladies from New York, purchased stock. Before making these sales, I called Mel Schaefer and George Begley to seek some advice because our bylaws required that existing stockholders be given the first opportunity to purchase shares from a new issue. It is called "pre-emptive rights." We agreed that we would set the share price at $500 and continue the practice of requiring the purchaser to loan an additional $500 for each share in return for a ten-year, 6% promissory note.

Arlene Mayer, a high school physical education instructor and Irene Voelker, a public school nurse, had been going to dude ranches for years and I picked their brains unmercifully trying to get their impression of our operation compared to the other ranches they had visited. They must have thought we were doing something right and maybe even better than our competitors, because before they left, they purchased two shares and promised to buy more each year. They made good on that promise.

I called for a special meeting of the directors and Jim Dodson, Mel Schaefer along with their families, traveled from Ohio to see firsthand what the heck was going on. The meeting took place on August 31, 1968 at 11:30AM and wasn't adjourned until 5:30. Mel, Jim, Dolly, George Begley and I attended. Schaefer was concerned about unpaid wages. The minutes read:

A review revealed that Elder was owed $21,830 for cash lent to allow continued operations and $21,970 for back wages since 1961. A note in the amount of $2,630 was due to Schaefer. Mr. Schaefer then moved that to clear the books as of the date of this meeting, the board issue to R. D. Elder 36 shares together with a $500 note for each share, and to Schaefer Roofing Company, 8.33 shares together with the required note.

Since Mel had purchased the entire Horton equity, George Horton was no longer eligible to serve as a director, so we elected George Begley to take his place.

I told the group about what we had done during the year and projected a gross sales figure of $41,000. From the middle of July until the end of August, there were significantly more requests for reservations than there were rooms available. I said that if the ranch was to continue to grow, new housing and supporting facilities had to be built. In order to pay for these things, I suggested a $50,000 stock issue.

We had some differences of opinion and a lengthy discussion about what should or should not be added to our facilities. Here's what was stated:

Mr. Dodson questioned the advisability of constructing a recreation building and suggested that same amount of money might be used to build an additional four-room cabin. Mr. Elder pointed out that in his judgment, it would be folly to predicate the expansion of this ranch solely on an increase in the number of guest rooms. He said his goal is to not only increase the total number of guests per year, but to develop with every increase in guest accommodation some supporting guest facilities, whether they be of a service or of an entertainment nature. He pointed out that the criteria of a top notch guest ranch is not in terms of how many guests they are able to accommodate, but how good a program, how well it is carried out and how much variety it offers the guests. He therefore argued strongly in favor of the recreation building as a necessary adjunct to current facilities and pointed out the real need for a "quiet" area for the adult guests, namely, the conversion of the present snack bar to a guest lounge. He pointed out that just as the new laundromat facility proved to be a great convenience and not necessarily a money producing operation, so would the lounge area create another such convenience and that is was the sum total of the conveniences along with other activities and programs that enticed the guests to return.

We discussed the pros and cons of building a swimming pool. I said that a pool served a two-fold purpose: One, to be able to state in advertising that the ranch had a heated pool had great promotional value because prospective guests look for a swimming pool when making choices. Two, a pool would positively enhance our programming flexibility and give the guests one more thing to do.

The board authorized me to implement the various projects I had suggested, contingent upon the outcome of the sale of the 50 share issue. Before the meeting adjourned, I asked them how much of those fifty shares *they* would agree to buy. To my surprise, Mel agreed to buy five, Begley said he would take fifteen and the board had authorized the sale of fifteen shares to Ken Hendrickson (a United Airlines pilot), so, thirty-five were sold right then and there. What a turn around when compared to my request for money just a few years before!

While the minutes of that meeting record the facts, they do not reflect the new energy that pervaded that meeting. As a business and as individuals, we had not witnessed anything like it since our early meetings in Ohio when we were all fired up but had no concept of what lay ahead. Suddenly, Mel Schaefer, sparked by Begley's and my enthusiasm, renewed his interest and participation.

It was during that meeting that I articulated my core convictions on a critical policy issue. It bears repeating because the statement gets to the heart of how I perceived our role and, frankly, our duty as a vacation destination. [Elder] *pointed out that the criteria of a top notch guest ranch is not in terms of how many guests they are able to accommodate, but how good a program, how well it is carried out and how much variety it offers.* The other significant point I made was the relationship of the ancillary facilities and amenities a guest ranch provides and their value not only in enhancing the recreation experience, but in their value as promotional tools. Gene Roberts, the owner of Wilderness Trails Ranch, recently reminded me that I had told him that the ultimate and obvious purpose of all advertising is to have the prospect select your ranch. That is accomplished, I said, by providing no reason for the prospect not to choose your ranch. From a marketing standpoint, the most logical reason for having a swimming pool is so the prospect cannot say, "They have no pool therefore we'll go to a ranch that has one." Later, when tennis was all the rage, I put in two tennis courts. Sure, it was an important addition to our sports program, but more importantly, the prospective guest would not have a reason to select another ranch that did offer tennis.

It was Jim Dodson who lined up and accompanied five hunters for the big game hunt in October. I didn't participate to any extent as I was busy with new construction.

There was one incident I recall from that hunt that you may find illuminating. One afternoon as it was turning dusk, one of the hunters excused himself from the camaraderie of the campfire to attend to an urgent call of nature. Striding off a respectful distance, he set about lowering his pants and squatting in the customary style. Suddenly, and without warning, a bear approached. The hunter tried to scream for help but he was so frightened that no sound escaped his lips. Then, as he later recounted, he must have fainted, collapsing on his own defecation. Not a pretty picture. Upon recovering and finding himself unharmed, he cleaned himself as best he could and returned to camp. There, sitting quietly amongst the men, he saw a large brown Airedale dog that had wandered into camp. It was, in fact, the very bear that had rendered our brave hunter unconscious.

Before the snow fell, I wanted to complete work on a four bedroom, four bath guest cabin we planned to name the X-Wing cabin. It got its name from the fact that it was built in the shape of a cross with each leg being a bedroom. I reckon we should have named it the cross cabin. Later on we changed the name to "Mountain Cabin." We also built a much-needed office building that we named "The Assay Office." The "Trading Post" was another project. It had a large game room and another room that served as our store where we planned to sell sundries, clothing, jewelry and assorted tourist type items. I found a 1940 model Liquid Carbonic soda fountain behind a café in Durango that we rebuilt for the snack bar. Homer Hartley built a counter with stools and three booths all out of pine. It was beautiful work. All of the buildings were designed by Homer and me to create the appearance of an early western town.

The 1,000 square foot room on the first floor of the lodge that had served as our recreation room and store was remodeled with walls covered by a wood wainscoting and brocaded wallpaper. We laid thick carpeting over the concrete floor, hung Tiffany style lighting and finished the ceiling with elaborate plastering. We called it the "Parlor." In due course it was furnished with antiques and become the "quiet" area that I talked about during our August meeting.

We purchased a new Dodge station wagon, put in more street lights, improved our water controls and graveled our drive from the Florida Road to the lodge. I had budgeted $51,519 to accomplish these and the other projects but our actual cost was under $44,000. With the help of Homer Hartley and another great carpenter, Fred Valencia, we virtually accomplished miracles for very little money.

When the work was done, we winterized the ranch, moved back to our home on Spruce Drive and went on vacation, spending a week with the Begleys on their farm near Richmond, Kentucky.

It was just after leaving the Begley home, where the two of them smoked constantly, that I quit cigarettes. I'll tell you why I quit: By the time we left the Begley home, my throat was raw from smoking. It seemed like every time they lit up, I did too. Now, I was a guy who had smoked since I was around fifteen, although I rarely smoked more that 10 or 15 cigarettes a day. Everyone smoked! It was no big deal, and no one said it was unhealthy. I remember being in boot camp right after I joined the Navy with hundreds of seventeen and eighteen-year-old boys, and *all* of them smoked frequently. The air outside our barracks would be blue with smoke, and the "butt cans" located everywhere were filled to the brim. I had developed a hacking cough which bothered me, particularly during my radio days. After leaving Kentucky, Dolly and I were on our way to Tennessee where we were to do a show. Dolly was driving and I was reading a book, a cigarette clamped between my lips. Suddenly, I felt a burning sensation on my chest and jumped. Startled, Dolly stopped the car and wanted to know what happened. The lit end of my cigarette had dropped off and fell on my shirt-burning a hole in it and me. I said, "That's it," and threw the pack out the window. I haven't smoked since, which is probably why I'm still alive and writing this at age seventy-five.

You'll have to excuse me, but I have to tell you one quick George Begley story. Darn near everyone in Richmond either knew or knew of the Begleys. George and I were driving back to his farm, passing through the "colored," as it was called then, part of town when suddenly he jammed on the brakes and backed up until he was in front of a little run-down church and exclaimed, "Dear Jesus!" On a tall ladder, apparently replacing a pane of glass, was an old gray haired man. "What in the world are y'all doing up there on that ladder?" Begley wanted to know of the man who he identified as the minister.

"I'm fixin' these windas Mistah Begley," replied the man. "I reckon some boys come along an' done broke a whole mess of 'em las' night."

George looking up, "Well, y'all got no business being up there on that ladder. You're too old for that kind a thing. Now, come on down and call someone to fix the windows."

"I reckon we don't have no money to be spending on fixin' these heah. Don't you trouble none, Mistah Begley. I'll take care of it."

"Well get on down anyway. I need to talk to you." George turned to me and whispered, "Lord have mercy, that old man don't need to be doin' that." Reluctantly, the old preacher carefully worked his way to the bottom. George reached in his coat pocket, pulled out a wad of bills and stuffed them in the top pocket of the old man's bib overalls. "Now, y'all git in the house and call up a glass company to fix those windows."

That's the kind of a guy George Begley was. I use the past tense because George died of lung cancer when he was only fifty-three. He was, among other things, a tobacco grower, and I'm afraid he used way too much of his crop. One day, Geneva Begley called to say that George was dying and that he wanted to see me. I immediately flew to Richmond and was at his bedside the last ten days of his life. Just before he died, he motioned for me to come close. I sat on the edge of his bed and placed my head close to his. "I'd be obliged," he whispered, "if you'd do me a little favor after I'm gone."

"Sure George. Anything at all. Just ask."

"I always would go visit my Daddy's grave and put some flowers on it. I was wondering if you'd ask my boys to do the same for me."

"Sure I will, don't you worry none. What kind of flowers would you like?"

He rolled his head toward me, his soft eyes losing their light and in a barely audible voice said, "Wildflowers would be fine."

CHAPTER FORTY SEVEN

I saw traces of yellow snow.

I was achieving some stature in La Plata County and that brought a certain degree of satisfaction, especially when I recall how hard it was for an *outsider* to be acknowledged by the *old guard*. Durango society was a tight clique and not many newcomers were accepted. I can't say that I was welcomed into Durango's inner sanctum, but they knew who I was and were aware of my presence in the community. I served on the La Plata County Fair Board. I was elected to the Durango Chamber of Commerce. I was an officer of the Durango Hotel-Motel Association and appointed, along with Ed Searle, to fill a vacancy on the board of directors of La Plata County Community Hospital.

The hospital was virtually bankrupt when Ed and I came on the scene, and in one year we salvaged it. The following year I succeeded Ed as President of the Hospital District and Chairman of the board. The hospital board was an elected office and at the end of my first term, I was re-elected by a large majority. Under my leadership, the hospital became profitable and underwent many changes, including a significant expansion. Interestingly, after serving six years, I chose not to run for reelection and within a few years, the hospital sank into debt again and eventually was bought by Mercy

Hospital. I was a diligent officer during my time with Community. I was at the hospital several times a week checking with doctors, department heads and service personnel. I had frequent, almost daily conversations with the administrator. I visited patients regularly and asked how they were doing and how we could improve our service. In short, I ran the hospital very much the way I managed Colorado Trails and the Lodge at Purgatory. The modern idiom would be, "I was all over it!" By this time, I was well ensconced in the daily life of a bona fide Durangoan.

During the summer, Ray Duncan called to advise that Durango Ski Corp. had decided to build a second restaurant a short distance from the top of Lift #1. Ray asked me to meet with George King, a Durango architect who told me that Duncan had instructed him to stay within a $20,000 budget for the building and equipment. After I reviewed King's preliminary building plan, I told Duncan that I wasn't interested in leasing the new facility because it was, in my view, a poor design that had been driven solely by budget constraints. There was no provision for substantial refrigeration and storage space which, given the restaurant's remote mountaintop location, was an absolute must. When I asked George King why no toilet facilities had been included in his design, he told me that Ray didn't think they would be necessary. Moreover, including toilets required an expensive septic system. The original plan had no provision for supplying water to the building. I guess the idea was that jugs of water would be packed up the mountain on mules. As my dad might have phrased it, the entire concept was *nuts*.

Ray Duncan listened to my reasons for rejecting his offer then asked me what was required. I listed the changes and additions I felt were necessary regardless of who ran the restaurant. Exasperated, he told me to go back to the architect, work out the details and revise the plan. I asked him about equipment in general and particularly about including a walk-in freezer/cooler. "Do whatever you want," were his final words. Thus was born the new mountaintop restaurant which we named the *Powder House* and, like a new puppy, it was a royal pain in the ass. Food and supplies were assembled at the lodge then sent up the mountain by snow cat or on the chair lift. I had to ride lift #1 to the top and ski down to the *Powder House* several times a day and that wasn't always convenient, particularly during holidays and weekends. Sometimes, I would make the trip on my snowmobile, a gift from a ranch guest who worked for the company that made them.

Practically everything that could go wrong did go wrong both during and after construction. Work did not start until fall and the building was not under roof until mid October, the start of hunting season. About the time we were ready to bring in the kitchen equipment, a very heavy snow covered the ground, making it almost impossible to get to the site. I recall the Oliger Sheet Metal Company bringing our range hood up to the building in a new panel truck that became hopelessly stuck. I had to use a four-wheel drive pickup with chains on all four tires to pull the truck up to the *Powder House*. By the time I dragged it up the mountain, that new truck was a wreck. I'm quite sure that Louie Oliger included the cost of repairing his truck to the price of the hood.

Bad things were bound to happen given the combination of poor planning, a late start, followed by a hurry up and get it done mentality. The ground was frozen by the time the concrete septic tank, leach field and underground pipes were laid. Almost every weekend, when we needed it most, the incoming water lines would freeze and the toilets would plug up, overflow and stink up the dining room. I had suggested that access to the lavatories should be from outside the building instead of from the dining room, but no, too expensive to change the design I was told.

One humorous Powder House story and I'll drop it. Well, maybe two stories. Bill Balliger, the head of our local health unit, skied down to the Powder House one bright Sunday and after lunch, suggested that we check out the new septic tank. The tank was located downhill, about fifty feet from the building. There was very little snow on top, as the heat from within kept it melted. We kneeled down, shined a light inside and much to our surprise, saw that the liquid level was only a few feet high. The water level should have been at the exit pipe near the top. Very strange, we concluded, but Bill said he'd come back again and take another look. Being, as I was, an old hand when it came to septic tanks, especially malfunctioning ones, I had a pretty good idea what the problem might be, but said nothing. A week or so later, while skiing a run called *Swire's Gulch*, which traversed an area some distance directly below the *Powder House*, I saw traces of yellow snow. As I continued downward, the traces became streaks, then large patches, until the entire run and surrounding area was overlaid in light brown. The six inch plastic sewer pipe that connected the toilets to the septic tank had broken. The heat inside the tank generated by the sewage caused the frozen ground to thaw just enough to allow the tank to settle a few inches, thus breaking the pipe. It didn't take the guys in the ski school and ski patrol very long to rename *Swire's Gulch*. I'm reluctant, however, to repeat that name.

One other story, con permiso: One of Bill Balliger's health inspectors was a man named Walter. Walter called to tell me that he wanted to inspect the new top restaurant. We set a date and when he arrived, I asked Keith Blackburn, the head of maintenance, to take us up in the Tucker snow cat. The Tucker had an enclosed heated cab and was quite comfortable. We took the "cat tracks" (narrow trails designed for maintenance vehicles) up to the restaurant where Walter and I got out. I told Keith he need not wait.

After Walter had finished his inspection, we got on the snowmobile, which I had previously parked there, and made the short ride back up the hill to the chair lift. I had the operator stop the chairs so that Walter and I could get on and ride to the bottom. If you have never ridden a chair lift *down*, let me counsel that it is a whole different ride than the ride *up*. Looking down the mountain can be very scary for someone who is taking his very first ride on a chair lift. This was Walter's first ride and he immediately freaked! He grabbed the center pole with one hand and my arm with the other. I thought he would pull me plumb off. "Just sit quietly," I told him. "Just hold on to the center pole and the arm rest and for Christ sake, let go of me before we both end up on the ground." At the bottom, Walter staggered to his car without a word. He never again inspected the mountain top restaurant and that was just as well, because if he had, I'm sure he would have shut us down.

If I have given the impression that it was all work and no play during my Purgatory years, I am sorry and hasten to correct that notion. Winters at the ski area, particularly after the holidays, found me on the slopes almost every weekday. I would get things organized for lunch then jump into my Head 360's or whatever the skis du jour were and be on the lift. I was quite keen to be among the first on the mountain after an overnight snow to 'cut' the fresh powder. There is something quite marvelous about skiing through knee-deep powder before it has been packed. Those conditions made me fearless as I pointed my skies down the fall line and let her rip. If you have never experienced a southwest Colorado day of skiing, you may have a problem understanding the exhilaration one feels, flying down the face of a mountain on that kind of snow.

There is no wind as you take the twenty-minute chair lift ride to the top. You become aware of the profound stillness, interrupted momentarily by the occasional shush of a skier carving turns in the snow below. The sky is intensely blue, made purple by the tint of your ski goggles. The sun beams warm your face and parka and though the temperature may only be 20 degrees, you feel warm, almost hot. Sliding off the chair at the top, you stop for a moment to adjust boot buckles then push off with your poles and just let it happen. When it's good, when everything is working just right, the feeling is wonderful. On those 'perfect' runs I would find myself singing as I navigated a course through the moguls. For me, it is the same sense of elation that I get while training a horse, when he gets the message and does the thing just right.

Paul Folwell, the head of the ski patrol, once declared, "A perfect run in the powder is better than sex and so is one that isn't perfect." I didn't fully subscribe to that hypothesis, but I would agree that he wasn't far off the mark.

CHAPTER FORTY EIGHT

*"He tackled the thing that couldn't
be done and he did it."*

The year 1968 was a good one for CTR and for me personally. Purgatory generated a nice profit and, for once, the ranch finances were such that I didn't feel compelled to dump some of it into the CTR coffers.

As the 68/69 ski season wound down, the pace of ranch activity increased. The usual ritual of hiring staff, increasing the tempo of promotions, writing and placing advertising and other matters were becoming less arduous and more productive. Having Dolly running the office certainly was a plus. She was a model of efficiency and organization. The years she had worked as an executive secretary gave her skills that greatly enhanced our office operation.

In 1969 we launched the first *Colorado Trails Ranch Round-up*, a four page newspaper with stories, information and pictures. A copy was sent to every former guest and it was included with each brochure we mailed. While it appeared to be a folksy recap of the events of the previous summer, the paper had great promotional value, with articles about upcoming events and planned improvements. The pictures of people and new buildings were selected to amplify the benefits of choosing CTR over another vacation venue. One of the features was the editorial, which gave me a pulpit from which I was able to expound my altruistic ideas about dude ranching in general and CTR in particular. My first editorial told how much we enjoyed the many letters our guests sent and included quotes from some of them.

Little Marilyn Moore wrote, "I miss the staff and you and the ranch so much. Another way of putting it, I'M RANCH SICK."

From the Moon family, "I can't express what a wonderful time we had. Your staff and of course both of you made us feel that our comfort and activity was of the utmost importance. Looking back on our stay, I cannot think of one thing which I could criticize and we all agree that the best part of all [their two week vacation] was the week we spent with you at Colorado Trails Ranch."

Crystal Novota said, "Whenever we come to your ranch, I always feel at home."

Including these flattering remarks in the *Round-Up*, along with recaps of the previous summer and updates on plans for the coming year, helped turn an inquiry into a reservation. It provided the prospect with increased confidence that by choosing CTR they were making an informed selection. I had no doubt that the *Round-Up* was a super advertising tool.

Some of the articles in that first edition carried these headlines: *Heaven can wait. We spend winter in Purgatory.* This article was written to let prospects know that Dolly and I had more going for us than dude ranching alone. Since our interests were diverse, someone selecting a ranch might infer that CTR had a wider social/recreational focus than did some others. *Inquiries—reservations set record for first Q.* Subconsciously, a person selecting a vacation place wants to be assured that his selection will be one that has been the choice of many others. *Laundromat a BIG Hit.*

Since the brochure didn't mention our laundromat, I wanted readers to know we did have one and that too might influence their selection process. *New wagon ain't hay*. Mel Schaefer told me that he didn't know anyone could make a story of nothing more than a hay wagon. A related story about how we changed the exhaust pipe on our Ford 8N tractor from the rear (that blew gases back on the wagon riders) to a vertical pipe (that eliminated the problem), got Mel's attention as well. *New exhaust, a gas* read that headline.

I came up with another promotional idea that was simply an extension of our informal visits to former guests whenever we traveled. First, we selected a city that had a number of "Oldtimers." We then selected those guests who we thought would be interested in helping us sell vacations to their friends. We mailed a letter to all of the selected names advising that we would be in their city on a certain date. The invitation declared:

There will be refreshments, ranch style sing-a-longs, comedy with Dick and Bob, a slide show plus a drawing for a free vacation, cowboy boots and other prizes. We encourage you to bring your friends so that they too can learn how much fun a vacation at Colorado Trails can be for every member of the family, be they five or seventy five. You'll hear all about what's new for next summer, what your favorite staff people have been doing and best of all, this will be a great time to renew friendships fostered at CTR.

In March of 1969 Dolly, Bob Bellmaine and I drove to Oklahoma City. On the way we laughed ourselves silly making up jokes, song lyrics and bits we would use during the "show." Several oldtimers arranged for the location and rallied the support of others. Most notable among our Oklahoma City advocates was Ken Bonds, who sponsored and paid for a lunch attended by a rather large number of ranch guests and their friends.

The three of us met with Ken, an officer at Liberty National Bank, at his office to review details of our upcoming event. He took us to the executive dining room where we enjoyed a lovely lunch prepared just for us. "Bankers know how to live well," Bob observed. In the elevator, filled with bank employees, Bob said in a whisper that he knew would be heard by everyone, "W. K., I think the presentation went quite well, don't you?"

Ken played along. "Yes. I thought the directors were impressed."

Bob, with a dead pan expression declared, "I think the thing they liked best was the Mickey Mouse cartoon."

The show went well. The people had an opportunity to visit with one another, renew ranch friendships and we filled June, normally a slow month. We tried a similar tactic in Los Angeles where we did three shows over two days in various hotel locations. One event was attended by so many people that we had to have the moveable wall opened so we could use the adjoining room. We had expected a hundred or so to attend but more than two-hundred people showed up. When the show was over, Dolly sat at a table to take reservations. Quickly, the prime weeks became fully reserved. Some people became irritated when she told them that the week they wanted was sold out. The good news was that they then agreed to reserve during a week that we normally had trouble filling. There was a lesson to be learned and we learned it! Concentrate on selling the hard-to-fill weeks first.

The summer of 1969 was the one I had dreamed of for a decade. The minutes of our August 31 director's meeting tells the story. Schaefer, Begley, Dolly and I attended. Jim Dodson, the fifth director, did not attend. Stockholders Geneva Begley, Ken and Marion Hendrickson also were present.

Treasurer George Begley reported cash on hand of $25,861. After making the August payment to SBA and *paying all bills and payroll including a bill for paving the driveway, we estimate a remaining cash balance of $10,500. The treasurer advised the manner in which the fifty share stock issue was distributed. . .*

By this time, I had sold all fifty shares authorized by the board in 1968. Henrickson had made good on his promise and now had fifteen shares. Begley and Schaefer each purchased fifteen, Novota, Mayer, and Voelker each took three shares and Robison bought six. At that point in time, we had 273 shares outstanding. I had 121, Dolly had 9, Schaefer had 63 and Begley had 55. Dolly and I were still minority shareholders owning 48% of the company.

The president indicated that a new policy of advertising and promotion had been adopted which included considerably more newspaper advertising. In addition to the ads in five major cities, there was a great deal of promotion through the Colorado Visitors Bureau, The Colorado Dude and Guest Ranch Association, the Dude Rancher's Association and the Durango Chamber of Commerce. The ranch mailed 2,923 brochures [to those organizations] and 1,000 were distributed around the country to United Airlines offices. We received 886 direct mail inquiries, every one of which was answered by a personal letter together with a brochure and a copy of the ranch newspaper.

In light of today's costs for print advertising, the following statement is pretty funny:

The newspaper ads were costly. They ran as high as $160 per insertion.

Our personal solicitation in Oklahoma City resulted in a substantially better June than we have ever had in the past. This year was the largest in our history. As of September 1, total income from summer activities plus anticipated income in September will be $72,000, compared to our total sales for 1968 of $42,830. Advance *bookings for 1970 equal $11,150. Another significant figure is the dollar value of the families that were turned down this year because we did not have space. Turndowns this year amounted to $18,475. If the ranch had additional housing facilities for guests, we could have had a $90,000 summer.*

In the span of one year, we almost doubled our income. With greater guest capacity, we would have more than doubled it. That was a remarkable achievement. But my view, what was more important than the dollar volume was the larger consideration of what we had done for our guests in terms of providing quality vacations. Though we had only been operating for seven years, we had become the predominate guest ranch innovators. CTR was offering more total programming with more variety than any ranch in the state or possibly in the west.

We had a comprehensive riding program that included more instruction, highly trained horses, and fully trained guides with more variety of riding opportunities than other ranches. The typical morning and afternoon rides offered by most other ranches kept riders in the saddle for three to four hours or more, a long time for folks not used to riding. I believed it was better to take shorter rides and do something more interesting than just walking along head to tail in line with a dozen or more horses. Our guests rode in sections of no more than six so that they could receive additional instruction on the trail and have more freedom of movement. The small groups permitted our riders to have more fun and, after instruction, they were allowed to canter their horses, one at a time, on trail rides. I also insisted that children ride in their own groups and not with adults, that adults of similar ability ride together so that the ride could move at a pace comfortable to all, and that guides take an active role in pacing the ride while teaching and interacting with the guests. Other ranches were content to give minimal instruction and take guests on long, butt-busting rides in much larger groups with little communication from the guide.

We offered outstanding home-style cooking and baking all made from scratch, nothing at all like a restaurant meal. Our staff-to-guest ratio of about two to one was easily on a par with the most expensive guest ranches anywhere. Most importantly, our children's programs kept the kids busy all day, every day, rain or shine. A majority of ranchers were willing to let their guests sit around most evenings on their own. We had a program every night, sometimes several programs going at once, geared to the differing preferences of adults and children. In short, we were making a name for ourselves amongst our peers in both the Colorado Dude and Guest Ranch Association and the Dude Rancher's Association.

During that director's meeting, I outlined my plans for continued improvements and expansion which I declared would cost about $40,000. The major items included were another X-wing cabin, remodeling of the Alpine cabins, a maintenance shop and a heated swimming pool. Quoting from the minutes:

An accounting was made of all of the ranch's holdings with land valued at $300 an acre which all agreed was a rather low figure in view of what land is selling for in the vicinity. On this basis, it was determined that new shares of stock should be sold for not less than $1,100 ($600 per share with a $500 promissory note). It was suggested that the workshop be incorporated into our trading post/swimming pool complex on the oval, using more of the early Western architecture, and be called the Blacksmith Shop. Elder advised that he would build it along those lines, using a dummy front, and will find a location that will be compatible with the long-range planning on the oval.

Begley moved and Schaefer seconded that the Board issue and authorize the sale of 25 units from its treasury stock at $1,100 a unit. The President advised that he is going to increase rates for the 1970 season between 8 and 12 percent.

My annual salary had been raised to $8,500. The total wages for all other employees was just under $8,000 which tells me that dear little Dolly only made a couple hundred dollars a month. What some people will do for love!

Gross income for 1969 was $72,000 with net operating profit before depreciation, of $19,600. Cash as of September 30 was almost $11,000. Money in the bank meant there would be no problem paying our SBA mortgage payment. Advanced reservations, coupled with more satisfied guests doing word-of-mouth advertising, a board of directors and stockholders fired up enough to become involved both emotionally and financially, boded well not only for the coming year, but for years to come.

CHAPTER FORTY NINE

Nothing succeeds like success.

The spring of 1970 found us at Purgatory waiting impatiently for the closing day. It was warm, snow conditions were poor and we had very few skiers on the mountain. Dolly and I, as well as the rest of the crew, were getting restless and eager to get the hell out of there. CTR had a big summer coming up with advance bookings running well ahead of my projections and I was keen to get to work on the construction projects we had started.

Ray Duncan's older brother, Walter, who owned a substantial interest in the ski area, was staying at his Purgatory condo. I enjoyed being around Walter, his quiet demeanor set him apart from his hard-charging brother. I came to know Walter a little better when Dolly and I were guests in his beautiful home adjacent to the fairways of the Oklahoma City Country Club.

Walter and I were alone in the dining room having an insightful discussion about the future of Purgatory. The question arose why the condos, built the previous year, had not been sold. The "Twilight View" condominiums were two buildings situated on the edge of a ridge that faced a mountain known as the Twilight Peaks. The view from those condos was spectacular, especially at twilight, when reflected rays of the sun created a phenomenon

called "alpine glow." The buildings were two-story struc-
tures, and each contained two large apartments. If memory serves, the asking price for a second floor unit was
$30,000 and the lower unit was $26,000. Regardless of
the seemingly low price coupled with the upper end
amenities that these condos afforded, they just didn't
sell. Walter asked if I would try to sell the three remain-
ing units. I had no desire to become involved, so I didn't
commit one way or the other. He said he had another
matter he wanted to discuss with me, but our privacy was
interrupted when some skiers drifted into the dining
room. I told Walter we would get together later on.

That afternoon, Ray Duncan cornered me. We were by
ourselves in the lounge on the third floor looking out at
the mountain. The lower end of the run, called
"Pandemonium," had a number of bare places that, for
safety reasons, had been covered with straw. Outside the
#1 lift shack, Chuck Johnson, the lift operator and my old
buddy from the Full House, had hung a large sign that he
had altered from the official *Think Snow!* to *Think Straw!*

Ray commented on the sign, we both laughed and
then he officially requested that I take over the sale of the
Twilight View condos. With the ski season almost over,
my chances of selling the units would be slim to none.
Regardless of my lack of enthusiasm for the project, he
asked me to take on the task. Then, abruptly changing
the topic, he asked, "What about your dude ranch? Are
you going to stay with it in spite of the fact that it hasn't
made any money after, what is it, ten years?"

"Well, hell yes I'm sticking with it. We've got a great
summer coming up and I think this is going to be the
year we actually do make some money."

Ray scanned the large bank of windows, then turned
his gaze in my direction. He had a certain look on his face
that I had come to know so well, a look that revealed that
he was pondering how to say the next thing. Stalling for
a moment he observed, "These windows could use a

washing." I agreed. "Listen Dick, Walter and I have been talking and what we would like you to do," he paused, then plunged on, "is sell that ranch of yours and devote full time to Durango Ski in a top management position."

Without thinking, I fired back, "Now, why in the hell would I want to do that? I just told you that we're going to have a really good year. Besides, I didn't leave Ohio and a very good paying job, to run a ski area. I came out here to build a guest ranch and, I might add, make it the best god damn outfit in the state."

When Ray became nervous or uneasy he would tend to stutter. He stuttered a little as he said, "We just don't think you can do both, that's why we're suggesting that you sell the ranch and devote full time to Purgatory."

"You're right! I can't do both and do them well, that's for sure." I softened my tone as I continued, "Ray, you and Walter and the rest of your family have been very good to me. When you gave me this job five years ago I really needed it and tried to show my appreciation by doing a first class job. I think I've done that for you. Purgatory may not be Colorado's finest ski area, but the food at Purgatory is as good or better than any day lodge in the state." Ray nodded in agreement. "But you have to understand, I'm on a mission. I intend to make Colorado Trails the best there is and nothing less is going to satisfy me. Certainly, you of all people can understand that, can't you?"

"Sure. I know." Ray sighed and turned his gaze toward the mountain. "I understand what you're saying. It's been the same for me with this damn ski area. Like you, I had a dream about this place, but it's been rough trying to get it done. Hell, I don't know if we'll ever get there. We just thought that getting you on board, you know, committed fulltime, might help." He looked at me thoughtfully. "But, why don't you and Dolly talk it over before you turn this down. I'm prepared to offer you a very good salary with bonuses and other benefits and . . ."

I cut him off. "Ray, although I already know what Dolly will say, I can tell you it wouldn't matter. I appreciate the offer, really! And I'm gratified that you and Walter have that much confidence in my ability, but the truth is, you are absolutely right, I can't do both jobs effectively." Now I paused, undecided as to what I was going to say next. "Okay, I was going to tell you this after we closed, but I may as well tell you now as long as we're talking about it anyway. This is the end of the line for me. It's been a great run and a lot of fun but I have to move on. The ranch has become a full time job and I just can't spend my winters up here anymore."

From the look on his face, it appeared that Ray was genuinely surprised. I don't think he had a clue that I was ready to drop my lease. However, he took the news with grace and wished me luck. To soften the blow a bit, I agreed to work on selling the condos. I showed them to a number of people before the area closed and I think I did sell one, or was instrumental in the sale.

It was a busy three months after we left Purgatory. With the help of Bob Bellmaine, George Smith and Ed Bruning of our staff, Homer and I finished work on the new X-wing cabin, then, in something like a week, built the Blacksmith Shop. From a kit I had purchased, and with some outside help, we erected an above ground swimming pool, then put porch roofs over the Alpine cabin entrances, completed an addition to the barn for horse stalls and transformed the room below the dining room into the "Parlor." We worked hard and we worked fast to get it all completed prior to opening day on June 7. The summer staff arrived and they all worked at painting, pounding nails, cleaning, fencing, you name it.

Shorty Mars returned as head wrangler and his wife Faye Mars was our baker. Louise Robinson, a local lady who worked as a cook at Purgatory, became our ranch cook. Jeanne Fullerton also returned and worked part time in the office and as head housekeeper. We had another half dozen or so staff returnees who helped train new staff, making my job much easier and freeing me up to attend to other things. I would rate that staff as one of the top three in our thirty-seven year history.

Since the end of our 1969 season, we had received 1,032 direct inquiries. Every inquiry received a brochure, a personal letter, and when the new 1970 edition of *The Round-Up* was ready in early February, a copy was also included. Additionally, we mailed over 3,300 brochures to individuals whose names we received from the two dude ranch associations, the Durango Chamber of Commerce and the Colorado Visitor's Bureau. I noted in my report to the stockholders that we spent several thousand dollars less than we had budgeted for print advertising because by the time the first ads appeared, we were already 80% booked for the summer.

We had a total of twelve bedrooms in Alpine cabins and twelve more in X-Wing cabins. If every bed was used, we had a capacity of 70. Practically however, I considered any week with all rooms filled as 100% occupancy. Since every weekly census had some singles, couples and families of three, 100% occupancy would be 55 to 65 guests.

We had only two rooms vacant the week of June 7. From the week of June 14 until August 30, we were fully booked. Significantly, because we were fully booked, we turned down $22,215.00 worth of business.

By September, we had advance reservations totaling $25,170.00 from departing guests. We learned another valuable lesson: it is much easier to sell a vacation to someone who has just spent a wonderful week with you than it is to go out and beat the bushes for new business.

Saturday evenings, after the chuck wagon dinner, we wound up the event with a final song, *Now is the hour when we must say goodbye*. Every member of our staff was required to attend and participate in the campfire sing-along that followed dinner. Staff was cautioned that during the singing of *Now is the hour*, they should not be horsing around but look solemn and even a bit sad as if close friends were going away. I explained to the staff that I wanted that moment around the campfire to be one that the guests would remember. After that song, both children and adults would have tears in their eyes as they said their good-byes to each other, to our staff and to Dolly and me. Guests would ask each other, "Are you coming back this same week next year?" When those kinds of conversations are being held, that is the time to talk about making reservations for next summer.

When guests came to the office after the program to pay their bills, we pointed to the big reservation chart placed in plain sight at the counter. Dolly, or whoever was collecting payment, would suggest that it would be a good idea to reserve for the following summer before all of the rooms were booked and they did! Ranchers that had been in business long before we came on the scene, were frankly amazed at the results we achieved. The important and significant point I would make is that our guests didn't return year after year because of what we now call "hype." We didn't get those repeat reservations year after year because of slick advertising, rebates, exaggerated promises or any of the typical methods used these days. As a brokerage firm commercial states it, "We earned it." We more than earned it! We knocked ourselves out for our guests, giving them not what they expected, but a lot more. Key to exceeding their expectations was our children's programs. By having the kids divided into groups, the younger kids would not have to compete with the older ones and the teens didn't have to put up with the little punks, as they called them. The adults loved doing the things they wanted to do while someone was taking good care of their children who were having the time of their lives.

It didn't take me very long to figure out that when a family is trying to decide whether to return to CTR or try another ranch, it is the kids who have the greatest impact on that decision. If the parents wish to return but the children do not, the children will get their way. No parent wants to spend a vacation with unhappy children. If the children are desperate, and I use that word advisedly, to return and the parents are indifferent, the family will probably return. It took a while for some of my peers to understand the validity of that self-evident truth, although some ranchers do not understand the concept to this day!

CHAPTER FIFTY

*It's the pot of gold some of us
are lucky enough to find.*

The minutes of the Director's meeting held on September 8, 1970, sums up what we had accomplished and what we hoped to achieve in the future. Here are excerpts from those minutes.

Discussion resumed on the proposed additions and improvement for 1971. There was an extensive conversation on our long-range plans and objectives, which in condensed form was a policy of constant refining of both plant and program. The goal was to become Colorado's best, but not necessarily Colorado's largest, ranch.

The President said that after the S. B. A. was paid off, that cash should be used to reduce our interest debt to note holders and when that is current, for paying off stockholder notes. Only when those obligations have been taken care of, should we consider paying dividends.

Mr. Begley had called long distance the previous day and asked that a motion be put before the board as follows: "That R. D. Elder's salary as president and general manager be 10% of the gross income of the previous year." Hendrickson made the motion on behalf of Begley, Schaefer seconded. Motion passed.

Good old George Begley always took care of me. He continued to be my angel and saw to it that I got most everything I asked for, including annual salary increases. When there was resistance, George would tell the directors, "Now, let's not get our greedy pinchers out. This is the man that made this ranch and we need to keep him happy if we all are going to do well here. Colorado Trails is Dick Elder, and that is something we should always remember." Then with a deceptive grin he would add, "And when Cochise moves his tent, I move my tent."

Just as I had predicted during my conversation with Ray Duncan, 1970 was the year when CTR made some money. Our gross income of $110,000 yielded a net profit, before depreciation of $33,000. I know that doesn't sound like very much money now, but back then it was a treasure trove, especially in light of what had transpired during the preceding decade.

In my annual report I listed the many improvements I wanted to make prior to the 1971 season and the reasons why I felt these were important to the growth and stature of the ranch. One of those improvements was to replace the metal shower stalls in the Alpine cabins with tiled showers and glass doors which I knew the guests would love. Then I stated,

I had a long and fruitful meeting with our staff recently and during that meeting I asked them to make suggestions for improving the facilities and program. They came up with some fine ideas that I will certainly use. Of the 26 staff employed this summer, 19 indicated that they would want to come back. It is very advantageous for us to have trained people who know the ropes.

I anticipate that 1971 will be a year for growth in management, particularly amongst our permanent employees, Bellmaine and Fullerton, and we should see dramatic improvement in our program together with some significant improvements in our physical plant.

We are seeing our corporate assets appreciate daily. We build a building this year and it is worth more the following year. We see land being subdivided on three

sides by private landowners. Just this past week I wit-
nessed the purchase of one acre of land on the river
across from us for $7,000. When we purchased this
ranch back in 1960, we could have bought that same
acre of land for $500 or less. We have received several
feelers in this regard and I know that were we interest-
ed, we could no doubt sell 300 acres for subdivision pur-
poses and come up with more money than we have
invested in the entire ranch with all its facilities.

In spite of the generally depressed stock market, we
still have any number of people eager to purchase our
stock at $1,100 a share. I think the day is not too far dis-
tant when shares of Colorado Trails Ranch will be in
demand for $2,000 a share and more.

Tourism is becoming increasingly popular in
Colorado, as indeed it is everywhere. More and more
people are discovering what a delightful and rewarding
experience a dude ranch vacation is. But with today's
astronomical prices for land and higher costs of con-
struction, very few new dude ranches are being built.
Therefore, those of us who have been doing a good job
should continue to fill up each season.

Last year I rated Colorado Trails Ranch as being one
of the 10 best dude ranches in Colorado. I have revised
that estimate. Based on what many guests have told us
relative to other ranches they have visited and what we
personally know about other operations, I now believe
CTR is one of the top three in Colorado. We have
already established ourselves as the best when it comes
to our riding program. I am talking about the quality
of our riding instruction, the level of training of our
horses and our humane approach to handling horses. I
anticipate that in the not too distant future, Colorado
Trails will be number one in this state in terms of the
overall quality of the vacations we provide for both
adults and children. We will never be the biggest ranch
and we have no desire to be. We may never be the best

profit maker, but from our point of view and more particularly from the guests' point of view, we shall not only be Colorado's Friendliest, but Colorado's Finest.

Wow! Those were some mighty gargantuan predictions, but they demonstrate how very confident I was about the future. I remember telling people that "If CTR is not number one, then we sure aren't very far behind whoever is."

Looking at the editorial I wrote for the 1971 edition of the *Round-Up*, I have to say that I don't think I could improve it because it's right on the money:

An old horse trader I knew some years back once gave me the definition of a Dude. "A dude," Sam Carson said, "was an ole boy who could look at a beautiful sunset then turn right around and ask you, "Which way is west?"

The Webster definition of the word (admitting that the origin is unknown) "is a man extremely fastidious in dress and manner, a type of dandy, a city man, especially an easterner in the west." Dude ranchers themselves have an endless variety of definitions. The word "Dude" means different things to different people, that's for sure.

At Colorado Trails we recognize the fact that there are dudes both on and off of ranches. You'll find people who fit the Webster definition at our ranch and a few that fit Sam's. Some ranch operators always refer to their patrons by the term Dude and talk about wrangling dudes. That's why our state association is called the Colorado Dude and Guest Ranch association. Some [ranchers] like it one way and some the other.

Regardless of what we might choose to call them, the fact remains that the folks who come to our ranch are guests, guests in our home, and that's the way we treat them. We are not a hotel, motel or resort, and we don't want to be. Guest ranches are unique and that is why there is no other vacation like it. It is the most memorable, most rewarding, most enjoyable, most downright old-fashioned good time a group of people can have. This is true at Colorado Trails, and at many of the ranches in the west. Don't let anybody tell you that some other type of vacation is just as good, because it just isn't so. No other vacation offers you the chance to get to know so many people so well in such a short span of time. That alone is worth the price of admission.

It seems to me like folks want to be in the west more than ever. To be a part of the western experience, to see blue sky and breathe pure air. They want to see the back country and mountain tops. They want to sing the songs and hear the stories, to live the cowboy life and ride the cowboy trails on the back of a good horse. They want to step out of themselves if only for the moment and be a part of it all.

My greatest satisfaction is helping our guests become a part of it all. Basically, our job is seeing to it that you forget yours and once you forget yours, you are on your way to relaxation and a great vacation. My kick is seeing a "Dude" climb on a horse for the first time, perhaps feeling just a hair edgy, but by the end of the week, seeing that same person go cantering on by with a big smile on his face. He's out west, he's a cowboy riding an ol' pony and he's having a ball! And you can sure substitute SHE, because it's the same for the gals.

Can you imagine my pleasure when I see our guests enjoying each other's company at a game of volleyball or while swimming, at the snack bar or wherever. At our weekly pow-wow, sitting in the parlor, your candle-lit faces looking into mine while in the far corners of the room the last strains of "Little Joe the Wrangler" are fading into history. I think to myself, how fortunate I am to have known these people. How is it possible that we became such good friends in only six days? The answer is, because we wanted to become friends. The usual barriers simply do not exist here and therefore it's easy.

Your faces at the pow-wow are the faces of people, not dudes. We visit you in your homes and you are individuals and not dudes, interesting people who in some way have made an impression on us as I am sure we have on you. So, what is a dude and which way is west after all? For the time you are with us, a dude is the most important person in our lives. And west? Why it's right here. It's the pot of gold some of us are lucky enough to find after a long and sometimes arduous trip across a rainbow.

DURING THE DECADE OF THE SIXTIES, I HAD PROBLEMS, THAT'S for sure. But I always managed to have some fun too. When asked, I used to quip, "It sure beats working." I can't think of anything I have ever done or ever will do that was anywhere near as enjoyable and rewarding as dude ranching. I was able to be anything I wanted to be. I was the head of a company, a creator of advertising, and both editor and columnist for our newspaper, *The Ranch Round Up.* I was a performing musician and writer of music, an actor, writer/director for staff shows and campfire programs. I was a horse trainer, a vet, a riding instructor, a riding guide, a hunting guide and outfitter, a building contractor, an architect, carpenter, plumber, electrician, heavy equipment operator, farmer, human resources manager, father confessor and that's not even half of it. How could I not have had fun? I loved performing, whether on horseback or on the stage. I enjoyed the attention and the status of being The Man, The Boss, the ranch owner and even, "The Brain." Most of all, I loved living my childhood fantasy of being a cowboy. That truly did happen when my Purgatory buddy, Benny Basham and I went into the cattle business. My hobby had become my life, with horses at the center of it, and horses were certainly the centerpiece of the Colorado Trails Ranch experience.

If all of that were not enough, I had the incredible opportunity of meeting people from all economic, social and ethnic backgrounds, many of whom became life-long friends. Working with the kids on staff, getting to know them, listening to their problems, helping them learn more about life, perhaps having some profound and positive impact on a young mind, was all part of it. How could I not love it?

One starry evening after a program for adults at the cookout area, they piled on to the hay wagon for the return ride to the lodge. It was plumb dark and the sky was filled with stars. Crossing the creek I pulled off of the trail and said, "I want you all to look up and just be quiet for a minute." They obediently complied. "When you get back home and you're having a rough day, just sit quietly for a few minutes with your eyes closed and remember this night, this beautiful night. Try to recall this star-filled sky and think back to how peaceful it was. Think of the friends you've made this week and the pure enjoyment you got from sitting around a campfire and singing. If you'll do that, you may come to understand that while there are many things in life that are pleasurable, it just may be that those moments that bring the greatest pleasure are those that are all around us and only require our attention."

Just then, a shooting star streaked across the eastern sky and from the wagon some thirty voices uttered, "Ahhhhh." Then it became very still, a group of strangers who had become friends, saying nothing, immersed in their own thoughts when someone started singing, *Twinkle, twinkle, little star*. Another voice joined in, then another and another until everyone was singing. It was a magical moment. Try to picture that scene in your mind, and if you can, you will understand why I loved my job so much.

If I had it all to do over again, sure, I might change some things, but not my desire to live the life I have lived. That trip across the rainbow, that elusive pot of gold, that search to find which way is west, was, after all, a journey of a lifetime.

EPILOGUE
And now, the rest of the story:

From the time my story ended in 1970, until we sold the outfit, we never again had a loosing year. We served about seventy-five guests a week (around a thousand plus guests during a sixteen-week summer season), had a staff of thirty-eight, offering a children's and adult program of sports, horseback riding and entertainment that was the best in the business. Major improvements to our facilities were completed each year, giving back to our guests some of what they helped pay for.

In 1989 we reorganized as a limited partnership, and soon thereafter, I bought out all of the partners. My guess is that none of them ever made an investment that paid off so handsomely. My one regret is that the Hortons and Dodsons, having previously sold their equities, were not able to participate.

While I miss the activity and excitement of owning and operating Colorado Trails Ranch, I have to say that I was ready to retire. All of the new and exasperating regulations, the specter of lawsuits, the difficulty of putting together a staff of young men and women with the right attitude and work ethic, made it difficult for me to maintain the level of enthusiasm I once had. In 1997, at the age of seventy, I ran out of steam and sold the ranch.

The personality of a dude ranch is an extension of the personality of the owner. As George Begley once put it, "Colorado Trails is Dick Elder. It follows therefore, that the Ranch is not the same outfit I once owned. The look and feel that we worked so hard to foster is no longer there. Maybe that's a good thing, then again, maybe not.

Now, let's find out what happened to the characters in this story:

In December, 1970 shortly after his 73rd birthday, my father died. In the 1971 edition of the Round-Up, I wrote a short piece about him.

Always scrupulously fair, my father treated each of his three sons alike, never doing for one that he didn't do as much for the others. In death as in life, he leaves each alike, his legacy: How to think, to lead, to be charitable, to be respectful and to be a gentleman. Perhaps most of all, to be a gentleman.

It seems strange when I think back on it. Dolly and I were in Ohio last October. When it was time to leave, Dad drove us to the airport. We thanked him for the lift then Dolly kissed him and said goodbye. For the past twenty years or so, Dad and I had taken leave of one another with a handshake, but for some reason, I put my arms around him and gave him a hug. "Goodbye Dad," I said.

"Goodbye Dick," he whispered, and drove off.

That was the last time I saw the man who kept for me, and for you, all of those letters written by the son he once called *nuts*. Well, he never said I was nuts, but he did say the idea of what we were doing and the ill-informed manner in which we went about it, was *nuts*. Still, I know that he was proud of me and what I was able to achieve. How do I know? He kept all those letters and made sure my brothers read each one. That's proof enough for me.

My Mother passed on at the ripe-old age of ninety-five, while brother Bob suddenly, and without prior warning, passed away at age seventy-eight. He was alive one minute, and dead the next leaving this world without a murmur. In my eulogy at the jam-packed church in Chagrin Falls, Ohio, I said that Bob had the perfect death, the one we all wish for. Not so for my partner and friend, George Horton who died after a long and arduous illness. He was seventy-seven. Donnie Horton lives in Ohio. We frequently talk by phone and recently, she came out for a visit. All things considered, she's doing fine and is still the wonderful and charming gal I remember from 40 years ago. Jim and Twila Dodson settled in Pennsylvania. Jim owned a trucking company, was one of the founders of the Christian Truckers of America and still drives a tour bus. Twila is working in retail sales. We communicate regularly.

Brother Howard is doing well, retired, and living in Sarasota, Florida with his second wife. George Begley, as you have read, is gone, but I stay in touch with his wife Geneva. I often talk to Bruce Begley, and remind him to place flowers on his daddy's grave. Mel and Jeanette Schaefer live in Willoughy Hills, Ohio. After selling his roofing business years ago, Mel was elected mayor of Willoughby Hills and was re-elected many times. He is reported to have done one hell of a good job. But knowing him as you and I do, that comes as no great surprise. I see Homer Hartley occasionally and we talk about the "good old days." He's retired now but still will take a job, if he feels like it.

Shorty, Faye, and Cecil Mars are all departed. Cecil died of some weird disease last year. I think he was in his early fifties. Over a hundred people, myself included, attended his funeral in Bayfield. Ray Duncan is no longer active at Purgatory but the last time I saw him, he seemed to be enjoying life.

Swede shows up occasionally and we have coffee. Jeanne is still working at Colorado Trails, and her husband Don Ross, is an interpretive guide at Mesa Verde National Park. As for Hilton Fix, Weldon Delany, Dave Sanchez, Vern Woodworth and some of the other characters you have met in this story, I have no knowledge.

My former wife, Marye, re-married but has recently become a widow. She has returned to Durango and lives in a new home built by my son Brad, a bachelor, who is a developer and contractor. Daughter Nancy sold her horticulture business in Los Angles seven years ago and took up residence in Quito, Ecuador. She too, is unmarried. Laurie lives just four miles from the ranch and works as a consultant. She is married, has two boys, and her husband is a detective with the La Plata County Sheriff Department. Mark is married, has a bunch of children and lives in Karachi, Pakistan. Why Pakistan? That's a long and fascinating story and, if I can get him to cooperate, perhaps his story will be the subject of another book.

You may be surprised to learn that Dolly and I divorced after ten years of what I would have to characterize as a good marriage. It was the same old story. I fell in love with a twenty-six year old girl on our staff and in 1977 we married. Ginny and I recently celebrated our twenty-fifth wedding anniversary so I think it is safe to say that I am now thinking with the right organ . . . finally! As for Dolly, she too remarried immediately after our divorce and as far as I know, she is doing okay, maybe, a lot better than just okay.

Ginny and I kept our home and thirty-five acres adjacent to the ranch. We live there in the summer and, having sold our home in the Santa Ynez Valley in central California, we will winter with our dog and two horses in our new home in Cave Creek, Arizona.

Although I'm retired, in my heart I'll always be a dude rancher, so if you would like to chat with me about horses or comment on this book, I would love to hear from you. My Email address is: Delder1927@aol.com.